LIFETIME ENCYCLOPEDIA OF LETTERS

Harold E. Meyer

Prentice-Hall, Inc.
Englewood Cliffs, New Jersey

Prentice-Hall International, Inc., *London*
Prentice-Hall of Australia, Pty. Ltd., *Sydney*
Prentice-Hall Canada Inc., *Toronto*
Prentice-Hall of India Private Ltd., *New Delhi*
Prentice-Hall of Japan, Inc., *Tokyo*
Prentice-Hall of Southeast Asia Pte. Ltd., *Singapore*
Whitehall Books, Ltd., *Wellington, New Zealand*
Editors Prentice-Hall Do Brasil LTDA., *Rio De Janeiro*

20   19   18

Library of Congress Cataloging in Publication Data

Meyer, Harold E.
    Lifetime encyclopedia of letters.

    Includes index.
    1. Letter-writing.   I. Title.
PE1483.M43   1983   808.6   82-13343
ISBN 0-13-536383-7

Printed in the United States of America

HOW YOU WILL BENEFIT FROM THIS BOOK

Do you sit down to write a letter and wonder, "Just what is it I'm trying to say and how should I say it?"

Is your letter clear enough that you can confidently omit the popular last sentence that reads, "If you have any questions, please call me?"

You have to terminate an employee. How do you write a letter that does the job and still remains a model of fairness?

Letter Categories

These and numerous questions of a similar nature are answered in the *Lifetime Encyclopedia of Letters* which covers 533 separate categories of letters, including: Apologizing: to an ignored customer; for failing to complete a project; for a missed meeting; for indiscreet behavior. Sympathy: to an accident victim; upon death of a child, parent, spouse, or relative; for a birth defect; from a business firm upon death of an employee. Welcome to new employees Invitations. Accepting and presenting a gift. Recommendations. Fund raising: for churches; for hospitals; for schools; for desperate children; for specific charities. Asking for a favor: of a business friend. Answering complaints: about a misunderstanding; about a faulty product; about a foreign object in packaged food. Thank you: for a job well done; for being our customer; for helping my career. Warning of possible termination of employment and the termination. Congratulations: on a promotion; upon graduation. Declining: a credit applicant; a donation; an invitation; employment. Reprimands: for lack of cleanliness; for misconduct. Collection letters from the first reminder to the notice of legal action.

If you should have questions about letter writing in some of these or similar areas, this encyclopedia will help you answer them.

How to's

Among the many other aids to easier and better letter writing, the *Lifetime Encyclopedia of Letters* will show you how to write an interest-arousing first sentence; to write a persuasive closing sentence; to be polite yet positive; to solve the problem of saying "no"; to be encouraging; to complain; to make a sales letter sell; to open the pocketbook of a potential contributor; to collect money; to organize your thoughts; to retain the reader's goodwill; to fire an employee; to express true sympathy; to take your guilt out of an apology; and to get action from your request.

Simplified Organization

One special feature of this encyclopedia that helps you organize your thoughts is the "How to Do It" section preceding each group of model letters. This feature is a step-by-step basic outline for your letters. Using these steps, you will remember all the essential parts of your letter and eliminate any unnecessary digressions.

As an illustration, the "How to Do It" section for needed encouragement lists these four steps:

1. Admit that an adverse condition exists.

2. Mention the condition or problem.

3. Indicate conviction that the condition can be overcome.

4. Suggest how to overcome the condition.

Now notice how smoothly the letter below fits the outline — without sounding as if it were chopped into four separate and unrelated pieces.

> Teaching at P.S. 24 is a difficult assignment for any teacher and even the most seasoned instructors often find that the integration process takes time. Thus, it comes as no surprise that you have spoken of submitting your resignation at the end of the school year.
>
> Discipline remains a problem for many new teachers here, as you have discovered. Students tend to "test" a teacher. However, once the test is passed, teachers often find themselves responding with enthusiasm to the challenge.
>
> Take a little time to reconsider your decision, then please see me to discuss the matter at your earliest convenience.

Beginning and Ending Sentences

Another special feature of the *Lifetime Encyclopedia of Letters* is the 379 suggested beginning and ending sentences for letters. Often, just getting started on a letter is all it takes to get you into the swing of it and then to carry you through. The starting sentences will accomplish this.

Chapter 2, "Declining Requests," suggests that one way to decline a request is to start with a thank-you. For example:

> Thank you for your recent request for a charge account at Liberty House.
>
> Thank you for your interest in Inland Steel.
>
> We appreciate your asking us to participate in your budget meeting.

This chapter offers statements of refusal, and the last step in the "How to Do It" section suggests offering help to the reader. Some encouraging statements are listed:

> I know you will find a suitable position soon.
>
> I believe the Abbott Company could give you more detailed information.
>
> We wish you great success.

In many letters, the last paragraph or sentence is a summary of the whole letter, an expression of appreciation, or a call for action. The chapter on sales letters illustrates this call for action:

> Your credit is good. Just tell us what you want.
>
> We've cut all the red tape — simply mail the card.
>
> Our supply is limited. Act now!
>
> If for any reason you're dissatisfied, simply return it . . . and owe absolutely nothing.

Soft Sell vs. Hard Sell

The variety of approaches within each category is another special feature of the *Lifetime Encyclopedia of Letters*. One fund-raising letter (which is a sales letter with a heart tug) consists of three short sentences:

> You make the difference between mediocrity and excellence.
>
> Think about it.
>
> Your considered gift to the Dartmouth Alumni Fund supports the Campaign for Dartmouth.

More common is a two-to-four-page letter with numerous appeals, one of which the writer hopes will elicit a response from the reader.

Another contrast in presentations included in this reference book is the soft sell offset against the hard sell, different approaches directed to different audiences. One real estate sales letter begins:

Peaceful . . .
Reaching a gentle rise overlooking a flowering meadow . . .

In contrast, another realtor starts off:

Another home SOLD . . . at 0000 Windmill Way . . .

Easy-to-Follow Models

All the letters in this encyclopedia are written in language currently in use. Letters of long ago that are considered standards of good writing but contain outdated expressions have been eliminated.

Many of the examples can thus be nearly copied. Only the change of a name or a few words is required to turn a sample into your own personal letter. You may wish to take a sentence or two from one letter and additional sentences from other letters, creating a letter you prefer to any of the models.

Because the model letters in this encyclopedia are standards and can be adapted to your requirements for many years, this book will become a long-term investment and companion. The range of topics and the variety of treatments within each topic make the *Lifetime Encyclopedia of Letters* a reference work that will indeed last a lifetime.

Analyses

For some situations, the explanations, analyses, and suggested outlines will make adaptation easy. The fund-raising letters, for example, may not fit individual needs as precisely as many of the sympathy letters. Sympathy letters are short and general, while fund-raising letters are long and specific. Money is requested for a particular cause, and many separate appeals may be included in one letter so that at least one appeal will touch the pocketbook of the reader. Fund-raising letters are outlined, then analyzed to point out what techniques are used in the appeals. This will enable the writer to list appeals, set them into the outline, and write the letter using one or more of the attention-getting techniques mentioned in the analysis.

Index

In this reference work, all the information found in the Table of Contents can also be found in the Index. Many letters are indexed in several ways: by topic; category within the topic; alternate names for the topic and the category; geographic location; and company name. Having read a letter once, you can locate it in the index by referring to one of several words. Double indexing is also used. For example, *reader's viewpoint* is indexed under both *reader's* and *viewpoint*.

Through the use of suggestions and model letters, the *Lifetime Encyclopedia of Letters* shows you how to write a letter that accomplishes your intended purpose.

Harold E. Meyer

CONTENTS

HOW YOU WILL BENEFIT FROM THIS BOOK   v

Chapter   1   REQUESTING FAVORS   1

How to Do It – 5
Closing a Request with Confidence —
Examples – 5
Additional Information – 5
Answering Questions – 5
Questionnaire – 6
Consumer Survey – 7
Response to Inquiry – 7
Procedural Change – 7
Rescheduling Order – 8
Time Extension – 8
Meeting Deadline – 9
Shorten Deadline – 9
Office Visit – 10
Manufacturing Plant Visit – 10
Share Experience – 11
Financial Statement – 11
Business Guidance – 11
Business Statistics – 12
Business Forecast – 12
Business Location – 13
Business Opportunities – 13
Sample Letter – 14
Quote from Article – 14
Obtaining Interview – 14
To Speak – 15
Getting Speakers – 16
Entertaining a Friend – 16
Alleviating Fear – 17
Board a Relative – 17
Job for a Friend – 18
Job for a Relative – 18

Chapter 2 DECLINING REQUESTS 19

How to Do It – 23
Begin by Agreeing – 23
Begin with a Thank-You – 23
Begin with an Agreement and Apology – 24
Statements of Refusal – 24
Close with Encouragement – 24
INVITATIONS – 25
Invitation to Dinner – 25
Invitation to Speak – 25
Join a Group – 26
Victory Celebration – 26
Football Game – 26
REQUEST FOR INFORMATION OR
MATERIAL – 27
Information Not Available – 27
Item Not Available – 28
APPLICATION FOR PERSONAL CREDIT – 29
Lack of Information – 29
Lack of Work Record – 30
Short Employment – 30
Slow Pay – 31
New in Area – 31
Current Information Lacking – 32
APPLICATION FOR BUSINESS CREDIT – 32
Financial Condition – 32
Credit Limited – 33
Company Procedure — Late Payment – 33
Guarantor Needed – 33
Previous Poor Pay – 34
Bad Risk – 34
Bad Risk — No Hope – 35
Franchise Refused – 35
Will Not Change Prior Understanding – 36
Credit Information Available Elsewhere – 36
DONATION – 36
Funds Limited – 37
Use of Name in Fund Raising – 37
Company Policy – 37
Budget Limitation – 38
Disagree with Charity Project – 38

EMPLOYMENT – 39
Position Unsuited – 39
Personal Information – 40
CUSTOMER ADJUSTMENTS – 41
Damaged Product – 41
Cash Discount – 41
Special Product – 42
Poor Workmanship – 42
Slow-Selling Product – 43
OTHER LETTERS OF DECLINATION – 43
Untested Sample Letters – 43
Special Assignment – 44
Business Meeting — Unnecessary – 44
Magazine Subscribers Limited – 44
Publication — Too Specialized – 45
Publication — Editorial Program – 45
Publication — Needs Reworking – 45
Refusing a Volunteer – 46
Freight Claim – 46

Chapter 3 SALES   **47**

How to Do It – 51
Model Openers – 52
Model Closings – 54
Investment — Real Estate – 55
Business Magazine – 56
Magazine — Elitist – 57
Mortgage Insurance – 57
Homeowner's Insurance – 58
Health Insurance – 59
Auto Insurance – 59
Book Club – 60
Real Estate — Homes – 62
Real Estate — Mountain Property – 63
Wrist Watch – 64
Camera – 64
Computer System – 65
Specific Customer — Roofing Tile – 66
Sales Promotion Book – 67
Gift of Food – 68

Bread – 69
Income Tax Consulting – 70
TV Service Contract – 71
Inactive Customer – 72
Collection Service – 72
Public Official – 73
Executive Recruiter – 74
Personal Credit – 74
Furniture, Retail – 75
Art Object – 76
Life Insurance – 77
Cost Savings – 78
Store Sale – 79

Chapter   4   FUND RAISING   81

CHARITABLE HELP FOR THE
DISADVANTAGED   86
Runaway Children – 86
Disadvantaged Girl – 88
Troubled Boys – 89
Destitute Children – 90
Mentally Retarded – 90
Crippled Children – 91
Handicapped Children – 92
Handicapped Youth – 93
Heart Fund – 93
Heart Disease – 94
Sclerosis – 95
American Veterans – 95
Cerebral Palsy – 96
United Way – 97
CARE – 98
Arthritis – 100
Lung Disease – 101
Cambodian Relief – 102
CHURCHES – 106
Secular Appeal – 106
Preparation for Fund-Raising Campaign – 107
Every Member Canvass – 108
Budget Can Be Met – 109

Delinquent Pledge – 110
Appeal to Faith – 110
Love Is a Reason for Giving – 111
HOSPITALS – 111
Updating Facilities – 112
Success Story – 113
Equipment for Senior Patients – 114
Need for Continuing Support – 114
Expansion Costs – 115
Maintain Quality Service – 116
Doctors Join in Giving – 116
Doctors as Business Persons – 117
Last Appeal to Doctors – 118
Using a Specific Example – 118
Replace Equipment – 119
Appeal to the Ego – 119
Join Hospital Foundation – 120
SCHOOLS – 121
Give More Than Last Year – 121
Library Needs – 123
Alumni Solicitation – 124
Haven't Given Yet – 124
Minorities Program – 126
Operational Funds – 127
Building Fund – 127
Student Union Building – 127
Religious Appeal – 128
Financially Disadvantaged Students – 129
Every Little Bit Helps – 129
Pledge Not Received – 130
Request for Small Gift – 130
Worthy Projects – 131

Chapter 5 COLLECTION 133

How to Receive a Prompt Reply – 137
How to Do It – 137
Attention-Getting Openings – 138
A Strong Close – 139
For Prompt Action – 139
To Build Goodwill – 140

To Soothe – 140
To Apologize – 140
To Reassure – 140
To Repeat – 141
To Promote the Future – 141
Series of Collection Letters – 141
Series One, Three Letters: General – 142
Series Two, Three Letters: Business Charge
Account – 142
Series Three, Three Letters: Past Due Freight Bill
– 143
Series Four, Four Letters: Make Account Current
– 144
Series Five, Four Letters: Loan Past Due – 146
Series Six, Four Letters: Charge Account – 147
Series Seven, Five Letters: Charge Account – 148
Series Eight, Five Letters: Charge Account – 150
Series Nine, Six Letters: Slow Pay Business
Account – 151
Series Ten, Six Letters: Business Account Delin-
quent – 153
The First Collection Letter Is a Reminder – 155
Credit Union Loan – 159
Middle Stages of Collection Letters – 160
Slow Pay — Terms Explained – 166
Final Collection Letters – 166

Confirmation – 178
Payment Instructions – 178
Continue Procedure – 179
Number Code Changes – 179
Repeated Instructions – 180
Distribution of Reports – 180
Confirmation – 180
Claim Against City – 181
Effect of Strike – 181
Insurance Policy Transfer – 181
Layoff – 182
Statement of Future Occurrence – 182
Test Run Assigned – 182
Policy Change – 183
Change in Items Used – 183
Address Change – 183
Will Contact You Again – 184
REQUESTING INFORMATION – 184
How to Do It – 185
A Report – 185
Accounting System – 186
Acknowledgment of Gift – 186
City Information – 186
Recent Sales Activity – 187
Strength Analysis – 187
Data for Newsletter – 187
Review of Claim – 188
Credit Information – 188
Credit Card – 189
Warranty Questions – 190
Making an Appointment – 190
Old Equipment – 190
Pollution Check – 191
Corporate Name – 191
Please Investigate – 192
Incomplete Files – 192
Office Furniture – 193
Life Insurance Questions – 193
Correct an Error – 193
Restricting Receiving Hours – 193
Using Credit Memo – 194
Procedural Change – 194

Keep Records – 195
Reporting Period Changed – 195
Personnel Evaluation – 195
Safety News – 196
Price Quote – 196
Where Is the Report? – 197
Chemical Hazards – 197
Physical Inventory – 198
Opinion Asked – 198
Survey of Consumption – 198
Claim Follow-Up – 199
Suggestions – 199

Chapter 7 COMPLAINTS—MAKING AND ANSWERING   **201**

MAKING COMPLAINTS – 203
How to Do It – 204
Transit Damage – 204
Cost of Purchases – 204
Incorrect Mailings – 205
Inadequate Explanation – 205
Messy Work Area – 206
Low Sales – 206
Sales Forecast – 206
Manufacturing Errors – 207
Manufacturing Problem – 208
Shipping Errors – 209
Billing Error – 209
Computer Error – 210
Catalog Order – 210
Misrepresentation – 211
Parking in Driveway – 211
Noisy Driver – 211
Meetings Out of Control – 212
Muddy Newspaper – 212
Delivery Person – 212
Barking Dog – 213
No Stop Light – 213
ANSWERING COMPLAINTS – 214
How to Do It – 214
Opening Sentences – 214

Closing Sentences – 215
Disturbed Retail Customer – 215
Our Mistake – 216
Misunderstanding – 216
Incomplete Instructions – 216
Misdirected Mail – 217
Late Delivery – 217
Shipping Error – 218
Delayed Order – 218
Delivery Method – 218
Damaged Merchandise – 219
Auto Defect – 220
Merchandise Guarantee – 220
Wrong Style – 221
Unsatisfactory Chair – 221
Unsatisfactory Recorder – 221
Foreign Object in Food – 222
Declining Responsibility — Frozen Food – 222
Pricing Error – 222
Billing Error – 223
Statement Error – 224

**Chapter   8   TERMINATION AND
RESIGNATION   225**

TERMINATION – 227
How to Do It – 227
Plant Closed – 228
Company Cutbacks – 228
Company Merger – 229
Financial Problems – 229
Indiscretions – 230
Project Completed – 230
Personal Friend – 230
Performance – 230
Classroom Procedures – 231
NOTICE OF EMPLOYEE LEAVING – 231
Resignation – 232
Retirement – 232
TERMINATION WARNING – 232
How to Do It – 233
Personal Problems – 233

Poor Performance – 233
Classroom Performance – 235
Tardiness – 235
Absentee Record – 236
RESIGNATION – 236
How to Do It – 237
New Position – 237
Seeking New Challenge – 237
College Training – 238
Ill Health – 238
Heart Problem – 239
Allergies – 239
Personal Problems – 239
Disagree With Goals – 240
Want Less Travel – 240
Credit Union – 240
RESIGNATION ACCEPTANCE – 241
How to Do It – 241

Chapter   9   SYMPATHY AND CONDOLENCE   243

How to Do It – 245
Sentences Expressing Sympathy – 246
Sentences Thanking the Reader for an Expression
of Sympathy – 247
Letters to Hospitalized People – 248
Other's Illness – 249
Death of Business Associate – 249
Death of Business Friend – 250
Death of Spouse – 250
Death of Relative – 253
Death of Others – 256
Belated Condolences – 257
Death by Suicide – 258
Death — From a Business Firm – 259
Birth Defect – 261
Divorce – 261
Marriage Separation – 261
Misfortune – 262
Personal Reverses – 262
Unnamed Tragedy – 262
Thank You for Your Sympathy – 263

Chapter   10 APOLOGY   **265**

How to Do It – 267
Sentences of Apology – 268
Reasons for an Apology – 268
Bad Behavior – 269
Billing Error – 270
Company Procedure – 270
Confusing Word Usage – 270
Declining Dinner Invitation – 271
Delayed Answer – 271
Delayed Credit – 273
Postponed Dinner – 273
Delayed Order – 273
Delayed Paper Work – 274
Delayed Return of Borrowed Item – 274
Delayed Thank You – 275
Indiscretion – 276
Ignoring a Customer – 276
Incomplete Instructions – 277
Incomplete Project – 277
Late Report – 278
Missed Appointment – 278
Missed Meeting – 278
Missing a Caller – 279
Project Failure – 279
Quote Error – 280
Shipping Error – 280
Slow Payment – 281
Small Reward – 281
Statement Error – 282
Wrong Information – 282

Chapter   11 CONGRATULATIONS   **283**

How to Do It – 285
Sales Volume – 286
New Customer – 286
Good Job – 286
Top Salesperson – 287
Exceeding Goal – 287
Graduation – 288

College Degree – 288
Specialized Teacher – 289
Handicapped – 289
Promotion – 289
New Position – 291
Service Award – 291
Retirement – 292
Golf Tournament – 294
Industry Award – 294
President of Rotary – 294
Anniversary – 295
Honorary Sorority – 295
President of Association – 295
Opening Store – 295
City Councilman – 296
Loan Paid – 296
Marriage – 296

Chapter   12 THANK YOU AND APPRECIATION 297

How to Do It – 301
Gift – 301
Pamphlet – 302
Information – 302
Materials Received – 302
Career Help – 303
Advice – 303
Recommendation – 304
Dinner Invitation – 304
Recognition – 304
Going Away Party – 305
Companionship – 305
Friendship – 305
Appreciation – 306
Sympathy – 307
Illness – 308
Job Well Done – 309
Being Our Customer – 311
Charge Account Request – 311
Sales Presentation – 312
Accounting Help – 312

Payment – 312
Referral – 313
Attending – 313
Visiting – 314
Departing Employee – 315

Chapter 13 OTHER BUSINESS LETTERS 317

GOODWILL – 319
How to Do It – 320
Season's Greetings – 320
Good Work – 321
Free Bulletin – 321
Golf Invitation – 321
To a Salesman's Wife – 321
Sales Agreement Ended – 322
To Parents of Young Employee – 322
Enjoyed Meeting You – 322
Real Estate Service – 323
Fishing Trip Invitation – 323
Gift Received – 323
Requested Information – 324
Sending Information – 324
INTRODUCTION – 324
How to Do It – 325
New Sales Representative – 325
Friend for Sales Position – 325
A Friend – 326
Academic Assistance – 326
For a Job – 327
INVITATIONS – 327
How to Do It – 328
Luncheon for an Old Friend – 328
To Do Advertising – 328
Use Company Hotel Room – 328
Ball Game – 329
Dinner Guest – 329
Accepting Invitations – 329
How to Do It – 330
To Speak – 330
Football Celebration – 330

Retirement Dinner – 331
Dinner Invitation – 331
Join a Group – 331
Declining Invitations – 331
ACCEPTING JOB OR POSITION – 331
How to Do It – 332
City Clerk – 333
Lions Club – 333
Purchasing Agent – 333
Store Manager – 334
Part-Time Job – 334
ACCEPTING JOB APPLICANT – 334
How to Do It – 335
Junior Accountant – 335
Office Clerk – 335
Foreman – 336
School Teacher – 336
Store Manager – 336
COVER LETTER – 337
How to Do It – 337
Expenditures Request – 338
Lists – 338
Agreement for Signature – 338
Warehouse Report – 339
Certificate of Incorporation – 339
Statement Requested – 339
Commodity Codes – 339
Savings Statement – 340
Insurance Renewal – 340
Price Increase – 340
Job Resumé – 341
FOLLOW-UP – 341
How to Do It – 342
Correct an Error – 342
Additional Information Requested – 342
Additional Information Provided – 343
Inactive Charge Account – 343
Power Lawn Mower Purchase – 343
Purchasing Position – 344
Retail Selling – 344
Accounting Position – 344

Chapter   14 OTHER PERSONAL LETTERS   347

WELCOME – 349
How to Do It – 350
To New Resident – 350
To New Member – 351
To New Business – 351
To New Customer – 352
To New Employee – 352
To Wife of Salesman – 353
GOOD WISHES – 354
How to Do It – 354
Season's Greetings – 355
Convalescing – 356
ENCOURAGEMENT – 357
How to Do It – 358
Sales Contest – 358
Low Productivity – 358
Promotion – 359
Research Paper – 359
Fund Drive – 360
Teaching – 360
COMPLIMENTS – 361
How to Do It – 361
Staff Help – 361
Expert Assistance – 362
Orientation Help – 362
Better Truck Loading – 362
Unusual Help – 363
Finding Error – 363
Getting the Facts – 363
Construction Bid – 364
Good Salesman – 364
Sales Volume – 364
Sales Increase – 365
Vote Getter – 365
RECOMMENDATION – 366
Recent Graduate – 366
Job Promotion – 367
Personal Referral – 367
Customer – 368

Secretary – 368
Accounts Payable Clerk – 369
Statistical Clerk – 369
Billing Clerk – 369
Domestic Service – 370
Inexperienced Worker – 370
High School Graduate – 370
UNCOMPLIMENTARY REFERENCE – 371
How to Do It – 371
REPRIMAND – 371
How to Do It – 372
Poor Work – 372
Poor Attendance – 373
Improper Language – 374
Outside Activities at Work – 374
Lack of Cleanliness – 374
Bad Behavior – 375
Travel Expense – 375
Lack of Cooperation – 376
Fire Insurance Increase – 376
Exceeding Budget – 376
Trespassing – 377
Inventory Records – 377
Sales Falling – 378
PRESENTING GIFTS – 378
How to Do It – 379
Friendship – 379
Advice – 379
Funeral Officiating – 380
Baptismal Officiating – 380
Hospital Patient – 380
Eightieth Birthday – 381
Illness – 381
Retirement – 381
ACCEPTING GIFTS – 382
How to Do It – 382
Chess Set – 383
Food Snacks – 383
Book – 383
Money – 384
Oil Painting – 385
Watercolor Painting – 385

Art Object – 385
Statuette – 386
Free Product – 386
Cooler – 386
DECLINING GIFTS – 387
How to Do It – 387
Company Policy – 387
Must Maintain Image – 388
Duplicate Gift – 388
Gift Too Valuable – 389
Expensive Gift – 389

INDEX **391**

1

REQUESTING
FAVORS

Many people find it difficult to make a request that seems to impose upon others. Often, the person asked feels complimented that he is considered capable of helping to solve a problem, so you should not be reluctant to ask—assuming the request is reasonable. When making requests of a sensitive nature, such as for a favor or for cooperation, you must indicate clearly and persuasively why the request is being made. Let the reader know why you came to him or her for help and how that help will be used.

A letter requesting only information can be short and direct. For example:

> We need quarterly SEC reports, our form C-140, for the year 19__ .
> Submit these by the 20th of the month following each quarter.

A more willing response, however, would be received if the letter were expanded just enough to include an explanation of why the request is being made. A word or two, such as "please" or "would appreciate" is helpful in eliciting the desired response. This is illustrated in the following request that is also short and direct, but adds the reason for the request and a polite tone:

> The year-end Tax Requirements report unintentionally omitted charitable contributions.
>
> We would appreciate it if you would provide us with a schedule of donations made during the year showing the donee and the dollar amount.

The key to getting results from a sensitive letter of request is having a persuasive and convincing explanation of the reason for the request. Think before you write: what will appeal to the reader? how are the writer's wants tied to the reader's interests? A request is more willingly granted if the practical psychology of give-and-take is recognized. The reader may ask, "What's in it for me?" Whenever possible, offer something in return.

One of the model letters asks for financial statements and offers prompt deliveries of future orders upon receiving them. Other letters ask for information, implying that the reader knows more than the writer, and all readers like compliments. One letter requests a stepped-up delivery date for part of an order, ". . . because we don't want to split the order with another supplier." This is not a threat of taking away promised business, but a suggested practical solution to a business problem, and of much interest to the reader. Another letter requesting a favor suggests an exchange of information about manufacturing plant operations. The reader of this letter is interested because he has an opportunity to receive information in exchange for giving information. In one letter a request is made by an alumnus doing research. Being an alumnus and doing research are both topics of interest to the college president to whom the letter is addressed. These offers of something in return or topics of personal interest to the reader can induce the reader to participate willingly.

When asking several questions in one letter, make the response easier by listing and preferably numbering the questions. In this way each specific question will result in a specific answer.

Another technique for getting a positive response is to write to an individual rather than to "Gentlemen." (The names of corporate officers can be found in reference libraries. Another method is to call the office of the person to whom you wish to write.)

When the request is mentioned early in a letter that includes an appeal of more than two sentences, repeat the request at the end. Make the reply easy for the reader by making the request specific and by providing an envelope or an address or a due date.

Never end a letter by saying, "Thanking you in advance" or the shorter "Thank you" or "Thanks." These phrases leave the reader with the feeling that the writer is terminating all interest in the request and that the reader is left to struggle on alone. Rather than ending with a curt "Thank you," make the reader happy to grant your request by clothing it with politeness and appreciation for the expected action. This can be done by using such phrases as, "It would be helpful," or "We would appreciate," or "Please."

Close the letter with confidence. Make no apologies. A letter ending with the statement. "I know you're awfully busy and I hate to ask you this, but maybe you could find time to check this report for me," is likely to draw the response, "You're right. I don't have time." The ending should indicate confidence that the request will be granted, and it must be stated politely.

How to Do It

1. Make the request specific, using a polite tone.
2. Explain persuasively the reason for the request.
3. Offer something in return.
4. Show appreciation for the granter's help.

Closing a Request with Confidence —Examples

Your answer will be gratefully received.

We appreciate your cooperation.

Please mail the financial statements today.

Receiving a sample drawing would be greatly appreciated.

Please let us know when you can do this.

We will expect your answer soon.

Even a short visit with you will be truly appreciated.

Your answers to the above questions will be of great help to us.

Your filling in the blanks below and returning this letter in the enclosed envelope will be greatly appreciated.

Additional Information

Dear Mr. Hoskins:

Thank you for the operating schedule you made for conducting the market survey we discussed in April. All the bases seem to be covered.

I would like, however, to have you add calendar dates and costs for the various steps you have listed. As we discussed, timeliness is essential. The cost is also important because we have a definite and limited budget for this project.

With the added information on dates and costs, we can make a prompt decision on how to proceed with the survey. We hope to hear from you soon.

Sincerely,

Answering Questions

Dear Ms. Carpenter:

Could you help us with a favor? We are considering the installation of a small computer to replace hand posting of our accounting records and the typing of financial reports and monthly statements. We have been told that you have experience with the Conrad 103 system. Could you help by answering the following questions? A brief answer is all we need.

1. How frequently does this system require adjustments or repairs to the machine?
2. Has the use of this system reduced your office staff?
3. Do reports and financial statements get to your managers at an earlier calendar date than before the system was installed?

We will greatly appreciate your answers to these questions.

Sincerely,

Questionnaire

Dear Mr. Dawson:

Because you are one of our past trainees who has become successful, we recently sent you a questionnaire asking about your work and personal background, your work experience, and your opinions on several related matters. We are anxious to have your reply in order to better understand the characteristics of those entering our training program, and to improve our program for future trainees.

If you have already returned your questionnaire, many thanks. If not, we hope you will do so soon.

Sincerely,

Dear Ms. Walker:

We are compiling a guide to the employment of women in top firms in the nation and would appreciate your cooperation in filling out the enclosed questionnaire.

Given the timeliness of the subject, and the involvement of both the Government and women's groups, the answers to our questions will be valuable to women seeking responsible positions.

Since we are already informally aware of your company's progressive policy, your response will be particularly encouraging.

Any additional information and comments you might provide will be appreciated.

Sincerely,

Consumer Survey

Dear Mr. Summers:

Thank you for taking the time to talk with us on the phone recently and for agreeing to participate in our survey.

We have sent one questionnaire to be filled out by each member of your household, twelve years of age and older. Please fill out the enclosed material and return it in the envelope provided as soon as possible. No postage is necessary.

We hope that you will enjoy participating in this survey. Your answers will become an important part of our scientific study.

Please accept the enclosed token of our sincere appreciation for your cooperation.

Sincerely yours,

Response to Inquiry

Dear George:

You should receive a phone call next week from our Washington headquarters. Please make every effort to supply them with the information they have requested from your branch.

The main office is drawing up a company profile. The exposure provided by our data should be beneficial for both the branch image and the individual personnel involved.

I look forward to seeing your responses.

Regards,

Procedural Change

Dear Andy:

It seems there is a breakdown in procedures between our departments. We are not getting all the receiving records for scrap that your department receives after our department orders it. When inquiries are made directly to your receiving clerk, he complains that apparently he doesn't get all the copies of our orders to match with his receipts.

We have learned that our orders are sent through the company mail with the receiving clerk's name written in no particular place on them. Now we have instructed our order clerk to mail these in an intracompany envelope. This should eliminate misdirection of the mail.

Could you have your receiving clerk mail the receiving records to our department in an intracompany envelope? Please send them to the attention of Bob Smyth.

Sincerely,

Rescheduling Order

Dear Carl:

On July 24 we sent you our purchase order number AC 3341 for 100,000 tomato boxes. The requested delivery date, which you confirmed, is September 4.

Due to forecasted changes in the weather, tomatoes will ripen a month earlier than expected, and we will need 50,000 of these boxes before August 4 and the balance by September 4. Could you reschedule your production line to work in at least half our order to meet the earlier delivery date? I know your production schedules are full at this time of the year, but a profitable harvest depends upon boxing the tomatoes as soon as they are ready. We would certainly appreciate your help because we don't want to split the order with another supplier. Please let me know immediately if you can do this for us.

Best Regards,

Time Extension

Dear Mr. Mullen:

Enclosed is a copy of our option on rental space at the Furniture Mart. The option expires March 23.

The decision to renew must be made by our Board of Directors, and it is not possible for them to meet until March 28.

Would it be possible, therefore, to extend the option renewal date to March 29? We will have the decision then.

Sincerely,

Dear Ms. Bradley:

Is it possible for us to obtain an extension of the initial trial leasing contract for the 150 copier?

I am aware that the three-month trial period was provided at a reduced rate. Unfortunately, we could not take full advantage of testing the copier because the office was shut down for three weeks of the lease period.

The performance of the machine has, thus far, been satisfactory. There is, however, one special run to be made next week that will determine our decision either to buy the copier or to return it to you and end the agreement.

Please respond as soon as possible.

Sincerely,

Meeting Deadline

Dear Mr. Hartfeld:

Because of an audit by the Internal Revenue Service on September 27, I will need a transaction-by-transaction listing of all my stock purchases and sales made through Sanders and Sanders, Inc. for the calendar year 19___ . Each transaction must include:

Name of stock	Date of sale
Date of purchase	Sales price
Purchase price	Brokerage sales fee
Brokerage purchase fee	

I know it will be a tight schedule for you, but I must have the report no later than September 26.

Your prompt attention will be greatly appreciated (by Uncle Sam as well as by me).

Sincerely,

Shorten Deadline

Dear Mr. Mays:

When we sent you the flat stock for 7000 formed steel channels, we told you that you could have 36 days in which to do the job. We now find, however, we cannot allow you that much time, due to the rescheduling of a U.S. Government bridge contract.

Can you get the job done by March 28? This cuts off 11 working days, unless you work Saturdays. Could you help us by shortening the deadline on this project? We really would appreciate it.

If this revised schedule is not possible, please ship back to us what you have completed and the remaining flat stock by March 18.

We hope you can do this favor for us. Please let me know immediately.

Sincerely,

Office Visit

Dear Ms. Jorgenson:

I understand you have a TM600 computer installed for use in your accounting procedures. We are considering several computer systems including the TM600.

I will be in Los Angeles September 25, 26, and 27. Would it be possible to visit your office then? I can arrange to come at any hour convenient for you. Even a short visit with you would be helpful, and greatly appreciated.

Sincerely,

Manufacturing Plant Visit

Dear Mr. Patterson:

We have had the Adenhaur starch-making system in operation at our plant for five months, and understand you have used this system for about two years.

I will be in Memphis during the week of November 19, and would like very much to visit your operation. We have found interesting solutions to some of the problems posed by the installation of this system, and we could exchange information that would benefit us both.

I can arrange to visit any day during the week of November 19. Please let me hear from you.

Regards,

Share Experience

Dear Ms. Wallen:

Your firm has the reputation of having a workable and fair personnel policy. We are revising some of our personnel policies and are rewriting our personnel manual.

Could you share with us a few of your successful procedures? I would like to discuss this with you within the next two weeks. A short interview at your convenience, during which time we could exchange information, would be greatly appreciated. Please call me.

Sincerely,

Financial Statement

Dear Mr. Bangor:

Thank you for your order dated August 20 for 5,000 pen and pencil sets. We especially appreciate orders from new customers. It will be shipped to arrive September 6 as you requested.

I would like to ask a favor of you before we fill your next order. We need a copy of your latest financial statements. It will take only a few minutes and will insure prompt delivery of your future orders.

Next month we will have pen and pencil desk sets available for a promotional program. Our salesman, John Harvey, will show you these soon.

I would appreciate your mailing your financial statements today.

Sincerely,

Business Guidance

Dear Allen:

With the recent reduction in our staff that resulted from current economic conditions, we are finding it impossible to complete the monthly reports required by our headquarters office on time. Several steps have been taken to consolidate scattered information, to redistribute work loads, and to eliminate duplicated efforts. Our staff members realize the importance of making every minute count and of continuing to discover quicker ways to complete our reports.

In spite of all our efforts, we are continually falling behind. I would like to ask a favor. I believe you can help us. Would you come here for a day, or even half a day, to review our reports and to suggest some that might be eliminated? Some reports can probably be combined. Then, perhaps you could persuade the headquarters office that these reductions on our reporting workload would not eliminate any necessary management information. We would certainly appreciate your coming here, and hope that the whole company will benefit. Please let me hear from you soon.

Sincerely,

Business Statistics

Dear Mr. Winters:

Our Manager of Marketing, Mr. Aaron Smith, asked me to write you for two statistics that he would like to incorporate in a marketing trend report for *Western Apparel* magazine. You will, of course, be given credit in the magazine for the information you provide.

To meet the magazine's deadline, we will need these figures by October 1.

What we would like is the following:

1. Number of leather jackets you shipped in 19__
2. Number of plastic and simulated leather jackets you shipped in 19__

Your help will be greatly appreciated. May we hear from you by October 1?

Sincerely,

Business Forecast

Dear Mr. Peterson:

Thank you for your help in making the year 19__ the most successful in our history. As you know, our sales exceeded all previous records, and because of the increased business we expanded our order assembly and shipping departments. We also added four delivery trucks to our fleet. With this, we will be able to offer even faster service than before. Your business played a big part in our expansion.

To help us continue our fast service, could you provide us with an estimate of your needs for 19__?

Please accept our best wishes for a prosperous 19__.

Sincerely,

Business Location

Dear Andy,

After listening to you at the Retail Hardware Association convention last fall, I have given serious consideration to our expansion plans. Your point about the price advantages of volume purchasing really struck home because our markup is low when we meet our competitor's prices.

I opened a branch store shortly after last fall's convention and it shows promise of turning a profit in a few more months.

I am now considering a third store in a new shopping development, but I can't decide definitely to go ahead with the project. I am bothered by the store space available for expansion and the projected population growth in that area.

Could I ask an extraordinary favor of you? Could you possibly come here for a day or two to look over the situation and give me your opinion? Or make it three or four days and enjoy a mini-vacation. I want you to stay with us, and of course bring Ethel with you. The lake and two golf courses are nearby.

Just talking over this decision with you would be a tremendous help to me.

Beth and I are anxiously awaiting your reply.

Best regards,

Business Opportunities

Gentlemen:

Please send me information regarding business opportunities in the Jacksonville area for an unfinished furniture store.

I am looking for a small but growing business community — and a place in which to live as well as work.

Any information you can provide to get my investigation started will be greatly appreciated.

Sincerely,

Sample Letter

Dear Mr. Hogness:

Could you do a small favor for an alumnus (1969)?

I am doing a research paper on charity contributions. What I need is a sample of a letter asking for a contribution to a worthy cause. You have probably written such a letter asking for money for the University of Washington. Any names and dates should be deleted from the copy or transcript sent to me.

Receiving a sample letter would be truly appreciated.

Sincerely,

Quote from Article

Dear Ms. Sanderson:

The immediate nature of your recent article on the subject of anxiety and performance makes it highly quotable. I would like permission to quote several paragraphs in my paper for the Psychology Association Workshop on psychological disorders most prevalent in affluent women.

As you are aware, too much misinformation has been common in the field. Thus, a well-written, logical evaluation of anxiety, such as you have produced, is extremely valuable.

Should you consent, full credit for your ideas will be given.

Your permission and any suggestions will be appreciated.

Sincerely,

Obtaining Interview

Dear Tim,

Can you help me obtain an interview with Dr. Jerson? I know you've worked closely with him for six months now, and you might at least be able to put in a good word or two for me.

The article I am writing is highly important to me because if it is successful, it will show that I really can handle investigative reporting. In addition, Dr. Jerson might feel relieved, at long last, to have the opportunity to tell his own story in his own way.

I'll be on edge until I receive your reply.

Sincerely,

To Speak

Dear Ms. Nylund:

You have taught a work-study course for legal secretaries for several years and have talked to me about it many times.

Would you be interested in sharing your obvious enthusiasm with the Alamo Business Women at their monthly dinner meeting? We will meet Friday, March 21, at the Sheraton Hotel at 6:30 P.M. A twenty- to thirty-minute talk would be well received by the group.

Please let me know. I can pick you up on the 21st shortly after 6:00.

Sincerely,

Dear Mr. Blackwell:

You are known in this area as a top salesman. Would you be willing to help some young people become better salespersons, to tell them some of the methods and techniques that have earned you your reputation?

The carriers for the Marin County Times are having a sales meeting Friday, February 22 at 7:30 P.M. at the Times office, 333 Silvera Way.

They would be thrilled (and I am sure educated) if you could speak to them for fifteen to twenty minutes and then answer questions.

I'm sure you will find the carriers an enthusiastic group. Please call me.

Sincerely,

Getting Speakers

Dear Jean,

Our seminar on the executive woman is scheduled for April and I'm in the process of putting together the list of speakers. Can you assist me here?

With your executive experience and your contacts with other women in the field, would you be willing to contact a few of them to speak at the seminar?

I would really appreciate it if you could use your influence to help me out. The more diverse our speakers, of course, the more productive the seminar.

My fingers are crossed in hope of your assistance.

Sincerely,

Entertaining a Friend

Dear Pete:

I would like to ask a tremendous favor of you.

Could you possibly spend part of a day with Jack Herald, who is one of our best customers as well as a personal friend of mine? He mentioned yesterday that he will be spending a week or more of vacation time in San Francisco, starting October 7. Jack is production manager for Aames Company here. He is still a bachelor, though I don't know how he manages to stay that way. Jack is an outgoing type but modest and extremely pleasant. He would just about match you in golf. He is a camera bug like you and will surely bring along his new Nikon. I'm sure he would like to take pictures from such spots as Coit Tower, Harding Park's 17th green, the Cliff House, and Twin Peaks. Jack would also enjoy one or two of the tourist-type nightclubs, but that is not his strong suit.

Can I have him call you when he gets to San Francisco? I realize this is asking a lot, but you know I will return the favor whenever I can do something to help you.

Sincerely,

Alleviating Fear

Dear Mrs. Miles,

I am sending this letter to your office for the obvious reason that Mr. Miles should not see it.

In my opinion, and in the opinion of Doctors Agnew and Danis, whose reputations as diagnosticians are excellent, Mr. Miles requires surgery as soon as possible.

It is understandable that you feel the way you do about surgery, Mrs. Miles. You expressed yourself clearly when we first met. We feel there isn't any other treatment, however, if you want your husband to recover his good health. Surgery isn't what it was forty years ago, or even ten, and you can be reassured by knowing that the mortality rate for this particular operation, when performed in time is less than 5 percent. The mortality rate for neglect of this condition is a certain 100 percent.

Please try to stop by my office with your husband Tuesday evening so that I may talk with both of you. If this is not convenient, please call my secretary this week for an appointment.

Sincerely,

Board a Relative

Dear Sue,

Is there any chance that you and Tom could have Jane stay with you for a month this summer? You've offered in the past, but the need has never been so great. I have the chance to take on a really big account that requires a month-long stay in Israel shooting fashion layouts and generally supervising the whole scene.

Jane has often talked of visiting with you, and I have felt that you would like to see more of her. If it can be arranged, count on me to take time off (I'll be due some if this goes through) to help you with the wedding in January. I already have some ideas.

Call me — even collect!

Sincerely,

Job for a Friend

Dear George,

Harry Watson recently graduated from Stanford Law School. I have known him for over seven years and can honestly say he is one of the few intelligent, ambitious, and likeable young men available. Had he studied engineering, I would take him in without a moment's hesitation.

I hope you can find room for Watson in your office. Someone will start him on his certain, brilliant career in law.

At the least, he will appreciate a visit with you because he greatly admires your work.

If you learn of any bright and ambitious engineers, send them to me. I'll be happy to return your favor.

Cordially,

Job for a Relative

Dear Tom,

Please review the enclosed resume of my nephew, John Wentling.

John is an intelligent and ambitious young man whose college performance and initial work experience have been admirable. His work with Grande Company should prove beneficial to you.

Could you check around a bit to see if there is a place for John in the company in the areas of interest he has indicated. Anytime I can return the favor, or assist you in further contacts, you know you can just call.

I look forward to some good news.

With regards,

2

DECLINING
REQUESTS

It is difficult to refuse or say "no." The key to the successful "no" is tact. In a letter of refusal, the goodwill of the reader must be retained, and if the letter is tactfully written, the reader's disappointment will be lessened.

A customer receiving a flat "no" to a request for an adjustment will often not complain: he will quietly take his business elsewhere. The customer has bought a product or service and now asks for an adjustment. He or she receives a rejection. The disappointment that started with the unsatisfactory product or service deepens into distrust and then anger. This lost goodwill must be salvaged. The writer's task is to explain the rejection in a tactful way and to offer an alternative. He or she must combine the refusal with help for the customer. This will not please the customer all of the time, but the chances of alienating the customer all of the time are considerably lessened.

One good way to start a letter of refusal is to agree with the reader on some point. This establishes a feeling of working together as opposed to an "I'm-right-you're-wrong" confrontation. For example:

We agree that a watch running only part of the time is useless.

Another recommended opening statement is a thank you. This sets a tone of courtesy, pleasantness, and consideration for the reader. An example:

Thank you for your recent letter requesting a donation to the Redwood Girls Club.

A combination of agreement and apology is a third introduction to model refusal letters. The message to be conveyed is that "we would like to help, but we can't." The use of this opening requires a reasonable and sincere explanation of why the request is refused. A strong alternative suggestion for obtaining help should follow the apologetic opening as in this example:

21

> We wish it were possible to provide door prizes for your annual
> meeting . . . Perhaps we can help by advertising in our store window.

After letting the reader know that you are aware of his or her request and have considered it from the reader's point of view, explain
the reason for the refusal. Explain the refusal before making it. This
takes the sharp edge off the refusal, and prepares the reader for the
disappointment which, to some extent, all refusals bring. The statements, "It is not company policy," or "For various reasons we cannot
comply," are only slightly better than completely ignoring the request. If it is not company policy, the reader would like to know why
it is not company policy. Perhaps it is that "Children under 12 years
of age are not allowed to visit our plant because the safety hazards
are too great to be covered by a reasonable insurance premium," or
"We cannot continue in business if we extend our free delivery policy
to purchases under $100." A request for credit may be refused be-
cause of lack of information or not meeting certain qualifications. A
request for a contribution may be denied because of lack of budgeted
funds. Company procedures may not provide the data requested. A
job applicant may be rejected because there is no opening, he or she
is underqualified, or overqualified. A pamphlet may be out of print. A
request for a refund may be turned down because of an obvious condition excluded by the warranty. Whatever is being refused, the explanation to the reader must be straightforward, definite, and
reasonable.

The next step is to state the refusal. The reader has been prepared by the explanation, and there is no reason to smother the refusal in a barrage of words. A few examples:

> I regret that we must decline this opportunity to help the Girls
> Club.
> I am sorry to inform you that we cannot supply the information re-
> quested.
> We hate to say "No" to your credit application but we do not
> have enough information to say "Yes."

Because the ending of a letter is the most emphatic position, a
tactful letter of refusal should end on a positive or upbeat note. Consideration for the reader suggests that a sincere effort to offer at least
some help or encouragement would be appropriate in offsetting the
unavoidable disappointment. This helps the reader to save face, it
gives him or her an out, it offers an alternative course of action, and

it reinflates the reader's ego. Closing statements like the following are encouraging:

> We wish you great success.
>
> We are interested in your business venture.
>
> Please keep us in mind for other ideas you may develop.

Many adjectives can be used to describe the proper tone of a letter refusing a request, but they are all brought together when the writer uses the persuasive power of a soft denial.

How to Do It

1. Agree on some point with the reader or offer thanks for the reader's interest.
2. Present reasons for the refusal.
3. State the refusal.
4. Offer a suggestion or an alternative that will help the reader.

Begin by Agreeing

Here are some agreeable beginnings for a letter of refusal:

> As you requested, we are enclosing a tally of the monthly purchases you made during 19__ .
>
> Your Junior Chamber of Commerce *Sports Annual* is a commendable project.
>
> A copy of the first quarter 19__ issue of *Semiconductor Science* is being mailed to you today.
>
> We like your approach to the consumer survey on garden tools.
>
> Your questions are most interesting.

Begin with a Thank-You

Using a thank-you is another good way to start a letter of refusal:

> Thank you for your recent request for a charge account at Liberty House.
>
> Your enlightening comments on our Direct Mail Selling series of letters are greatly appreciated.
>
> Thank you very much for giving us the opportunity to consider you for employment.
>
> Thank you for your interest in Inland Steel.

We are pleased that you thought of us as a source of information.

We appreciate your asking us to participate in your August meeting.

Begin with an Agreement and Apology

Agreeing with the reader while at the same time apologizing for not granting a request is a third beginning for a letter of refusal:

We would be happy to comply with your request for a sample of our new loan forms. May I suggest you write directly to our headquarters office.

We would like to grant your request for a copy of our booklet *Animal Husbandry* but our supply has been exhausted. More will be available next year. To help you now, may we suggest you write to the Superintendent of Documents in Washington, D.C. asking for publications on this subject.

We are sorry to learn that the paint work on your car was not to your satisfaction. I have talked to Bob Anderson and he suggests you bring your car in next Saturday for a complete inspection.

Statements of Refusal

Direct but polite statements of refusal include these:

At present, however, your financial condition does not quite meet Barrow's requirement.

He believes that meeting would not be helpful.

We do not have a position open that fits your qualifications.

I am sorry that we cannot accept the chairs for credit.

I am sorry we cannot provide the information you requested.

We hate to decline granting you credit but we need additional information from you.

We regret declining this opportunity to help the Bay Area Youth Council.

I am sorry we cannot grant your request.

Close with Encouragement

A statement of encouragement for the reader is an effective goodwill gesture to offset the natural disappointment of a refusal. Some examples:

Thank you for thinking of Carl & Henderson.

I know you will find a suitable position soon.

I believe the Abbott Company could give you more detailed information.

Have you thought of asking Tom Anderson?

We will be glad to receive other ideas from you.

We are interested in your proposed new business.

We wish you great success.

We wish you continued success.

INVITATIONS

An acceptable declination of an invitation includes three important points. The first is brevity. Long explanations turn into excuses that become confused and hard to believe. The second is a polite thank-you for the invitation. Let the inviter know you are pleased to have been considered worthy of an invitation. The third is a plausible reason for not accepting — a reason that is believable by the person you are refusing.

Invitation to Dinner

Dear Andy,

Thank you for your personal invitation to attend the Old School dinner meeting on October 22. I regret that only yesterday I accepted an invitation to a meeting with a business group to which I have belonged for the past few years. Perhaps I can join you and our Old School gang next year. Thanks again for your invitation.

Sincerely,

Invitation to Speak

Dear Jon Larson,

Thank you for your invitation to speak to your fund-raising committee about our success last year. Unfortunately, I have been scheduled to lead our sales meeting in Atlanta that week. I would have enjoyed discussing our problems, solutions, and eventual success of last year's campaign. Perhaps Ron Lentler can help you. He was involved in all the details and could offer many suggestions. I sincerely appreciate your asking me.

With regards,

Join a Group

Dear Mr. Adams:

I appreciate your asking me to join the Morgan Hill Toastmasters. I was a member of the Toastmasters a number of years ago but dropped out because of conflicts with my tax work.

I am new in town, am buying a new house, and have a new job. With all this piling up on me, I don't believe I could do my fair share as a participating member.

I will keep your kind invitation in mind, and hope to join you at a later date. Thank you for asking me.

Sincerely,

Dear Mr. Rogers:

Thank you for inviting me to join the Delta Cost Accountants group. I am sure the monthly meeting to discuss mutual problems and solutions would be most helpful.

I have been on the job here only four weeks and am up to my ears learning the job and cleaning up the backlog of work. I would like, therefore, to decline your invitation at this time. After another year, please contact me again. I think the group is an excellent idea.

Sincerely,

Victory Celebration

Dear Joan,

Thank you for your invitation to Dan and me to celebrate the Viking's conference victory at your house.

If we had not promised the AOPi sorority that we would chaperone their ski club that day, we would be there.

Sincerely,

Football Game

Dear Bob,

I am sorry Barbara and I cannot attend the Cal-Stanford big game with you this year. We have a previous commitment in Los Angeles that weekend, but I will have the radio tuned in. I am sure you can find another couple to share the excitement and the tickets you won.

Again, we appreciate your thoughtfulness.

Sincerely,

REQUEST FOR INFORMATION OR MATERIAL

Refusing a request for information, of whatever nature, should be done politely. The request may be inconvenient or seem useless or silly to the receiver of the request, but the fact that the requester has gone to the trouble to single out one company or person indicates that the request is of importance to the person making it. Respect for and a show of interest in the person asking for information can go a long way toward building goodwill for the organization or person answering the request — or refusing the request.

Information Not Available

Dear Mr. Newton:

At the present time, Tractor Mechanics, Inc. does not have an accounting system program for its members, but we did in the past and would certainly recommend it for your review. If you are interested, contact Mr. Robert Strong at Menson Accounting Systems. Their address is 000 Wescott Way, Portland, MA 00000.

We are in the process of compiling the type of data you requested. Initially, this information will be made available only to those who participated in the survey. It is hoped that the survey will be completed by the end of the year.

Sincerely,

Dear Ms. Darlington:

We are enclosing a tally of the monthly purchases you made during 19__ . We are sorry we cannot provide details of the monthly totals, but our accounting system does not retain itemized purchases beyond one month.

I am sorry the information is not as complete as you asked for, but I hope it will be of some help to you.

Sincerely,

Item Not Available

Dear Mr. Johnston:

We would be happy to comply with your request for a sample letter asking for contributions. However, Honourman Medical Center has just now received its full tax-exempt status, making us eligible for tax-deductible donations. Because we were not tax-exempt until now, we have not had an active fund-raising program and are only now reaching the final stage of our plans.

I would suggest that you contact Mr. George Appleton, Foundation Director, Boulder River Hospital, for sample letters. Boulder River has had an established and active fund-raising program **for** several years and could provide you with several examples. The address is: 111 Round Plaza, Boulder, California 00000.

If I may be of further assistance, please let me know.

Sincerely,

Dear Miss Conrad:

We would like to grant your request for twenty-five copies of our booklet, *Live Oak Tree Diseases*, but we have run out and will not print any more this year.

To help you now, we suggest you write to the Superintendent of Documents, Washington, D. C. and ask for publications on this topic.

Cordially,

Dear Professor Roland:

Your enlightening comments on our series of sales letters are greatly appreciated. We plan to use many of your suggestions as we continue the series.

This series was planned for a list of advertisers with only a few allocated to instructional institutions. The value of these letters as teaching material rather surprised us. We therefore do not have available the number of copies you requested, but two copies have been mailed to you today. Perhaps you can circulate these or make copies for your students.

After using these letters in class, we would appreciate your views on how to improve them for use as teaching material.

Very Sincerely,

Dear Mr. Woodward:

I have read your letter requesting copies of drawings for the Number 5543 Ward Press. I am sorry we no longer have these drawings.

I would suggest you contact Mr. Leonard Brown, Managing Director, Society of Historical Businesses, 000 - 15th Street, Washington, D. C. 00000. His telephone number is 000-000-0000.

The Society has many drawings of machinery manufactured in the 1800s.

Sincerely,

APPLICATION FOR PERSONAL CREDIT

Always show an interest in the person applying for credit. Even if credit is refused now, potential future sales should never be overlooked. Let the customer know that thorough consideration was given to the application. Then state the reasons for refusal, clearly but politely. End with the fact that cash purchases or layaway plans are available or that credit will probably be available later.

Lack of Information

Dear Mr. Ames:

Thank you for your interest in Rankin's and your request for a line of credit.

Based on the information you supplied us and that from our normal sources, we are unable to grant you the open credit you requested. If you can supply us with additional references, however, and current financial statements, please do so, and we will be happy to reconsider our disappointing decision.

While waiting for this additional information we will welcome any orders accompanied by a cash payment.

Sincerely,

Dear Mrs. Lawn:

Thank you for requesting a Capper's charge account. We appreciate this expression of your goodwill.

As you probably know, a routine credit investigation is the usual procedure before new accounts are opened. Since the available information in support of your credit application is incomplete, we shall appreciate your assistance.

When you have a convenient moment, will you please call at the Credit Office on the second floor? No doubt you can furnish the information we need to reconsider your request.

We are looking forward to talking with you, and welcome this opportunity to meet you personally.

Yours sincerely,

Lack of Work Record

Dear Ms. Alward:

We appreciate your interest in Bowen's Department Store and your application for a credit card.

Your lack of a permanent work record at this time prevents us from approving your application. Your part-time work references are good, and as soon as you establish a permanent work record, we will be happy to reconsider granting you credit.

Sincerely,

Short Employment

Dear Ms. Lindstrom:

Thank you for your recent application for a charge account at Fordham's. Your application has received careful consideration and we find the information furnished by you does not meet our requirements for granting credit. Perhaps in the future, when circumstances have changed, we can again consider your request for a charge account. Our decision is based on the following reasons:

Length of employment
No credit file

I regret we could not be more helpful at this time. Meanwhile, our quality selections are available for cash, and you can take advantage of our layaway service.

Sincerely,

Slow Pay

Dear Mr. Snowden:

Thank you for your credit application. We appreciate your interest in Abbott's.

For your own protection, however, we feel that your credit approval should be delayed for another six months. By then you should have less difficulty making prompt payments on your open accounts.

Until then, remember that cash purchases have no monthly interest charge.

Please contact us again in February.

Sincerely,

New in Area

Dear Mr. Lawrence:

Thank you for your interest in Matson's Department Store and your request for a credit account.

We notice that you have been in this area only a few weeks and have just begun to work here. When you have lived and worked here a little longer and have established a bank account, we will be happy to review your application. We hope to open a credit account for you when you apply again in another two months.

In the meantime, please take advantage of our Annual Sale next month. We carry many lines of quality merchandise, and are especially proud of our men's shop.

Please let us hear from you again.

Sincerely,

Dear Mrs. Ballard:

Thank you for your recent request for a charge account at Ford's. Your confidence in our store is appreciated.

Although we are not in a position to open an account for you just now, perhaps we will be able to do so when your residency has been established for another six months.

Meanwhile, please visit us often and enjoy the many conveniences of shopping at Ford's. Every effort will be made to serve you well.

Sincerely,

Current Information Lacking

Dear Ms. Esthers:

We appreciate your request for a Golden credit card.

It is a standard procedure with all companies issuing credit cards to check on the applicant's past payment record. We have found that you usually require more time to pay than our 25-day terms allow.

If we have not received current information, perhaps you could furnish us with the names of two or three firms from which you are now buying on credit. We will be happy then to reconsider your request for a credit card.

Meanwhile, we find that more and more of our customers prefer to pay cash and thereby avoid the high cost of interest on unpaid balances.

Sincerely,

APPLICATION FOR BUSINESS CREDIT

Future business must not be lost when refusing business credit. Be appreciative of the applicant's request. State any favorable elements in the application before explaining clearly the reasons for refusal. End with encouragement and suggestions that he or she may use to qualify in the future.

Financial Condition

Dear Mr. Colson:

Thank you for your application for credit at Barrow's. We appreciate your interest.

Your personal references are exceptionally good, and your record of hard work indicates that your business prospects are good for the near future. At present, however, your financial condition only partially meets Barrow's requirements. Therefore, we cannot extend the $5000 open credit you requested.

Please come in and talk to me at your convenience. I am sure we can set up a program of gradually increasing credit that will benefit both of us. Meanwhile, remember that deliveries on cash purchases are made within two days.

Let me hear from you soon. We are interested in your business venture.

Sincerely,

Credit Limited

Dear Mr. Snelling:

We appreciate receiving your order of January 29 for 50,000 boxes.

This is our slack season and we would like to receive several orders of this size. However, you have only been in business since October, and we feel that until we have had a little more experience with you, your open line of credit should be limited to $5000. This limit can be raised as your business improves and expands.

We hope this is satisfactory as a starter, and we thank you for the opportunity to be of service to you.

Sincerely,

Company Procedure —Late Payment

Dear Ms. Arthur:

We received the copy of the past due freight bill No. 278-089799 that you sent Wednesday, November 21. We have matched it with our purchase order and will mail it today to Central Freight Payment, Inc. in Atlanta, Georgia for payment.

Although the bill is overdue because we did not receive the original bill, our corporate procedure requires that Central Freight pay the bill. This procedure speeds payment in practically all instances and includes an audit of all paid freight bills. We cannot write you a check from our local plant as you have requested.

We are sorry for the delay. You should have your money in less than a week.

Sincerely,

Guarantor Needed

Dear Mr. Almond:

We greatly appreciate the order you gave our Mr. Robbins. You will find that we have reason to be proud of our quality products.

We want to work with you and help you get established, but from the information we have been able to gather, you appear to be undercapitalized, which would make it difficult for you to meet payments on our terms.

One temporary solution we might suggest is for you to find a person or firm that would guarantee your open account with us. We have found this arrangement to work well with other customers until they become established. This could take care of your immediate needs. Later, we can work together on other arrangements.

Please let us hear from you soon.

Sincerely,

Previous Poor Pay

Dear Mr. Pappas:

It is pleasing to learn that you are still interested in Allen's high quality tools. We received your order on October 22.

You may recall that when you last purchased goods from us, we had a difficult time getting payment from you. In fact, some of your account was turned over to Dun & Bradstreet's collection department.

We realize, however, that times and conditions change, and we should probably not be concerned. To relieve the concern we do have, please send us a few current credit references and a recent statement of your financial condition.

If you are in a rush for the tools you ordered, please send us a check for $928.50. We still maintain the prompt delivery service you are familiar with.

Thank you for considering us again, and we hope to hear from you soon.

Cordially,

Bad Risk

Note that this letter follows an outline nearly the reverse of that suggested in the **How to Do It** section.

Dear Mr. Bankhead:

I am being completely honest when I say that many of our customers prefer to pay cash. This relieves them of any anxiety about having to make late payment charges. I would like to suggest this method to you, because, as hard as I have tried, I just can't find a way to add you to our list of credit customers at this time.

The information we have gathered indicates that your payments have consistently been getting further and further behind during the past year. This may have been a bad year for you, but we cannot see adding to your outstanding debts. We hope that conditions soon improve for you.

We do, however, appreciate your considering us as a supplier. We will be most happy to do business with you on a cash-with-order-basis. You will find both our service and products outstanding.

Sincerely,

Bad Risk — No Hope

Dear Mr. Blair:

We appreciate your interest in Sampson's and your desire to establish credit with us.

However, based upon reports from our numerous sources of credit information, we can make shipments to you only when cash is received with the order.

We are sorry for this, but we are sure you understand. If we can be of any further service to you, please let us know.

Sincerely,

Franchise Refused

Dear Mr. Goodall:

We greatly appreciate your interest in obtaining an American Chicken franchise. Our present expansion rate exceeds our most optimistic expectations.

We, of course, make credit checks on all potential franchisers, and our information indicates that you might have difficulty meeting our payment terms for merchandise and supplies to be purchased from us. These payment terms must be met as well as those for the expected loan on the purchase price.

Past experience can be temporary, and we hope your financial condition improves soon. Perhaps we can review another application from you in the near future.

Sincerely,

Will Not Change Prior Understanding

Dear Mr. Donaldson:

We are very sorry to learn of your unsatisfactory experience with our Mr. Hanson's letters, but the bearings that we manufactured and delivered to you in Waterford became your property.

When Mr. Hanson and I visited you on February 17, 19__, there was no question that these bearings were left on consignment at your Waterford warehouse until 19__ and were used at that time by your customer, Central Trailer. The only unanswered question on your part was the problem of your pending bankruptcy and when you would be able to settle all the outstanding items. This was stated in your letter of February 24, 19__.

As far as we are concerned, Mr. Donaldson, these bearings were purchased by you and used by your customer. Our position has not changed, and this invoice, No. 43332, in the amount of $3,459.90, is still outstanding.

Sincerely,

Credit Information Available Elsewhere

Dear Mr. Bagley:

Referring to your letter of May 25, 19__ , if you phone Mr. Apply at our Billings, Montana plant (000-000-0000) he will be able to give you general information about our credit experience with Zenno Corporation. He has credit responsibility for that account.

It is our policy not to provide written information about our customers. However, I am sure Mr. Apply can help you.

Sincerely,

DONATION

Start this type of refusal with a thank-you, apology, or complimentary statement about the organization or event you are asked to help. Offer a plausible reason for the refusal, and end with alternative help or at least best wishes for success.

Funds Limited

Dear Mrs. Alberts:

I am sorry I cannot contribute to the Children's Fund this year.

I am involved in several charities, including some for disadvantaged children. Your needs are real, I recognize, but my funds are limited and I have to make my own choices about the distribution of those funds.

I wish you well in your program to help these children.

Sincerely,

Use of Name in Fund Raising

Dear Mrs. Lansing:

Please accept my sincere regrets for having to decline the use of my name as a sponsor of Belmont Boys Home. I feel a little insincere about sponsoring something I am not actively involved in. I work with a number of charities now and just don't have the time to consider any more at present.

Your cause is worthy, I know, and I wish you well in your endeavor to obtain prominent names for your sponsor's list. Thank you for asking me.

Sincerely,

Company Policy

Dear Ms. Wells:

Thank you for your recent letter requesting a donation to the Redwood Girls Club. In a company like ours, with fifty-five divisions throughout the country, it is impossible to support the many worthy causes in each area. Instead, the company makes an annual contribution to the United Way Fund, which in turn supports many organizations.

I am sorry to have to tell you that because of this policy we are unable to contribute locally to the Redwood Girls Club. It is a fine project, and we wish you great success.

Cordially yours,

Dear Mr. Sundston:

We wish it were possible to provide door prizes for your fund raising meeting. Your cause is commendable. We find, however, that as a national company, we are asked quite often for donations of merchandise for worthy organizations. We feel that if we give to one good cause, we should give equally to all good causes. I am sure you recognize that this is not practical, and therefore we do not make door prizes available.

Perhaps we can help in another way: by advertising in our store window or preparing an advertisement for the newspaper. Let us know if we can help in this way.

Sincerely,

Budget Limitation

Dear Mr. Bates:

Your Junior Chamber of Commerce *Sports Annual* is a commendable project. We do budget for special advertising, but unfortunately, the money has been spent for this year. I am sure you can understand that we must operate by our budget to stay in business.

If you plan to make this publication an annual event, contact us earlier next year. We will try to consider you in next year's budget. The Junior Chamber of Commerce will receive our full help and co-operation.

Sincerely,

Disagree with Charity Project

Dear Ms. Eggmont:

I agree that St. John's University is badly in need of a new gym. I think, however, that this is an inappropriate time to request contributions for a building fund. The basketball team has not won a local conference championship in twelve years. I recognize that the gym is used for many activities besides basketball, but basketball is all the public hears about — and they haven't heard much about that in recent years.

When the team has won a local conference championship and a state championship and is headed for a national meet — then you can go to an enthused public and meet little resistance. Big donors will also give more willingly at that time. Everyone loves a winner.

This may seem an unkind attitude toward a school in need of a new gym, but I feel that a team must earn its right to a new facility. Best wishes for success in your campaign.

Sincerely,

EMPLOYMENT

The first two letters that follow are standard letters rejecting an applicant for employment. Each can be used for almost any situation or position. They show an interest in the reader even though the reasons for rejection are general and vague. Both could be made better by adding, before the last paragraph, an explanation that covers the particular applicant. Whether or not this is necessary depends upon the likelihood of wishing to consider the applicant in the future.

The third letter is written for a particular applicant and explains with specific details why the applicant is being rejected.

Position Unsuited

Dear Mr. Wilson:

Your interest in Stanford Corporation is appreciated. I read your resumé with considerable interest and it has been carefully evaluated by our personnel and marketing departments.

Your qualifications are excellent, but I regret that we do not now have a position open that fits your obvious abilities.

We thank you for considering Stanford Corporation, and I know you will find a suitable position soon.

Sincerely,

Dear Mr. Jones:

Thank you very much for giving us the opportunity to consider you for employment.

After carefully considering your background and qualifications, we find that we do not have an appropriate position for you at the present time. Should one develop, we shall be in touch with you.

We appreciate your interest in Evans Corporation and wish you well.

Sincerely,

Dear Mr. Lattler:

Thank you for sending your resumé and giving us the opportunity to consider you for the accounting manager's position.

Our personnel and financial officers have thoroughly reviewed your qualifications. They are excellent but do not quite fit the position we have in mind at the present time. Your technical experience is notable, especially in the area of tax accounting, but right now we need someone who is stronger in supervisory experience.

We will keep your file active, and when promotions create an opening to fit your qualifications, we will write or call you.

Yours sincerely,

Personal Information

Dear Ms. Andrews:

I am sorry we cannot provide any information on Miss Jean Peterson except that she was employed here from October 1974 until December 1978. We treat personal data about our employees as confidential material.

Sincerely,

Dear Mr. Culver:

Your letter to Mr. James Purser was referred to me for reply.

I'm sorry to inform you that we cannot supply you with the information you requested. Jones & Hamilton does not permit the release of personnel data.

Thank you, nevertheless, for your interest in J & H.

Sincerely,

CUSTOMER ADJUSTMENTS

Customer adjustments must be made with tact. It is difficult to refuse the customer's request while retaining his or her goodwill. Open with something agreeable, a point you can agree upon or a thank-you for letting you explain your point of view. The explanation that follows must be clear and definite but not curt. Take enough time and space to make a complete and logical explanation. Completeness is important to the reader. Then let the reader know what he or she can do, or what you will do to make an adjustment satisfactory to the reader.

Damaged Product

Dear Miss Gerald:

We agree that a watch running only part of the time is useless. And we guarantee trouble-free operation of Serra watches for a year from the purchase date.

Your watch has been thoroughly examined by our service department. They report a dent near the winding stem, perhaps too small for you to have noticed. This indicates physical damage to the case which is not covered by our guarantee. The dent is deep enough to touch the main spring regulator when it expands in warm weather. This can cause the occasional stopping of the watch.

Although not covered by our guarantee, we can repair your watch at factory cost and extend the warranty for a year from the repair date. The cost to you is only $8.50.

If you wish to have the repairs made, please return the enclosed card and attach your check for $8.50. We will repair your watch and return it promptly.

Sincerely,

Cash Discount

Dear Mr. Allsworth:

Thank you for your letter of February 28. You ask about our billing you for the 1 percent cash discount you took with your payment on February 17.

As you know, our terms for several years have been 1 percent 10 days, net 30 days. We offer these terms because we save interest on borrowed capital when we receive cash within 10 days. This is a savings we can pass on to our customers, but we have no savings to pass on when payment is received after the 10-day period.

The dollar amount involved in this case is small, only $32.10, but when multiplied by the number of our customers, the total is significant.

Our policy has always been to treat all customers equally well, with discounts as well as service and reliable merchandise. I am hopeful that you will see the consistent fairness in our bill for $32.10, and that we can both benefit from our 1 percent 10-day cash discount policy.

Sincerely,

Special Product

Dear Mr. Mills:

Your memo requesting credit for the gear housing we made for you in October has been given to me by our sales engineer.

Although we realize that machinery rebuilding plans are sometimes changed at levels above that of the purchasing agent, we are sorry we cannot accept the gear housing for credit. It was cast to your specifications and there is no market for it among our other customers.

If we do get an inquiry for this type of casting we will get in touch with you immediately. I'm sorry we can't do more for you.

Cordially,

Poor Workmanship

Dear Mr. Wilson:

We are sorry to learn that your application of Thickwall to your house was not completely to your satisfaction.

Applying Thickwall is a specialized job, and that is why we request all our dealers to make this part of our warranty clear to each customer. Mr. Bob Johnson, salesman at your dealer, Appley Building Supplies, recommended application by John Sanders, a specialist who works with Appley Building Supplies. Our warranty states clearly that Thickwall must be applied by a specialist.

I have talked to Bob Johnson and he suggests that John Sanders inspect your house and make recommendations for correcting the work. Mr. Sanders can then make necessary repairs at a reasonable cost or perhaps suggest how you can make the repairs yourself.

Please talk to Mr. Bob Johnson at Appley Building Supplies. I am sure you can work out a satisfactory arrangement for getting the application of Thickwall corrected.

Sincerely,

Slow-Selling Product

Dear Mr. Lunsford:

Thank you for writing us about the Country Gentleman chairs you purchased on September 3, and wish to return for credit. These are the chairs you ordered. In fact, you paid for them early and took our 2 percent cash discount.

As I understand the situation, you wish to return them because of slow sales. I am sorry that we cannot accept the chairs for credit. We discontinued this line six months ago, but most of our dealers found them to be good sellers during the winter promotion we sponsored. We are sending you additional promotional material and ideas that proved successful with others. If there is anything else we can do to help you sell these chairs, please let our salesman, John Ballard, know. He will be calling on you next month, and will have some helpful suggestions.

With regards,

OTHER LETTERS OF DECLINATION

The following letters cover a variety of refusals, from sample letters to a church volunteer. They follow the general outline: agreeing with the writer or showing appreciation for the writer's interest, offering a plausible reason for refusing, and ending with an alternative or an expression of goodwill.

Untested Sample Letters

Dear Mr. Adams:

We have received your request for sample fund-raising letters.

Even though Emerson Society has had an ongoing development program for several years, it is only recently that we have developed direct mail fund-raising letters. Since these letters have not been thoroughly tested in terms of response, I would be reluctant to offer them as teaching material.

Thank you for your interest.

Sincerely,

Special Assignment

Dear Mr. Wilshire:

I deeply regret the amount of time that has passed before responding to your letter of November 26, 19__.

After careful consideration and the exploration of some possibilities, I find that we cannot handle this particular assignment.

Please accept my best wishes for your success in this endeavor.

Sincerely yours,

Business Meeting — Unnecessary

My Dear Mr. Ames:

Mr. Sanders has carefully considered your request for a meeting to discuss a change in your property settlement. If a personal meeting would be of benefit to you, he would be happy to arrange an appointment. He has asked me to write and tell you that he believes another meeting at this time would not be of any help to you.

With regards,

Magazine Subscribers Limited

Dear Mr. Ludwig:

A copy of the first quarter 19__ issue of *Semiconductor Science* is being mailed to you. Please accept it with our compliments.

Your interest in our publication is appreciated, but we discourage subscription by those who are not directly engaged in the production of semiconductors. This quarterly manual is highly technical and expensive to produce. We find that those outside the industry do not continue their subscriptions, and this makes the printing difficult to schedule and unduly costly.

I am sure you understand our position, and we sincerely thank you for your interest in *Semiconductor Science.*

Sincerely yours,

Publication — Too Specialized

Dear Mr. Saunders:

Thank you very much for giving us the opportunity of considering your manuscript, "Tombs of Egypt."

We regret that we cannot extend publishing interest in your material because it is too specialized to fit into our present publishing program.

We wish you success in finding the right publishing house for your work and do appreciate your thinking of Wilson Publishers.

Sincerely,

Publication — Editorial Program

Dear Mr. Smythe:

Thank you very much for inquiring about Wilson Publishers' possible interest in your proposal for a textbook: *Essentials of Psychology.*

I very much regret that we must decline the opportunity of publishing this interesting work. Our editorial program is, unfortunately, unable to accept an addition of this kind.

Please understand that this response to your idea is the reaction of only one company. Opinions vary widely among publishers, and I hope you will continue to develop your material towards a successful publication. I also ask you to keep Wilson Publishers in mind for any other textbook ideas you may have.

Sincerely,

Publication — Needs Reworking

Dear Professor Nelson:

Enclosed are three reviews of your proposed COST ACCOUNTING text. I share them with you for the benefit of the text's development.

Based on the reviews, you have the basis for a fine text. While the concept of a brief book is sound, it is my opinion that it does not go far enough, which limits the value and marketability of the text.

Should you be willing to expand the text's coverage and appeal, I would be pleased to reconsider the text for publication. I would also appreciate receiving more information on how your text would compare to existing competing books.

Cordially,

Refusing a Volunteer

Dear Ms. Lester,

We appreciate very much your volunteering to head the Junior Youth Fellowship for the coming year. Looking at the overall program, however, we believe you could serve the Church better working with Mrs. Holbrook and the Senior Youth Fellowship. She is in need of someone with your background and willingness.

We hope you will consider working with Mrs. Holbrook. The Seniors need your helping hands.

Yours in Christ,

Freight Claim

Gentlemen:

Please refer to your Claim No. 00000:

Our records show your bill of lading 0000 signed August 29, 19__ . Your claim is dated June 20, 19__ .

Section 2(b) of the Bill of Lading Contract Terms and Conditions requires that claims be filed in writing within nine months from the date of delivery or, in case of failure to make delivery, within nine months after a reasonable time for delivery has passed.

We are sorry we cannot honor your claim. We have checked all possible sources for a prior filing, and can find no record of an earlier claim related to this shipment.

If, however, you can provide proof of an earlier filing, we will be happy to reconsider your claim.

Sincerely,

3

SALES

A sales letter is only one of many factors in the sale of a product or service. A need must exist — or be imagined; the customer's interest must be aroused and a choice must be made from competing salespersons and products. A sales letter probably won't accomplish all these things, but it can persuade the reader that he or she will be helped by buying the product or service.

One technique for persuasion is to use POWER words. Using words to make people DO things is the key to business success. Listed here is a sampling of power words, effective in pepping up a sales letter:

able	free	powerful
absolute	great	professional
advantage	guarantee	proved
brilliant	hard-sell	quality
confidence	help	quickly
controlled	immediate	results
delighted	impelling	satisfaction
detail	insight	scientific
different	instant	solved
economical	know	stunning
effective	largest	successful
electronic	latest	super
emphasis	lowest cost	today
expert	money-making	tremendous
extensive	new	value
fact	now	volume
fair	oldest	you
flare	persuasive	yours

As will be observed in the models, sales letters also take advantage of visual aids. These include such devices as CAPITAL LETTERS, "quotation marks," underlined words, dashes —, dots . . . , short paragraphs, phrases punctuated as sentences, indented paragraphs, exclamation points, and postscripts.

The purpose is to hold the attention of the reader, who thus becomes eager to read on to find out what is interesting enough to earn this special presentation.

Insurance sales letters and advertisements often emphasize fear — fear of what *could* happen — so you had better be prepared with *our* insurance coverage. Fear is one basic appeal. Other basic appeals, which are general themes or topics running through the letter, include love, pride, greed, ambition, sex, hate, and loyalty. An emotional appeal is usually more effective than an intellectual presentation.

A word of caution when appealing to these various emotional feelings: don't belittle the reader, exaggerate, trick the reader, be flippant, or abuse competitors. A little puffing of your item or service is good, but respect the intelligence of your reader.

However intelligent the reader, he or she has a limited attention span. Cover only a few selling points in each letter (or preferably only one). Trying to tell everything only confuses the reader.

What you say should be directed toward the audience you have chosen. Sell an elitist magazine to college educated people, sell farming equipment to ranchers, sell wrenches to mechanics. Your audience can be targeted geographically down to specific postal Zip Code numbers.

The reader will want to know *why* he or she should buy; not what the product or service can do, but what it will do *for the reader*. This statement can be strengthened by a guarantee. Present a testimonial from a well-known person, offer a free trial period or a money-back guarantee. Let the reader know you are interested in his or her welfare.

The proper length of a sales letter is debatable. One theory is that no one reads past the first page, so don't make it any longer. Another theory is that if the first page gets the reader's attention, the fourth page will clinch the sale. One standard suggestion is to tell the story and then stop, regardless of length. Another standard is to tell only enough to make the reader ask for more information. The proper length, in the final analysis, will be determined by the writer's best judgment of the presentation to which the majority of the selected readers will respond.

Selling the reader must begin with a strong statement of interest to your particular audience, be he or she a druggist, accountant, housewife, business executive, dog lover, or doctor. Also, the first sentence must relate to the statements that follow.

There are many types of attention-getting opening sentences:

- Reference to a previous personal contact
- A sentence encompassing who, what, when, where, why
- A question
- An unusual remark
- A story
- Invoking a well-known personality
- A well-known quotation
- Using the reader's name (if not obviously inserted into a blank space that doesn't fit the name)
- Use of gimmicks, such as enclosing a stamp, pencil, or address labels; or a question on the envelope that is answered inside

Endings are also important. Having presented your sales story and gotten the reader interested, he or she must be moved to action. Tell the reader exactly what to do and when: "Mail the enclosed card today"; "This offer ends June 30"; or "Phone us right now at 888-888-8888." Of most importance, make the action easy: "Phone us toll-free at 800-000-0000"; "Use the enclosed postage-paid envelope"; or "We are open 7 days a week."

When reviewing your written letter, a few checkpoints may be helpful:

- Are the sales points presented clearly and simply?
- Are enough *facts* presented to make the letter convincing?
- Are the strong points emphasized in short, two-or-three-line paragraphs?
- Is the appeal enthusiastic? A great salesperson is one who sets into motion the contagious emotion of enthusiasm.

How to Do It

1. Use an effective attention-getting opening.
2. Develop a central selling point.
3. Be vivid and specific in talking up the product.
4. Present proofs of your statements.
5. Close by moving the reader to specific action.

Model Openers

The following are ideas and suggestions for sales letter openers:

It's your money that's involved, and the stakes are HIGH!

Here's an indispensable invention for anyone who . . .

Strength in numbers may be good for the military, but not for the fashion-conscious woman. Barbara's Exclusive Fashions promise what the name implies.

This letter is unlike any we have written before.

Select any three books from the list below. I'll send you two of them *free*.

If you're not sure you want _____, I can understand.

If we have selected our prospects as carefully as we think, you qualify on two accounts.

Have you looked at mountain property and failed to buy because . . . ?

We would like you to select any three important professional books — value to $72 — for only 99¢ each.

We nurses can never know enough about IV therapy, can we?

I wonder if you have ever had an experience like this one —

Here are nine hard-sell secrets to triple your advertising results.

This may be your last chance to . . .

You're hard to find, Mr. Anderson.

Levitz has opened a great new store in . . .

Just a little note to say HELLO, and to let you know what's happening at Todd Valley.

A mortgage is a wonderful thing.

You don't know me from Eve.

Today I feel like a salty sailor.

I feel a little like the flinty old mule skinner.

Has your eye ever been caught by a picture so beautiful you couldn't look away?

Mark Twain once remarked, "Always do right. This will gratify some people and astonish the rest."

The two most abused words in manufacturing sales are *quality* and *service*.

This letter will keep you from being fined . . . severely penalized . . . or deprived of your livelihood under the 19— Tax Reform Law.

You can well imagine the kind of quandary we are in.

Would you like an estimate of the present value of your home?

The average home is now for sale every three or four years.

You couldn't have chosen a better time to request the enclosed booklet.

I am most grateful to loyal customers like you who have made 19— the greatest year in our history.

We live in an age in which there seems to be a club for just about every purpose you might imagine.

The San Francisco area has long been known for its cosmopolitan tastes.

You probably get a lot of mail like this — and it goes in the round file — but don't be too hasty!

Do you know Socrates' chief attribute? Pertinacious curiosity — and with it he came to represent the highest achievement of Greek civilization. This quest for answers has drawn Zellwell Chemicals into the search for relief from the common cold.

You can buy a Stone's Lifetime battery today, next month, or probably ten years from now. But not at our special price of $55.20. That price ends February 28.

Have you ever looked in the mirror in the early morning and said, "There has to be a better way"? We have said that too. And we can help you. Jones Correspondence Courses can prepare you . . .

Did you know that the average person uses a mere 10% of his or her brain power? Why not double that, or even triple it? You can. Our new book tells you how.

So many of us are tired of the day-to-day dull routine of a salaried job. Now you can do something about it! Chicken Little Franchises offers . . .

Too many expenses have doubled in recent months. Why not double your income? Our training courses has doubled the salaries of a great many men and women. It can do the same for you.

As chairman of the Board of Trustees, I'd like to personally invite you to . . .

When General Electric calls on us for information, that is something to be proud of.

Wilcox and Associates has changed its name. We thought you might be interested in the story.

Model Closings

Here is a list of suggestions to spark the reader into action:

So do the right thing for yourself — mail the card today.

Your credit is good. Just tell us what you want.

Won't you take advantage of it *now* — to put a quick stop to cost-ly losses?

Save yourself some time. Just initial this letter and return it in the business reply envelope enclosed.

Allen Albright, a fellow you are going to like, will be around Tuesday morning to show you samples and to write your order.

Your copy of this interesting publication is ready for you. Just initial and mail the enclosed card.

Send no money. Simply mail the card.

We take all the risk. You enjoy the food.

This letter is your guarantee. Keep it but send us the card — today.

The enclosed order blank should be mailed immediately.

Do not delay — send the order blank now.

Simply check the card and put it in the mail today.

Remove the coupon below and mail it with your order at once.

Mail your check today in the convenient envelope enclosed.

We've cut all the red tape — simply mail the card.

Break out of the summer slump. Return the order blank right away.

Don't write a letter. The enclosed check-off card is for your convenience.

Before you put it aside, sign and return the card.

Just sign the card and have your secretary mail it promptly.

Our supply is limited. Act now!

Send no money. If not satisfied, don't pay.

There are no strings attached to this offer. It is simple. Just mail the enclosed, postpaid card.

Put the card in the mail to start the ball rolling.

It's your move. Telegraph orders are filled overnight.

If for any reason you're dissatisfied, simply return . . . and owe absolutely nothing.

When it comes to service, ABC Corporation produces results.

We will be happy to assist you. Please give us a call.

Investment — Real Estate

Dear Friend:

Although their incomes have climbed during the passing years, many people today are living beyond their means. Some try to help themselves by taking on extra work, but there is a limit to what a person can earn in an eight- or even twelve-hour day.

An excellent solution is to make a sound investment that will provide enough READY CASH for increasing future needs. Listed below are a few of the more popular types of investments:

STOCK MARKET . . . . Considered somewhat unstable, a speculation on the general economy

SAVINGS BANKS . . . . Yields up to ___% annually: the bank then often takes YOUR money and invests it in Real Estate

REAL ESTATE . . . . One of the safest, surest investments that can offer substantial profits if the following rules are observed!

1. LOCATION . . . . As close to a MAJOR CITY as possible

2. POPULATION . . . . City requires a past and present history of growth

3. HIGH GRADE
   PROPERTY . . . . Not desert or swamp, but good, usable land

4. UTILITIES . . . . Water, roads, electricity, phones, gas

5. PRICED RIGHT . . . . Buy UNDER comparable land prices, if possible

We would like the opportunity to prove to you that even as little as $___ monthly may bring you substantial returns over the years. Billions have been made with land located in the path of progess. In these days of high taxes, the opportunity *to keep big profits* is due to the many favorable tax concessions allowable in Real Estate.

Mailing the enclosed card may open your eyes to a new path leading to attractive long-range profit opportunities for you and your family in years to come.

Sincerely,

Business Magazine

Dear Executive:

This letter and enclosure offers you an opportunity to discover if you have been missing a source of invaluable information —*Small BUSINESS REPORT*.

The best way for you to judge this would be for us to place a copy of *Small BUSINESS REPORT* in your hands, so that you can decide for yourself if this report is applicable and beneficial to you and your business.

And that is precisely what we have done. Please read the enclosed complimentary issue of *Small BUSINESS REPORT*. If you feel that it may provide you with positive solutions to your business problems, *return the enclosed reservation card*.

Then, to further prove that this report will give you practical how-to advice, we will send you the next current issue. At the same time, a one-year introductory trial subscription will be entered in your name. You risk nothing and there is no obligation to subscribe.

If, after reading the next issue, you agree that *Small BUSINESS* is the kind of business publication that can be of use to you, you may pay our invoice of $____ and receive eleven additional monthly issues of *Small BUSINESS REPORT*.

If by chance *Small BUSINESS REPORT* does not fill your needs, simply write "cancel" on our invoice, and return it. No more issues will be sent . . . you owe nothing . . . you risk nothing. And the issues you have received are yours to keep with our compliments — our way of saying thank you for looking over this offer.

Fair enough? Then I urge you to mail your reservation form today. See for yourself — *Small BUSINESS REPORT can* make a dramatic bottom line difference in your business.

Sincerely,

Magazine — Elitist

Dear Mr. Deskins:

History teaches us that the punishment, indeed the price, for exceptional talent and intelligence is the indisputable fact of solitude.

But history also teaches that being alone is quite different from being lonely.

In fact, the mind's most ingenious revenge against its own limits is the limitless, joyful creation of mirrors — in music, in movies, in mathematics, in cities, and in great ideas.

I would like to invite you to experience firsthand the friction and intercourse of exceptional (but not necessarily similar) minds in the pages of Harper's Magazine.

In fact, out of 200 million Americans, fewer than 1 million read it.

But for those who do, Harper's is like a monthly visit from an exceptional array of companions; as such it can be both aggravating and exhilarating. And Unforgettable.

Since time is what all of us have the least of, I am enclosing a simple, postpaid trial subscription certificate.

You may examine your first issue and then cancel, if you like, at no cost whatsoever.

However, Harper's is so different from other magazines, I suspect you will decide you don't want to be without it.

Yours,

P.S. If you decide to join our select group of subscribers, you'll receive free a 19__ calendar consisting of twelve rare and handsome Edward Penfield reproductions. Our business people insisted I point out that the calendar will be sent immediately if payment is enclosed.

Mortgage Insurance

Dear Mr. Hodges:

A mortgage is a remarkable obligation.

Do you have a mortgage? Most families do. Few families could afford to live in their comfortable homes without a mortgage and its monthly payments spread out for twenty to thirty years.

You are making regular payments from your salary and your family is secure. But what would happen if suddenly you were no longer there? Who would continue the payments? Would the family continue to feel secure?

We have the answers. We can provide you with a simple insurance plan that in the event of your death will pay off the mortgage. Your family can continue living in their home. They can retain their feeling of security.

All this is available for only about one percent of your mortgage annually.

Surprising? Yes.

Simple? Yes.

Your neighborhood representative, Mr. Al Hoerner, will phone you soon to arrange a time to allow you to see how this plan works — how simple it is — and how inexpensive — especially when you consider the potential benefits.

Sincerely,

Homeowner's Insurance

Dear Neighbor:

YOUR HOMEOWNER'S INSURANCE POLICY WILL SOON BE DUE FOR RENEWAL. BEFORE IT IS, PLEASE ASK YOURSELF THESE QUESTIONS:

DO I KNOW MY AGENT PERSONALLY?
DO I HAVE THE RIGHT KIND OF COVERAGE?
DO I HAVE THE RIGHT AMOUNT OF COVERAGE?
IS THE PRICE RIGHT?

IF ANY OF THE ABOVE QUESTIONS DISTURB YOU, PLEASE CALL ME FOR A RATE QUOTATION. THERE IS NO OBLIGATION, EVER.

Sincerely,

Thanks to George Spellman, State Farm insurance agent, Concord, California.

Health Insurance

Dear Mrs. Ashland:

You probably get a lot of mail like this.

And it goes right in the round file . . .

. . . But don't be too hasty!

Especially if you're the kind who lives dangerously and doesn't have a health plan — this could be a very important piece of mail for you. Vital!

If your present health plan pays less than $200 a day and you haven't looked it over lately, you might just take a good look at it and compare it to the plan we describe in the enclosed folder. The average daily hospital charge that Blue Cross pays is now running closer to $500 a day — and intensive care is well above that.

Surprised?

Some health plans (like yours, perhaps) pay a fixed amount for surgical and medical services and when health care costs go up, you're still getting the same benefits you had before. That means you pay the difference. And if they go up again — it's on you, again!

This Blue Cross health plan (ours) doesn't work that way. We pay on a percentage basis. And that means that when health care costs go up — your benefits go up right along with them. And Blue Cross pays the difference.

Now, isn't that better?

Read the enclosed folder carefully — then fill out the card and send it in. We want you to have the best possible health protection we can give you.

Sincerely,

Auto Insurance

Dear Mr. French:

JCPENNEY HAS A NEW WAY TO HELP YOU SAVE MONEY!

The next time you're in your favorite JCPenney store, look for something new: the Insurance Center operated by JCPenney Casualty Insurance Company. You'll find that it's the place where you can buy auto insurance at rates significantly below those charged by most other auto insurance companies.

But, in keeping with the long-established JCPenney tradition, price alone is not enough. Value is the ultimate measure . . . and we're sure you'll find that JCPenney Auto Insurance gives you the kind of value you've come to associate with the name JCPenney. We're confident that we can show you that not only can you buy for less, but you'll actually be getting more protection for your money, and more in the way of service too.

Lower cost. More protection. Better service. How can we do it? Modern, efficient marketing techniques is one reason . . . but the big reason is the drivers we insure. Because we want to be sure that we can always provide auto insurance at lower-than-average rates, we have to be careful to insure only better-than-average drivers. If you have a clean driving record to prove that you're a good, responsible driver . . . and the other drivers in your family measure up to that same high standard . . . you have a great deal to gain and nothing to lose by asking us for a personal rate quotation that will show you exactly how much you could save by switching to JCPenney Auto Insurance.

While not everyone will save money on our auto insurance, we estimate that our typical policyholder is saving from $30 to $50 a year.

If you can't wait to find out how much you could save by switching to JCPenney Auto Insurance, just pick up the phone and give us a call at any of the Insurance Centers listed. If you can give us the information called for on the enclosed request for rate quotation card, we can give you exact figures right while you're on the line.

If you're going to stop by to meet us, you can save yourself a little time by filling out the enclosed form in advance and bringing it in with you. Or, if you don't expect to be in a store soon and can't conveniently call us, just complete the form and drop it in the mail. In that case, we'll have the postman deliver your personal rate quotation.

Cordially,

Adapted, with permission from and thanks to JCPenney Casualty Insurance Company.

Book Club

Dear Writer:

SELECT ANY THREE BOOKS FROM THE ENCLOSED LIST.

I'LL SEND YOU TWO OF THEM *FREE* WHEN YOU BUY THE THIRD AT A HUGE DISCOUNT!

Regardless of the retail price, you pay only $5.95 for the third book.

THIS IS OUR GIFT TO YOU FOR BECOMING A MEMBER OF THE ONLY BOOK CLUB EXCLUSIVELY FOR WRITERS.

And . . . this is just the beginning of your FREE books. After buying four books as a Club member (at discounts up to 20%) you'll be eligible for our bonus·plan:

EVERY TIME YOU PURCHASE AN ADDITIONAL FOUR
BOOKS. . . . YOU SELECT A FIFTH BOOK
FREE!

Frankly, short of stealing, there probably isn't a more economical way of building a valuable library of outstanding writing books. And you do it without risk. The books you order today, as well as in the future, are covered by our unique NO-RISK Guarantee.

We know that occasionally a writer buys a book that doesn't quite fit his needs. But if you order such a book through the Club, you can return it within ten days. No questions . . . no bills . . . no orphan stuck on your bookshelf.

Sure . . . I know what you're thinking. Return the book and hassle with a computer for three months. But not with our Club. At Writer's Digest you deal with *people*.

HERE'S HOW YOUR BOOK CLUB MEMBERSHIP WORKS:

Every four to five weeks, you'll receive a Club bulletin listing over 40 books on various aspects of writing. This list will include a main selection and an alternate, both of which will be fully described.

If you want the featured book, do nothing. It will come to you automatically.

If you want the alternate selection . . . one of the 40 or so other titles . . . or no book at all . . . just return the selection card enclosed with your bulletin. That's it . . . EXCEPT FOR ONE BIG MONEY-SAVING EXTRA!

If you send your check or money order in advance for the books you want, they'll be shipped free of postage and handling. This benefit alone can save you a lot of dollars every year.

And remember: every year you'll be able to buy WRITER'S MARKET and PHOTOGRAPHER'S MARKET at a discount.

Pick up a pen and print the numbers of three books of your choice on the enclosed membership application.

Remember, you're getting over $40 worth of books for only $5.95.

Within a short time, you'll be receiving your books and current Club bulletin.

Join now! WRITER'S DIGEST BOOK CLUB can help you become a more successful writer.

Sincerely,

Real Estate — Homes

Dear Mr. and Mrs. Henshaw:

Another home SOLD . . . at 0000 Windmill Way, Saratoga. Please stop by and welcome your neighbors.

SOLD by Nolan Associates, your neighborhood realtor.

We offer top $$$ for our SELLERS • Speedy sales for our SELLERS • Personalized, professional service for our SELLERS • 98% of homes listed are SOLD!! • We don't just collect listings . . . We service what we list!

We offer speedy sales—courteous service—and a free evaluation of your home.

Please use the enclosed GOLD MARKET ANALYSIS CERTIFICATE for a market evaluation of your home.

Please phone today: NOLAN ASSOCIATES, 000 Hamilton Ave, Saratoga, FL 00000. Phone 000-000-0000.

Sincerely,

Dear Mr. and Mrs. Sutherland:

Peaceful . . .

Reaching a gentle rise overlooking a flowering meadow you come upon a secluded setting of prestigious homes. The tree-covered slopes are fenced and guarded, insuring protection and peace of mind.

The custom-built homes are designed by A. I. A. architects and are priced from $595,000. Homesites of from two to five acres are also available from $200,000.

These are the Wallingford Estates of Saratoga — telephone 000-000-0000.

Sincerely,

Dear Property Owner:

In the next twelve months some two million Americans will sell their houses, with varying degrees of success — or sacrifice.

With a bit of showmanship and some time-tested techniques they should be able to sell satisfactorily — and fast. Home buyers shop by comparison; they look for charm, comfort, convenience, and location, and they want a bargain too! Helping owners give real estate buyers the best "show" for their money is my business.

From a modest beginning some ten years ago, Security Pacific Real Estate has grown to be the largest real estate brokerage company in Contra Costa County, California. This growth is due to our firm belief in providing competent service, fair dealing and professionalism in all our business relationships. We hope that when the time comes for you to make a move, we can earn the right to represent you in the sale of your property.

If you would like an accurate idea of what your property would bring in today's market, why not take advantage of the enclosed Free Market Evaluation Certificate? There is absolutely no obligation.

Sincerely,

Real Estate — Mountain Property

Hi Folks:

Just a little note to say Hello, and to let you know what's happening in Todd Valley Estates.

The property values in Todd Valley Estates are still going up every month; we now have over four hundred homes in the valley.

The Todd Valley office is still going strong and our Foresthill location is now a five-person office, with a total of over forty years in sales.

It is a proven fact that buyers looking for mountain property seek out a real estate firm in the respective area that is well acquainted with that property. We feel that, as we have grown up with the development of this area, we are especially well qualified.

As local residents and people who are really interested in the area, we know that our *two* offices can serve you best, whether you are interested in selling or buying property. It's hard to believe that most real estate people from out of the area will *not* come up to Todd Valley to show property.

We realize that you are probably sick of all the real estate mail you receive. But we feel that our track record in sales here in Todd Valley is what you are looking for if you really want to sell your lot. We hope to hear from you soon.

Sincerely yours,

P.S. If you are interested in selling your lot or know of anyone looking for mountain property, please feel free to call collect 916-367-2890.

Wrist Watch

Dear Mr. Farnsworth:

Elegant, sophisticated, unerringly right.

That describes the new Seiko Dress Quartz Collection.

It is Seiko's continual striving for technological achievement that has brought together all the distinguishing qualities a man wants in a dress watch. That is what makes Seiko Quartz such an outstanding and exciting possession for any man.

The strong good looks, and the lightweight, veri-thin elegance make him proud to wear it anywhere. All this is accomplished without compromising the legendary quartz accuracy and dependability he expects from Seiko.

There's such a wide selection to choose from, you're sure to find just the perfect design, either classic or contemporary. Seiko Quartz is the watch a man will be proud to own.

On the attached list, you will find the name and location of local dealers. Visit one soon for a watch equal to your own self-esteem.

Sincerely,

Camera

Dear Ms. Vaught:

Action pictures!

If you see it happening, you can capture the action with your dependable Minolta XG-1. Why is it so simple?

Because the Minolta XG-1 electronically measures the light for the correct exposure — and does it continuously and automatically as the amount of light changes. Your action photography is nearly fool-proof.

You set the focus, and then your compact, lightweight XG-1 does all the work while you get all the credit for a beautiful picture.

You can increase the range of your creative ideas by adding any of the more than 40 precision ground, computer designed lenses and other low-cost accessories.

Your local dealer will be pleased to explain the Minolta XG-1 to you.

Information is also available by writing to Minolta Corporation, 101 Williams Drive Ramsey, N. J. 07446.

Action photos are fun. Make them lasting memories with a Minolta XG-1.

Sincerely,

Computer System

Dear Mr. Graham:

The 5120, our newest entry in IBM's family of small computers, can be ideal for your growing business. It has more power for less money than any IBM small business system, ever . . . costing less than $13,500.

You need only an hour for a complete demonstration.

The 5120 is designed to be run by the people who work for you right now. Reliability and ease of operation are built in.

It has a simple keyboard, display screen, diskette storage, and print-er — all for under $13,500. Installation support aids make start-up easy. There's even an IBM Hot Line to answer your questions.

The 5120 is available with the most commonly needed programs — to do the jobs you need done, the way you want them done.

A key step in your growth could be the installation of the IBM 5120 System. A small computer can make a big difference.

Why not call for a demonstration today? Our phone number is 800/XXX-XXXX.

Sincerely,

Dear Mr. Bowers:

No longer need haste make waste.

The Xerox 9700 electronic printing system is both amazingly fast and precise.

That is why the Xerox 9700 is used by such companies as Fast-Tax, a computer firm that processes hundreds of thousands of income tax returns each year. Up to a million pages of returns are processed in one day. The Xerox 9700 converts the input data and uses laser beams to precisely print the tax forms — and even collates the forms automatically.

That is managing information the way it should be managed: accurately, with a minimum of waste and a maximum of haste. It is all done with the Xerox 9700 electronic printing system.

Call your local representative, Mr. Alvin Goodman, today at 000-000-0000. He can explain this and other Xerox systems — one of which will meet your needs and do a better job of managing your information.

Sincerely,

Specific Customer — Roofing Tile

Allen Company

Dear John:

This confirms our conversation concerning Allen Company's plan to close down their roofing tile operation in Oakland, California and go to the open market for their tile requirements.

The Johnson Corporation is in a very good position in the Bay Area to be a dependable long-range source of supply for roofing tile. Johnson has two tile plants in the immediate area of the Allen Company's housing developments. One plant is in Dublin, which is 30 miles east of your development, and the other is in San Jose, which is 35 miles south of your current operation. These two tile plants are under one Resident Manager who correlates the two operations to give the best possible service to our customers.

At your convenience I would like to arrange a tour of our Bay Area operations for you and for anyone else from your company who would be interested in seeing what Johnson has to offer as a source of supply.

You stated that your National Director of Purchases will visit Oakland the week of December 6 to discuss with you the procedures and guidelines for acquiring quotations on your tile requirements. You also asked me to contact you the following Monday, December 13 to further discuss what our next steps should be.

If, during your Director of Purchases' visit, he would like to see some of Johnson's operations, we would be more than happy to make any arrangements that would be convenient. If not, John, I look forward to talking to you on December 13.

Best regards,

Sales Promotion Book

Dear Mr. Elender:

How would you like to make big money through the incredible power of the hard-sell approach? . . . literally be able to double, triple, or quadruple the power and the effectiveness of your ads, your sales pitch, or your merchandise technique?

Literally be able to look at any ad or promotion with absolute confidence and say, "Yes this has it" . . . or "No, this is no good because . . .," and then know exactly what to do to make it a winner?

You can quickly learn more about what advertising — and selling — is all about than 99% of the so-called experts! You can quickly, easily acquire a brilliant insight into the ABCs of the persuasive, hard-sell approach it takes to sell goods and services these days. You can write powerful, super-selling advertising and promotions, and you can put this new knowledge to work immediately — to give you a tremendous advantage over your competitors.

An acknowledged expert puts that information right at your finger tips in lucid, specific, how-to plain language in a brand new 312-page book that tells you precisely what to do and how to do it, to produce dynamite advertising, and powerhouse sales pitches, and super-effective hard-sell merchandise approaches.

This book is THE $10 BOOK THAT CAN MAKE YOU RICH, by expert Joe Bart, and it includes a detailed, line-by-line analysis of seven of the top money-making mail order deals of all time, PLUS seven rules for writing Impelling Sales Letters, and much more — all for only $10!

Money back if not absolutely delighted beyond your wildest expectations.

Rush the enclosed postpaid card today!

Sincerely,

Dear Mr. Capel:

You can Boost Sales . . . Slash Selling Costs . . . Perk up Profits . . . with this rich storehouse of tested and proven sales promotion ideas!

Modern marketing places more and more emphasis on effective sales promotion as a sure way to boost sales volume and reduce the cost of selling. And, one of the best sources of good promotion ideas is a close working knowledge of what others in creative sales promotion are actually doing. This handbook brings that goal within your reach.

The SALES PROMOTION HANDBOOK is virtually brimming over with hundreds of practical techniques for getting ideas, training dealer personnel, measuring results, exploiting every possible sales outlet for your products and services. For example, if you are looking for ways to build up stronger selling effort on the part of salesmen — your own or dealer representatives — you will have at hand some of the best motivational programs ever developed.

If your daily problems involve old sales territories, allocating budgets, or writing effective promotion copy, this handbook will provide you with many examples to stimulate your own thinking and imagination.

Without cost or obligation, see how the new Dartnell SALES PROMOTION HANDBOOK can help you boost sales and profits.

Read the SALES PROMOTION HANDBOOK for 15 days with no obligation. The all new 6th edition contains 1206 pages of stimulating sales promotion ideas. It is fully illustrated and indexed. The cost is $45.50.

Just fill in and mail the enclosed card today.

Sincerely,

Gift of Food

Every year 'bout this time . . .

we start feeling downright sentimental . . . start taking time to think of the special ladies in our lives. Lots of other folks do, too — and that's why we've put together this special booklet of gifts for Moms of all kinds, on their day.

Harry and I picked these gifts especially for Mother's Day. We think there's something special here to please every Mom you want to remember at this special time of year. You'll find truly original gifts of the finest quality — such as our tangy Royal Gala Apples, imported fresh from New Zealand . . . flowers and exotic foliage

plants she can grow in her home . . . our new Sweets and Senti-
ments, a delicate hand-crocheted pouch filled with a box of our lus-
cious Mint Truffles . . . and our famous homemade food gifts from
the kitchens here at Bear Creek!

Best of all, our prices include everything . . . all the extras you usually pay for at stores. Harry and I will gift pack and deliver in the nic-
est way . . . and every gift will be sent with your own personal
greeting.

Mother's Day is May 11 this year . . . and that's just around the
corner. Harry and I need your instructions just as soon as you can get
them to us. So please fill out your order right away . . . and return it
in the special postage-paid envelope enclosed. We guarantee *you'll*
be pleased . . . and so will *she!*

David

C Reprinted by permission of Harry and David, Medford, Oregon.

Bread

Greetings:

The San Francisco area has long been known for its fine food and
cosmopolitan tastes. Many varieties of foods from around the world
are available here.

The most universal part of any meal is bread. To go along with the
many different kinds of tastes here, Earth Grains has created the largest line of different kinds of bread and rolls in this area.

Earth Grains came to the San Francisco area last year with the
most modern bakery and a team of baking specialists dedicated to
making the finest quality and most consistently good bread products
you can buy.

To help you sample this wide variety, we have enclosed a six-part
coupon redeemable for your choice of more than a dozen different
products from premium white and wheat to ryes and extra sourdough
French.

We value you as a good customer and firmly believe that once you
have tried Earth Grains, you will appreciate the quality that we put
into our products.

Sincerely,

Income Tax Consulting

Dear Ms. Wharton:

I would like to have the opportunity to save you time and money in preparing your income tax returns. An experienced tax consultant who is willing to spend a few extra minutes with you can often save you a considerable amount of money. Generally, if your return is itemized, I can find enough missed deductions to at least pay my fee.

Listed below are several advantages in having me prepare your tax returns, and some answers to a few questions you may have:

1. You get personalized service. You are treated as an individual by a person who realizes that no two people will have identical tax returns.
2. I charge a reasonable fee — $___ for itemized state and federal returns. Business schedules, stock sales, and other complications are in addition to the basic fee.
3. You will get fast service and a private interview. There is generally no waiting for your appointment and most returns are completed in one week.
4. My business is locally owned and is open twelve months during the year to serve you more conveniently.

I feel that a satisfied client is my most valuable asset and I try to make you happy with my work. My continued business growth is based on client satisfaction.

Please place this letter with your other tax papers and call my office for an appointment when you are ready to complete your returns. I would appreciate having you as a valued client.

Sincerely,

Dear Mr. Tiffany:

You're probably going to pay too much in personal income taxes this year.

You are, if you're the kind of totally involved executive we think you are.

With everything else on your mind, there's a good chance you may fail to take some perfectly appropriate steps to minimize your taxes.

This makes it all the more important that you get the advice and counsel of the professionals at Deloitte, Haskins & Sells.

To start with, we'll systematically review your current financial picture and our returns for previous years. (Who knows? We may very well find refunds you've overlooked.)

Then we'll go further, and help you devise financial strategies to meet your long-term business and family needs — your needs for trust arrangements, perhaps, or the sale of a family business, or exercising some stock options.

At Deloitte, Haskins & Sells, we think income tax and estate planning is a very personal matter.

When we say we don't stop at the bottom line in serving clients, we include thousands of businessmen and professionals among them.

They're individuals who look to us for planning for the years to come — just as much as for our help in filing this year's return.

Of course, not everybody requires our kind of help. But if you do, perhaps we should talk.

The sooner, the better.

Call our local office at 213-628-8282, or write 114 Avenue of the Americas, New York, New York 10036.

Sincerely,

Adapted, with permission, from a magazine advertisement.

TV Service Contract

Dear Mr. and Mrs. Cody:

Just a reminder that your TV Service Contract will expire soon.

Don't let it!

Actually, your service contract is more valuable to you as your set gets older. That is when repairs get more complicated and are therefore more costly. One service call may cost as much as the annual contract.

Renew your contract now. You will save time and money and be assured of fast, efficient service from Terry's TV.

We are enclosing a renewal contract for one year. You can sign and return it in the enclosed, postpaid envelope. You pay only $___ for our low cost renewal policy.

Don't worry any longer about uncertain TV repairs — that are always needed at an inconvenient time. You may use your Master Card or VISA card for easy payment.

Why not sign and return the contract today?

Sincerely,

Inactive Customer

Dear Andy,

The loss of a business friend may not seem as tragic as the loss of a personal friend, but still a part of one's self fades away when a friend is gone.

We seem to have lost you as a business friend, and we feel the loss. Is there something we have done, or something we have *not* done? As a personal favor, could you give us, briefly, the reason for apparently leaving us. Just a short sentence or two on the back of this letter is all we ask. You can mail it in the postpaid envelope enclosed.

We have recently expanded our warehouse capacity and increased the variety of paper and stationery items to serve you better. A request for a quote or an order for a carton of Scotch tape would be most welcome. We will do everything possible to become a business friend of yours again. Please let us hear from you.

Sincerely,

Collection Service

Dear Mr. Caplan:

Tylenol may be replacing aspirin as a headache remedy — but headaches remain. Especially collection headaches. Perhaps your collection remedy should be changed.

If you are plagued with "headache" accounts, let us help you. We have many years of experience and an outstanding track record of clearing up old accounts.

Our method is as simple as it is effective. First, we send out a letter that is both imaginative and skillful. It commands respect. And it gets results. Most collection problems are solved at this point.

For more reluctant debtors, we send a trained expert who is tactful and persuasive and can hold your goodwill.

Give us a try. Send us a list of your past due accounts. If the first letter succeeds, you pay us nothing. We must, however, charge a modest fee for sending our personal service representative. If we collect nothing, you pay nothing.

With nothing to lose but your "headache" accounts, and the probable recovery of your inactive assets, give us a call today at 000-000-0000.

Cordially yours,

Public Official

Dear Mr. and Mrs. Baker:

I would appreciate your serious consideration of my candidacy for City Council when you vote on April 8 this year. You have been among the few who take the time and interest to vote in Municipal elections, which indicates your concern about local government.

Forecasts show that I have an excellent chance of winning a seat in this forthcoming election, as my years of volunteer involvement in community affairs and present position of Planning Commissioner have provided the name recognition and background that is necessary to be a viable candidate in _____.

As it is physically impossible to contact every voter personally, and as the press gives only equal and therefore minimum coverage to any candidate, I have to communicate by using signs and mailed campaign literature. To reach every voter with just one message requires over $7,500.

I hope to be able to provide each voter with sufficient facts upon which to base his or her selections on April 8. If I miss your house, it's because I did not have the funds to supply all the literature and postage necessary to mail it to you. If this happens, please understand. I cannot spend any campaign funds unless they are donated by supporters who want to see me on the City Council.

If you really want to help me and yourself for the next four years, $1 or more now and your vote on April 8 will do it.

I have always said that the way to keep an elected public official honest is to have his campaign financed by $1 each from 7,500 people rather than $7,500 from 1 person. I am sure you share that opinion.

Sincerely,

Executive Recruiter

Dear Mr. Butler:

Is your valuable time wasted in interviews and background checks of potential executives who later prove unqualified for the job? Has questionable information by a candidate slipped through the hiring procedure only to surface when the performance record of an executive is called into question weeks or even months later? Do you find too few qualified individuals from which to choose?

James and Jordan can assist you in recruiting qualified candidates for your available positions — and often with less cost to you in both time and money.

Here is why:

- James and Jordan's executive search service covers the nation.
- We have referral agreements with other recruiting agencies.
- We are on top of the current salary market: what is being asked and what is being offered.
- We know the latest labor and fair employment laws, rulings, and court decisions.
- We refer to you only qualified and motivated candidates.
- We practice complete confidentiality.
- We approach our work from our client's viewpoint.
- We have a large number of satisfied clients to whom you may refer.

In taking over the search for executives, James and Jordan completely eliminates one of your business problems.

Further information is available by returning the enclosed postpaid card. We look forward to working with you.

Sincerely,

Personal Credit

Dear Mr. Nordstrom:

Very likely you have heard about Individual Financing. This is our bank's special financial service created for people with an above average income and credit standing. It occurred to me that you might be interested in hearing a bit more about it.

With Individual Financing you enjoy the remarkable independence of administering your own long-term credit needs. If your annual net income is $25,000 or better and you also qualify in other respects, you'll have a credit line of somewhere between $5,000 and $25,000. Use it whenever you want to for personal, family, or household purposes simply by writing a special check of $500 or more.

Individual Financing can give you the flexibility you want through these valuable benefits:

1. There is no charge until you use it.
2. You can pay more than the minimum monthly payment, if you wish, thereby reducing the amount of future financial charges.
3. No collateral is required.
4. There are no prepayment penalties.
5. No bank visits are necessary each time you need a loan.
6. Credit life insurance of up to $25,000 is available.

Please take this opportunity to complete and sign the enclosed application and financial statement. You can be sure this information will be handled in confidence. By signing this application, you are under no obligation. Mail it in the prepaid return envelope provided. Soon after we receive your application, either a loan officer or I will call you.

Cordially,

Furniture, Retail

Dear Mr. Mosland:

Levitz has opened a great new store in Contra Costa County at 1695 Willow Pass Road. Although we're new to this area, Levitz has been satisfying home furnishing needs since 1911. These years of experience have shown us that when you shop, you want selection, availability, and value. Levitz can offer you all that, and more!

We have expanded our selection of 200 room groupings to include our new Classic House Gallery. This collection features American of Martinsville, Hibriten, the Burlinghouse Globe Collection, Thomasville, and the many other famous name brands that complete our three million dollar inventory.

As an introduction to our new Concord store, we're offering you a 20% discount on ALL regularly priced merchandise. In addition, we have a get-acquainted gift for you. It's a beautiful piece of imported crystal, absolutely FREE with any purchase of $100 or more. And you have a choice of five beautiful pieces from which to choose.

To make shopping at Levitz even more convenient, we're inviting you to open a Revolv-A-Charge account today. With this card you can charge your purchases and never have to worry about a down payment, or tying up your credit lines on other charge cards. And your card will be welcomed at any of our seventy-two locations across America.

All you have to do is complete the coupon below and return it in the enclosed postpaid envelope. It's so easy, why not do it today?

Sincerely,

Art Object

Dear Alumnus:

We are pleased to announce that the University of Washington Alumni Association has commissioned world-renowned Reed & Barton Silversmiths to create in rich and precious metals a Limited Edition Damascene Insculpture (metal etching) of our famous landmark — the Rainier Vista.

This uniquely beautiful metal etching, handcrafted in pure silver, 24kt. gold electroplate, burnished copper and bronze is being produced exclusively for Washington alumni — and for no one else. It is being offered at this time only, through this single announcement, and will never be issued again.

Each richly detailed Damascene etching of the Rainier Vista will be faithfully recreated by skilled artisans in Reed & Barton's famous patented process. The rare art medium of Damascene involves more than 20 separate hand operations in the creation of each metal etching through the painstaking blending of silver, gold, copper, and bronze.

Mounted to produce a handsome three-dimensional effect, each Insculpture will be in an antiqued gold and silver leaf frame, dramatically displayed against a rich velveteen background, as depicted in the attractive brochure enclosed.

A Certificate of Registration will be affixed to the reverse side of the Rainier Vista frame, and will bear your name, your class year, and your limited edition number.

Since this is the only time that the Rainier Vista Damascene Insculpture will ever be offered — and since only Washington alumni will receive this information — these exquisite works of art are almost certain to become collector's pieces.

Reed & Barton will honor all orders postmarked on or before March 31. They cannot guarantee to honor orders postmarked after that date.

The original issue price of this framed etching is just $125, including delivery. We have made arrangements to have all orders entered directly with Reed & Barton Silversmiths. You may pay for your University of Washington Insculpture with a $25 deposit, if you prefer. After you have received your Insculpture, the unpaid balance of $100 will be billed at the rate of $25 a month for four months. All of these details are described on the enclosed postage-paid Reservation Form.

Please mail it before March 31.

Sincerely,

Life Insurance

Dear Wells Fargo Master Card Customer:

As you know, Wells Fargo Bank, known for its service to Californians since 1852, makes available to you many financial services including your convenient Master Card account. We are pleased that Wells Fargo has selected us to add to these services by making available to you a product design for the protection of your estate and the future security of those dependent on you.

You are undoubtedly aware that what you can buy with one dollar today is hardly more than half of what you could buy with that same dollar ten years ago. The other half has been lost to inflation.

With this in mind, we offer you a unique Term Life Insurance Plan that is competitively priced, has a special anti-inflation Benefit Protection Option, and features convenient premium payment through your Wells Fargo Master Card Account.

Let me tell you about the highlights of this special plan:

Adults under 60 can select up to $50,000 of Term Life Insurance benefits.

You and your spouse, if under age 60, can protect your insurance benefits against inflation by including the Benefit Increase Option in your coverages. This option will automatically increase your insurance benefit until the total benefit doubles.

You can cover the balance in your Master Card account with your insurance benefit.

You have the convenience of having the monthly premiums billed to your Wells Fargo Master Card account.

Medical examinations are not required to apply for this insurance.

You will own your policy — it is your personal property.

You can have lifetime protection, regardless of any change in your health, because at any time prior to age 60, while your coverage is in force, you can convert this policy to a whole life or endowment policy without evidence of insurability and without a medical examination.

We are proud to offer this Term Life Insurance Plan to you and to support it with the strength of our company, a member of Fireman's Fund Insurance Companies group which, for 117 years, has provided Californians with quality insurance plans at competitive rates.

I urge you to read the enclosed material which further explains the Plan, then evaluate your insurance needs, complete the enclosed application, and mail it to us today.

Sincerely,

Cost Savings

Dear Customer:

Over the past several years, VALCO CINCINNATI has experienced a substantial growth record. Our increased production volume now allows us the opportunity to pass a cost savings on to the customer. These savings are offered to you in two forms:

1. A price reduction on selected spare parts most commonly used
2. A one-half price exchange program

For an itemized list of parts that qualify for these two programs, please refer to the attached sheet.

We hope these two programs will enable you to upgrade your present gluing system and at the same time save you money. We look forward to being of continued service to you in the future.

Sincerely,

Store Sale

Dear Mr. and Mrs. Letterman:

Just a note to let you know that we at Staples' Family Store are already having our After Christmas Sale — before Christmas — so you may enjoy your savings before the holidays.

These will include shoes, shirts, blouses, slacks, and everything in the Children's Department.

This is Staples' way of wishing you the best Christmas ever.

We look forward to meeting you during this season of good cheer.

Sincerely,

4

FUND RAISING

A written request for a contribution to a charity is a sales letter with a heart tug. Like a sales letter, the fund-raising letter first arouses the interest of the reader, then convinces the reader of the need for buying the product or service (or making the contribution), next tells how the product or service will help the buyer (or giver), and finally makes positive action by the buyer (or contributor) easy. The heart-tugging part is the second step — convincing the reader of the need to give.

Let us follow the steps in order, using the first letter in this chapter to explain them. The opening sentence excites the reader's interest with the intriguing statement:

> Right now, the people best equipped to help runaway kids are pimps.

The first three phrases are straightforward and suggest a problem of interest to many people, but the surprising last word of the sentence snaps the reader awake and arouses his curiosity. The reader is eager to read on.

Another letter begins:

> This is the story of Ella.

Because stories hold the promise of being interesting, the reader looks for that promise and finds:

> Ella is lonely.

Now the reader wants to know *why* she is lonely. A startling first sentence is not mandatory in a good fund-raising letter, but the reader's interest must be aroused if the writer expects the letter to be read. Here are more interesting first sentences:

> 3:00 A. M. is a rough time to be needing a ride to work . . .
> CARE hasn't shipped a food package in fifteen years.

Put a "little" life in your life.

Why should you give $25 to the Heart Fund?

Difficult choices must be made during difficult times.

Having captured the reader's interest, the heart-tugging second step begins. The reader must be convinced that the cause is good and just, and worthy of opening his or her checkbook. Referring again to the first letter in this chapter, how a pimp can help is mentioned, as well as why the children seek anyone's help. What happens to the child is described, arousing the sympathy of the reader, who also becomes emotionally involved with the helplessness of the runaways. Here are children as young as nine, searching for love, but hooked on drugs, selling their bodies, cast off by society, beyond the reach of family or government, helpless in the hands of brutal pimps. Any one of these treatments is reason enough to open the pocketbook of the reader.

The third step in a fund-raising letter is a statement of the benefit for the giver. The community problems of juvenile prostitution and pornography will be alleviated through the organization REFUGE. Most fund-raising letters, including this one, indicate that one of the reader's benefits will be the personal satisfaction of helping someone in need. Many letters mention the deductibility of the gift for tax purposes — definitely a direct benefit.

Making positive action by the giver easy is the fourth step. In our model letter, the chore of deciding how much to give is done by the writer when he suggests five or ten dollars. The assumption is that less will gladly be accepted and that more is hoped for. The *postscript* requests that the contribution be mailed in the enclosed envelope and states that the postage is prepaid. Envelopes and stamps are small items, but they can be exasperating inconveniences when not provided. The giving must be made easy.

Positive statements should be used in any request. Imagine the potential giver's lack of enthusiasm when reading, "We can't build a new Intensive Care Unit if you don't contribute something." It would be better to say, "Your contribution, added to those of our other donors, will assure starting our Intensive Care Unit early next year." A positive attitude in the letter promotes a positive attitude in the giver.

The first model fund-raising letter may seem emotional — and it is intended to be that — but in it, several unemotional techniques are used to induce the reader to give. A friendly, conversational tone is carried throughout the letter. Three devices are used to accomplish this: informal language, short sentences and questions, and contractions. Some contractions used are *it's, isn't, we're, can't,* and *won't.* **The** short sentences and questions include *It's ironic, isn't it? It really doesn't have to be that way;* and *We need your financial support.* Informal language also adds to the conversational tone: the use of the word *kids,* phrases such as *maybe get hooked on drugs, it's an ugly scene,* and *beat the pimps on their own turf.*

Additional sales techniques are used in other letters, and some recommended techniques even contradict others. How effective any particular one is depends on the audience to which it is directed. Here are some examples:

- Be brief.
- Fully state the need.
- Avoid gimmicks.
- Attract attention with an unusual letter layout.
- Prod the reader into fulfilling his pledge.
- Remind without undue pressure.
- Have the letter signed by the highest official of the organization.
- Make examples specific.
- Make the request specific.
- Have a specific use for the donation.

As these persuasions are used in the model letters, they will be mentioned in the introductions to the various sections.

Many of the model letters have a *postscript.* This is not an afterthought, but a planned part of the letter. The reason for using a *postscript* is to attract attention. This is accomplished by placing the added remarks outside the body of the letter and at the end, where emphasis is strongest. Just how much emphasis is added is a matter of choice. Some writers of sales letters use it consistently and some not at all, but it does add a little punch to the end of a letter.

One fact of direct mail solicitation should be noted: it is one of the least effective solicitation methods. If five percent of the letters elicit a response, the mailing is highly successful. This fact does not diminish the dollar importance of this method, however, because a large number of small donations can add up to as much as a few large donations. The return percentage can be improved by directing specific letters to specific groups. For example, a series of three letters in this chapter were sent to doctors who work in the hospital making the solicitation, and the appeals were directed toward the doctors' involvement in that hospital. Many solicitations by colleges are addressed to alumni with the appeal made to their interest in the college. In spite of limitations, fund-raising letters do bring in large sums of money.

The following are thoughts from successful fund raisers. Keep them in mind when preparing a campaign or a letter:

- In general, ninety percent of giving is done by ten percent of the donors; therefore spend ninety percent of your time on that ten percent.
- Always assume that your prospect has more money than you estimate. Flattery may get you somewhere.
- It is reported that when one millionaire was asked by an alumnus why he gave a large donation to one college but only a small one to his own alma mater, he replied, "Because no one from your school asked for a large donation."

How to Do It

1. Start with an interest-arousing first sentence.
2. Explain convincingly the need for the donation.
3. Indicate how the giver will benefit.
4. Make positive action by the giver easy.

CHARITABLE HELP FOR THE DISADVANTAGED

Runaway Children

The letter to Mr. Longworth from REFUGE appeals to the reader's sympathy. The sales (or pleading) techniques, describing the dangers to runaways, tax deductibility, and informal language have been described above. The letter is directed toward a wide, general audience, as indicated by the conversational style and the mention of many reasons for the reader's being sympathetic, at least one of which should appeal to any reader.

My Dear Mr. Longworth:

Right now, the people best equipped to help runaway kids are pimps.

A pimp can come off like a father figure to a kid who never had much love at home, particularly when she's scared, lonely, and right off the bus.

All he needs is a week to break her in, maybe get her hooked on drugs, and put her out to work the street. It's an ugly scene, and it's getting worse all the time.

Keep in mind that these are kids we're talking about, both boys and girls as young as nine who sell their bodies in the squalid marketplace of commercial sex.

It's wrong for these kids to leave home, of course, at least for most of them. Some can't really be blamed: they leave separated parents, alcoholic parents, or drug abusing parents. Sometimes the child just can't cope with the inconsistent confusion of present-day pressures. Is it any wonder they run off, searching for the love many don't even know they're seeking?

They're society's castoffs, beyond the reach of family, church, school, or government. It's ironic, isn't it? In the richest nation on earth, the people best equipped to handle runaway kids are pimps.

It really doesn't have to be that way. We think it's time to take the responsibility for their futures out of the hands of the pimps, and put it where it belongs: in the hands of people who care enough to give them a second chance — people like you.

With your help, REFUGE can make the difference. REFUGE is a nonprofit program to help communities cope with the growing problem of juvenile prostitution and pornography.

REFUGE is based on a simple idea. Every community has at hand right now the resources to help runaway children. Through REFUGE, these resources can be integrated into a network of critically needed services that will start these kids back toward useful lives.

Given enough support, we can beat the pimps on their own turf, with street-work counselors, crisis housing, professional guidance, medical care, and psychiatric care. The point is to reach these kids before they fall prey to the pimps, advocate for their rights, and get existing institutions to take an interest.

We need your financial support.

Five or ten dollars won't make much difference in your life, but it will make a big difference in the life of some runaway child.

Do it now, please! You'll be giving us a weapon no pimp will ever have on his side: simple human decency.

Sincerely,

P. S. Please mail your tax-deductible check in the enclosed envelope. It is for your convenience, and we pay the postage.

With thanks to the National Office for Social Responsibility, Alexandria, Virginia.

The following letter about Ella is an intriguing story of a teenage tragedy. The story technique leads the reader easily to the last two paragraphs, where the request for help is made. The appeal is to the reader's sympathy. Requests for contributions using teenagers as the basis of the appeal are most effective when directed to people who have or work with teenagers.

Disadvantaged Girl

Dear Mr. and Mrs. Wallan:

This is the story of Ella and a teenager's loneliness. Ella does not feel isolated from her friends, but she feels trapped — as though confined inside a crowded bus: the doors are locked, the driver is missing, and no one speaks. Each turn of her head reveals only blank faces. Confusion swells inside her mind, struggling desparately to release itself when she hears voices at the other end of the bus. For a moment hope dawns — but each word is contradicted by the next. The voices seem to say one thing but obviously mean quite another.

Ella's life is like that. She is no longer a child, but not yet an adult. She is experiencing the struggle of an adolescent for identity. Actually, she is searching for a solid base upon which to make her own decisions. But in this era the search is so often in vain. Her father tells her to attend college and find a career she can happily follow, but he implies that a woman's place is in the home. Her parents say, "We'll teach you to drink in our home," but the obvious message is, "Stay away from bars and drinkers." Her mother says, "I'll help you get birth control pills," but the thought is clear: "Sex is sinful."

Because a solid base for decisions cannot be found at home, Ella turns to her peers and friends. They have a simple solution: if it feels good, do it. She tries alcohol, she tries sex, she tries marijuana. These become intriguing, then comfortable, then compulsive.

Ella is still locked inside a crowded bus with strangers talking only in contradictions, but she is coping — she thinks.

You are one who can help unlock the doors. Youth Service Groups has psychologists and counselors, some volunteer and some paid, working with adolescents like Ella. Your dollars are needed to help these youths who are trying so desparately to find a solid base upon which to build their lives — lives that will become self-rewarding and self-supporting. Well-chosen guidance for Ella now will forestall a future of institutionalized care.

Please use the enclosed, postage-paid envelope to make your contribution to Youth Services Groups. Even a small donation helps.

Ella is waiting.

Sincerely,

Troubled Boys

Dear Friend:

While our youngsters prepare to observe our thirtieth birthday in December, those of us privileged to actually live and work with them have been looking back with fond memories at Hanna Boys Center's past and ahead with great hopes for its future.

I assure you that we have thought with affection and pride of the more than 1,700 troubled boys who found a measure of love and care here, and we have thought with gratitude and admiration of the literally thousands of warm-hearted people who have made our home possible through their support.

The boys who come to us are troubled and face problems too difficult for them to resolve without help. They are going through hard times. They are struggling with feelings of worthlessness, confusion, frustration, sadness, and anger. Successes are few and far between. The danger of their developing a delinquent behavior pattern is real. Unaided, they will have difficulty moving from childhood, through adolescence, and into manhood.

Our job here is to provide assistance — to extend the helping hand our boys and their families need at a crucial moment. The help we offer is available around the clock, provided by a skilled and understanding staff working to develop an effective program for each boy and his family. It is help that they have been unable to find in their home communities. The staff has worked closely together to improve the quality of child care, counseling, academic and vocational education, and recreation.

We have the capability of providing a large measure of love and badly needed special care for some lads who few other individuals and organizations can help. This is true only because of the support given to us over these many years by so many people having compassion for these children. This support is principally in the form of modest gifts and bequests. Any contribution you could make to our work would be most welcome and most appreciated.

Sincerely,

Destitute Children

Dear Friend:

Help wipe away a little boy's tears.

Sometimes, Tommy cries because he misses his dad; or because he's hungry. But the other day, it was because his mother told him Santa might not visit their house this Christmas.

Tommy's dad left the family six months ago. His mother's been working hard to make ends meet. But with three growing kids to feed and clothe, she knows there'll be no money left over for presents.

If you've ever looked into the bewildered, tear-stained eyes of a young child like Tommy, you'll know instantly why we're asking you to help youngsters and others like him this Christmas.

A contribution of $57.38 could provide a happy Christmas for this deserving family; $5 would buy a nice toy for a boy like Tommy; $10 could buy a warm jacket. And $50 could provide a bountiful Christmas dinner, plus a pair of shoes.

Larger donations of $75 to $100 or more will help those in our community year round — whenever disaster or tragedy strikes.

Please help those who are less fortunate than you by mailing your tax-deductible donation to The Salvation Army today. When you bring comfort and joy to those in need, you will surely receive God's blessing in return.

Thank you,

P. S. Please take time now to join your friends and neighbors who support our work in the community. Mail your check today.

Mentally Retarded

Dear Mr. and Mrs. Conrad:

Your past generosity has been most helpful in continuing the Young People's Center. The fight against mental retardation is long and hard and neverending. Recent research breakthroughs, however, do give us some hope that future generations of children may be spared the handicap of birth defects.

We have done much with the funds available. We have a day care center, and a training center for those who respond to our heartfelt assistance, and although slow, the results are so rewarding.

We sincerely ask you for another generous contribution to continue this essential work. Please use the postage-paid envelope enclosed.

If they could, these retarded youngsters would give you a most appreciative thank-you.

Cordially,

Dear Mr. and Mrs. Cantrell:

Mentally retarded children may have no braces, no scars, no physically observable defects. But these handicapped children desperately need our help.

With proper training, many can be helped to perform small tasks and thus become more useful citizens of our community. Our training center has done much in the past and will continue to do as much as our funds permit.

Another need is research. That is the only hope for future generations. Much more needs to be learned about the causes of birth defects, and progress is being made.

I know you must consider many requests for donations, but the needs of the mentally retarded are greater than ever.

Please give this request serious thought. Your contribution, added to that of our many other contributors, can add up to real help for those otherwise so helpless.

The enclosed envelope is for your convenience. Please use it today.

Sincerely,

Crippled Children

Dear Mr. and Mrs. Jackson:

Sameness can be monotonous; it can also be wonderful — when it is the same people each year giving to the Crippled Children's Home.

You gave last year, and we feel sure you will want to give again this year. Perhaps you can give more than last year. We have more children to care for and operating costs just won't stay down.

In addition, we are expanding our physical therapy program. We have some new equipment and need more. We need another professional therapist as well as more volunteer assistants.

All this takes more of that same commodity: money.

The children respond well to our help and their parents are appreciative of the benefits from your contribution.

Please be as generous as possible, and use the enclosed envelope for your tax-deductible gift. Do it today.

Cordially,

Handicapped Children

Dear Friend:

This is our fortieth year of continual assistance to the needy handicapped children of Contra Costa County. Our help is available when there is not any other.

As has been our custom for the past forty years, our All Volunteer, Nonprofit organization now asks for your financial support.

Your entire contribution, except for our expenses of postage, printing, and telephone, provides:

EQUIPMENT – corrective shoes, braces, wheelchairs, walkers, crutches, glasses, hearing aids.

TREATMENT – speech and physical therapy, medications, eye, dental and surgical care.

CAMPERSHIPS – for the Blind, Diabetic, Mentally Retarded, and other disadvantaged.

We are counting on your contribution to help us help an unfortunate child.

Memorials may be contributed throughout the year.

Very Sincerely,

P.S. Checks, tax-deductible, may be made out to: C.C.C.C.C. Soc., Inc. (Contra Costa County Crippled Children's Society, Inc.)

Handicapped Youth

3:00 A.M. is a rough time to be needing a ride to work . . .

Some jobs nobody wants.

Frank Bozzini is confined to a wheel chair. Driving him to work at the San Francisco Produce Market at 3:00 A.M. is one of those jobs nobody wanted.

Nobody except a kid from Enterprise.

There are others. An invalid needs help getting to bed at night. A church group needs protection from vandals. An 88-year old retired English teacher needs someone to clean her house and prepare her meals.

They're all jobs nobody wanted. And today, they're all filled by kids from Enterprise.

Enterprise is a nonprofit organization that helps teenage San Francisco students get jobs. Enterprise teaches young people the mechanics of looking for a job, and then actually helps them find one.

Enterprise is simple, and it works. From a small neighborhood operation, it has grown into a citywide service. Last year alone, Enterprise referred over 1,240 students to 2,157 jobs. And they did it all with private contributions and donations.

Enterprise helps the community, and it helps the kids in the community. Now, Enterprise could use some community help. If you have a job for a teenage student, please give us a call at (415) 673-7615. If you don't have a job, but you'd like to help us keep going, please send a contribution in the enclosed envelope.

Sincerely,

Heart Fund

Dear Mr. and Mrs. Gooderham:

Why should you give $25 to the Heart Fund?

If you have had heart trouble you already know why. If you have relatives or close friends with recent heart problems you will appreciate our request for money.

If you have been fortunate thus far, let me explain our need for your $25 donation.

Over 670,000 people each year in the United States have heart attacks, more of them men than women. One-fourth of all heart attacks hit people under the age of 65. Preventative measures, however, can reduce the probability of a heart attack. These preventative measures include reduced smoking, regular exercise, controlled diet, and regular checkups by a doctor.

This knowledge is the result of research that requires money, and your $25 donation (or more if you can) will assure continuation of this research.

When your contribution is received, we will send you an illustrated booklet outlining steps that can be taken to reduce the chances of a heart attack, how to recognize the symptoms of a heart attack, and what should be done when the symptoms appear.

It's your life we are concerned about. Please use the enclosed envelope so we can help you.

                                              Sincerely,

Heart Disease

Dear Ms. Trail:

A 20% reduction in heart and blood vessel diseases since 1950 for persons under 65 years of age is the result of your gifts. But the battle is not over. You could be one of the million deaths caused by cardiovascular diseases next year.

This startling statistic can be changed — through American Heart Association support of vital heart research and programs that bring the application of new scientific knowledge in the prevention, diagnosis, and treatment of cardiovascular diseases to heart patients as well as the general public.

Your tax-deductible gift to your American Heart Association will enable us to carry on this important fight against America's leading cause of deaths — heart and blood vessel diseases.

Please use the enclosed card to dedicate your gift. You may charge the gift by using your credit card.

We appreciate your gift and your sincere concern.

                                              Sincerely,

(c) *Reprinted with permission, American Heart Association*

Sclerosis

Dear Mr. Addison:

Reggie Jackson is batting for Lou Gehrig.

There are a couple of things you probably know about Lou Gehrig: that he was one of the greatest Yankees who ever lived, and that he died in the prime of his life.

What you might not know is that the disease he died from is Amyotrophic Lateral Sclerosis, that since it killed him in 1941, millions of Americans have also died from it, and that it is the most demeaning destruction of human life that we know.

There is no known cure.

If I am successful, and every fan sends money, a cure might be found. If I strike out, thousands of people may die this year.

So please, send whatever amount you can to the National ALS Foundation.

The enclosed envelope will help make your giving easy.

Sincerely,

American Veterans

Dear Friends of AMVETS:

Today you and I — all Americans — have reasons to be thankful. The guns of war are silent. Our nation is at peace.

But walk the wards of any VA Hospital. Visit the men who served those agonizing years in Vietnam — in Korea — in World War II. Then you'll know why their battle is not over.

Time does not cure what a mortar shell does to a man's legs — or what two years of P.O.W. interrogation does to his mind.

- AMVETS offers a nationwide counseling service to any veteran, widow, or dependent *entirely without charge.*
- In 48 of the 50 states, there are AMVETS Service Officers, and their job is to help veterans. Whatever the problem involves, hospitalization, compensation, vocational rehabilitation, or any of a hundred other things, AMVETS are ready to give them the hand they need.

– AMVETS volunteers reach the 75,000 veterans who are hospitalized today. More than tax dollars are needed to fill the lonely hours that sometimes stretch into years.

As Americans, we must remember and be willing to help, even beyond tax-supported hospitals or a pension check. The support you give to AMVETS is one way to show how much you care.

Whatever you can give — $3, $5, $10 or more — means so much to those who gave so much, and please remember, YOUR CONTRIBUTION IS USED DIRECTLY BY VETERANS TO SERVE VETERANS — and our nation.

Please don't forget. These are the ones who paid a high price for the peace we enjoy today.

Sincerely,

Cerebral Palsy

Dear Friend:

You probably don't think of a trip to the market as anything special, but for my friend Sue, it is a learning experience.

Sue and I are attending the Cerebral Palsy Center for the Bay Area where we are learning skills to help us lead more independent lives. Through these classes, my friends and I are learning how to travel, cook, manage money, and shop — things common to you perhaps, but that are new horizons for us.

The funds raised during Capella Auxiliary's annual Carrousel Capers helped make it possible for us to attend these classes. Now in its fourteenth year, Carrousel Capers is three days of fun, carnival rides, family entertainment and, of course, good food. Capella Auxiliary is again sponsoring its country fair benefit September 21, 22, and 23, and I hope you will attend.

If you can't attend, you can still help. This year's grand prize is a new Mercury. This car, donated by a generous friend, could be yours simply by filling in the enclosed ticket stubs and mailing them with your donation of $5, $10, $20, or whatever you can. Your ticket might win you a new car.

Your donation will help make it possible for us to receive important vocational, recreational, and daily living training. Although no contribution is required to win the car, please remember your dollars do make a difference.

We are looking forward to your coming to Carrousel Capers, but if you can't, won't you still help by sending your check today?

Sincerely,

P. S. This unique Center is one of the oldest health agencies in the United States serving the cerebral palsied and others with developmental disabilities. It is independent of any other organization. Please make your checks payable to Cerebral Palsy Center for the Bay Area. Your contribution is tax-deductible.

The following letter to Dear Fellow Employee takes advantage of a specific situation to make an appeal for the United Way Campaign. The specific situation is a labor dispute during which office employees are doing manual work normally done by "blue collar" employees. The third paragraph is a transition from the labor dispute to the request for a contribution.

United Way

Dear Fellow Employee,

I recently read a publication that stated "Colfax people are pretty special." Never has this been any more evident than during our current labor dispute when almost everyone has had the opportunity of learning more about how our plants operate and of becoming more physically involved in the actual operation.

We've all discovered new uses for our eyes, arms, and muscles in our dedication to keep the plant going. It is hoped that most of the original aches and pains have disappeared and our muscles and senses are toned up, putting many in the best physical condition they have experienced in recent years. This is one of the fortunate aspects of the labor dispute in addition to our need to help one another.

Some of the local residents do not have the eyesight to learn as we do. Some do not have the muscle control to wrap a carton, push a broom or even push a button. Most of these good people, and I've personally seen many of them recently as they attempted to contribute to a working society, would give a fortune to walk, run, talk, write, or see as you and I do each living day. We can help them and others feel that they have a place in the sun, a place to meet and work and earn, and offer them some means of upholding their dignity.

One of the unfortunate aspects of the labor dispute is that it prevented us from early participation in the United Way Campaign, which enables us to help our neighbors and local communities. I now plead with you to help our plant contribute 100 percent to this cause by whatever monetary means you feel is fair. By single payment or regular payroll deduction beginning in 19__ , you can support the local agencies through United Way. If you wish, you can designate the agency to which your tax-deductible donation is given. This is a new option, so feel free to make your choice on the enclosed card.

Your support is appreciated.

Sincerely,

The first CARE letter is directed to a wide, general audience. Numerous programs and ways of helping the underprivileged are mentioned or briefly described. The intent is that at least one of these programs will appeal to the reader. The second CARE letter is for the same audience, but the pleading technique is a story of success accomplished against great odds.

CARE

Dear Friend:

This coming holiday season, CARE will feed and help more than 25,000,000 men, women, and children in Asia, Africa, Latin America and the Middle East.

But there are still *others* in grave need. What of millions of children untouched by CARE? Those who wait for help but cannot get it because of a lack of funds? What is in store for them? Poor nourishment! Inadequate food! Too few jobs! Little education! A lack of clean water! Untreated sickness!

Without your contribution, their hopes for a better life shrivel and grow dim. Won't you help them see a better tomorrow?

CARE's nutrition programs are the *first* step in aiding the destitute. They are directed to the most vulnerable groups: infants, young children, pregnant and nursing mothers. Without proper nourishment, these helpless ones fall prey to disease and fail to develop. Weakened, they cannot help themselves.

MEDICO, CARE's medical arm, provides nations with a practical way to meet their own needs. An example is the 68 auxiliary public health nurses who were trained by MEDICO in Honduras last year. A year later, they are healing and training their own people.

And when catastrophes such as floods, drought, and earthquakes strike, CARE is there.

Initially we care for the victims' immediate needs: food, blankets, shelter, and cooking utensils. Then reconstruction starts. We help villagers build simple, low-cost dwellings to replace those destroyed or damaged by floods or earthquakes, and assist farmers in restoring the fertility of their land. We help repair damaged schools and water systems. In short, we provide a wide range of services to victims wiped out by disaster.

Please join CARE's 19__ Holiday Food Crusade today and start the *first* phase of helping people to help themselves! For example:

$25   will train a village leader to teach other farmers how to grow more food, or

$250   will provide a core medical library for medical training purposes, or

$1,000   builds a day care and feeding center for preschool children.

All you have to do is include your tax-deductible Holiday contribution with the special contribution form in the enclosed, postage-paid envelope and return it to us today. There is no doubt, I'm sure, that you will always be glad you cared enough to share.

May peace and happiness surround you and yours in this holiday season.

Sincerely,

Dear Friends,

CARE hasn't shipped a food package in fifteen years.

We ship more now, however, than we ever did. It is just that the small package is not an efficient way of distributing food. Our emphasis now is one of the Food-for-Work program. In Bangladesh last year, 600 villages participated in earthwork projects and workers were paid more than 55,000 tons of wheat. One example:

The drenching, summer monsoons sweep the Indian subcontinent. The villagers of Harta, a small community in southern Bangladesh, anxiously watch as flood waters swell across their rice fields. Too much water now means disaster. Twice each day, the tidal surge from the Bay of Bengal pushes upstream, overflowing the banks of the Juffura River and inundating the fields. The slender rice stems break and the unripened heads rot.

Village chairman Kashiswer Roy submits a proposal for a protective earthwork embankment via CARE's Food-for-Work program. Only a few of these many proposals can be acted upon each year, but this year Harta is fortunate. With winter the rains have stopped. More than a thousand unemployed workers converge on the banks of the now quiet Juffura River. Digging the hard earth with hand tools and carrying their filled baskets on their heads, the dike begins to rise. Over 3 million cubic feet of earth are moved. For each 70 cubic feet of earth put into the project, a worker is paid 6 pounds of wheat.

In only 18 weeks, the new protective embankment is complete: 6 feet tall, 26 feet at the base, 8 feet at the top, and 6 miles long.

The following May the monsoons return, moisture-laden clouds move up from the Bay, the river rises, the tides come and go, but the embankment holds. By August, rice seedlings have been transplanted and stalks bend as the heads grow plump.

This is the Food-for-Work program helping others to help themselves. But they need a starter, someone to provide the wheat so they can work to help themselves. And it is only through your generous help that we can start these people on their way to self-sufficiency.

Your tax-deductible contribution in the enclosed, postage-paid envelope will give many people the *start* they need. I am sure you will be thankful you cared enough to share.

Sincerely,

Arthritis

Dear Friend:

The East Bay Branch of the Northern California Chapter of the Arthritis Foundation is having its sixth Annual Drawing to be held the same evening as the companion Domino Tournament on April 18, 19__ , at the Claremont Country Club.

There are a number of wonderful prizes for winning ticketholders. The drawing prizes are listed on the back of each ticket.

Your past support of this worthy cause is greatly appreciated. We hope we can again count on you this year to purchase for yourself, or to sell to your friends, the enclosed tickets for our drawing, and thereby help us fight the crippling disease, arthritis. The tickets are $3.50 each or a book of ten for $30.00 and the cost is tax-deductible.

Please complete and return the stubs to our Oakland office in the enclosed envelope together with your check, made payable to the

Arthritis Foundation, East Bay Branch. Winners need not be present at the drawing, but will be notified.

The East Bay Branch of the Northern California Chapter of the Arthritis Foundation sincerely appreciates your tax-deductible contribution, which will help support our programs of education, research, and care for those stricken with arthritis.

Sincerely,

Lung Disease

FIGHT LUNG DISEASE WITH CHRISTMAS SEALS

For more than seventy years, people have used Christmas Seals as festive additions to their holiday mail. But their real purpose goes far beyond decoration.

Your contribution means vital support of Christmas Seal programs against Emphysema, Bronchitis, Air Pollution, Smoking, TB, and Asthma.

Your gift will bring victories that will enable children to breathe better on long nights and develop into healthy grown-ups — victories that will help you, and millions of others, enjoy healthier lungs in later years.

Strengthen this work. Use Christmas Seals.

It's a matter of Life and Breath!

Please use the enclosed envelope. Your gift to the American Lung Association is tax-deductible.

Sincerely

P. S. Just $1 will help a lot! Won't you enclose a dollar and return it now — to help fight Emphysema, TB, and other lung diseases!

The following group of letters is a series of four soliciting funds for the refugees of Cambodia. These letters present a good example of how the continuing progress of a fund-raising campaign can be used to promote the campaign. As contributions are received, comments about the givers and their gifts provide persuasive material to include in follow-up letters to prospects who have not given or who might give more.

This basic concept is used by successful professional fund raisers for churches that are making a big effort to get pledges from every member. The big donors are contacted first, the total amount of their pledges is advertised, the hold-backs see that the campaign is off to a great start, and they realize that their gifts can actually help their church reach its goal. If presented correctly, this technique will persuade the $60 pledgers to now pledge $80 or even $100.

The appeals in each of these four letters is sympathy and guilt—sympathy for the starving and diseased refugees and guilt for being so comfortable in contrast to the refugees' suffering.

Cambodian Relief

Letter One

Dear Friend:

Are you tired of hearing about self-fulfillment — about taking care of No. 1 — about self — about me — me — me ?

Are there no others in the world?

Yes, there are. There are many Cambodians who so far have survived the atrocities of the Vietnamese Khmer Rouge in spite of the familiar story reported by a former U. S. Embassy interpreter, Somreth Bunkytek, that he had seen 70,000 people in his village, only 50 kilometers from the capital, die of starvation.

And the hysterically sobbing mother who had just seen her two children killed by gunfire. And the bewildered little boy pathetically hugging a puppy in a deserted refugee camp.

"When I think about the people who spend hundreds of dollars on self-satisfying programs such as est and Lifespring, I wonder if they might not be happier with themselves if they sent that money to those starving in Cambodia. I, too, have problems — and I don't have much money, but before I spend it on SELF, I would be happier in mind if I sent it to those who really need it." With this comment, Julie Craig of Cotati, California sent a check for $10 to the Cambodian Emergency Relief Fund.

Brian Collins of Sacramento, California sent a check for $1,000 with this note: "Someone ought to lay a guilt trip on all of us who are spending dollars on gifts we don't need when these people need to eat. I spend five times that amount in the bars in Sacramento every year." (That contribution was good for the liver as well as the soul.)

Your contribution is needed, whether small like Julie's or large like Brian's. The checks do add up, and we hope soon to reach our goal of $1 million.

Please use the enclosed, postage-paid envelope. A bewildered little Cambodian boy in a deserted refugee camp will thank you.

Sincerely,

Letter Two

Dear Friend:

Everyone is helping.

Although sponsored by agencies in San Francisco, the Cambodian Emergency Relief Fund received a donation from Patrick Powers, who wrote, "This is probably the only check you have received from Iowa, but I really care about what you're doing."

We know the donor of $25 through a stark bureaucratic form that accompanied a check drawn on the State of California. The form stated, "Dear Warden, I hereby request that my Trust Account be charged $25 and authorize the withdrawal of that sum from my account." The return address revealed that this donor is an inmate of San Quentin Prison, someone who has drawn on meager funds, given up cigarettes and potato chips and candy bars and other simple things most of us don't give a second thought to, to feed four Cambodian infants for a month. We appreciate this gift from a prisoner who knows better than most of us what it is to be troubled and is reaching out as best he can to people who are severely troubled: the refugees of Cambodia.

A flea market was held in Berkeley last Saturday by Darien Ross and Elisa Moran who raised $675, a spectacular success for that sort of event.

We have a note that says, "The Mission Delores 7th Grade Basketball Team hopes our small contribution will help the cause." And we have one from Oak Grove Intermediate School in Concord.

We have a contribution from the student body officers of the Alvarado Middle School in Union City. They sold handmade holiday cards. And there is a sizable check from Concord's Carondelet High School, where the students held a "no junk food day."

Debbie Wong says, "Here is my contribution. I will never know how its feels to be in their place, but I hope my contribution will lessen the pain they are facing."

Deborah Ford of Dixon sent a contribution with this note, "I was born into a family that was quite poor materially, but very rich in humor. Making do was easy enough because we had the right attitude:

use what you have and thank God for everything. My tastes are simple and I am easily pleased. This check is about all the pleasure I can stand. May it benefit others as much as it has me."

Checks have also been received from the Kensington Senior Citizens Center and the Officer's Wives Club of Beale Air Force Base.

Kathleen Marshall of Cupertino held a cheese and bread lunch at home, charging $5 each to attend. Another note, addressed to our hard-working Joan Baez at the Fund said, "Good luck to you from your garbage man when you lived on the top of the hill on Page Mill Road."

Fulfill your own life. Join these widely diverse people in their sincere effort to aid the Cambodian refugees.

The enclosed envelope will make mailing your tax-deductible contribution easy.

Sincerely,

Letter Three

Dear Mr. and Mrs. Morgan:

The Cambodian refugees say Thank You.

As told by Kristin Jackson, a member of the Bay Area Medical team, "One mother, whose child died, came back to thank us for having been there to care for her child and trying to help."

The need is great and intensely felt by the fly-infested, wounded, and bleeding teenage soldiers. And by the children struggling to recover from malnutrition, disease, and utter despair. They are crying for a chance to live, to hope.

The refugees are making the best of their squalid existence. There is an unexpected cheerfulness, the mischievousness and appealing curiosity of the youngsters, and the eager willingness of the people to improve their lives.

One would expect them to be miserable and apathetic — which was the case when they first stumbled up to the Thai border, grimy and gaunt from disease and hunger.

After a few weeks of medical treatment and food, provided by contributions already received, their smiles returned. One observer said when he saw them enthusiastically preparing to stage a concert one night and watched them roar with amusement at candlelit comedy skits, "I couldn't hold back the tears."

He also reported watching a little girl in a hospital ward who hadn't uttered a word since being abandoned by her parents, skillfully sewing dresses hour after hour. A few weeks later he was honored with a shy smile and lowered eyes as she whispered a phrase picked up from other children, "O.K., bye, bye."

Your gifts have provided a chance for the refugee children to recover from malnutrition, disease, and despair. There can be nothing more beautiful than to have a parent come up to you, take your hand, and smile in thanks when her child is finally well, or to have an orphan give you a hug when she leaves the ward.

Their thanks is for the help received from you.

The enclosed envelope will make contributing easy. Please use it now to mail in your share of help for the Cambodian children.

Sincerely,

Letter Four

Dear Friend:

Small contributions can add up to a large sum, but large contributions add up faster.

Our goal for the Cambodian Emergency Relief Fund is $1 million. We will reach it — with contributions from large donors, as well as the heartfelt gifts of lesser amounts.

The suffering of the Cambodian refugees is almost beyond the imagination. With few exceptions, all the half-million refugees who fled Cambodia in the past few months have lost members of their families from starvation, executions, or war. These include starving children with matchstick limbs, bellies swollen with worms, and huge, blank eyes that mirror the human hell of Cambodia.

The refugees have been getting help — limited help for food and medicine — limited by the money available. They desperately need more.

Among those who have already given are the Fireman's Fund Foundation with $10,000. And $20,000 was received from the Holy Order of Mans, who had previously raised $20,068.93 by holding a two-day Christmas Fair under less than ideal weather conditions at the Hall of Flowers in Golden Gate Park. And one man from Sacramento sent a check for $1,000, realizing that the Cambodians were hungrier than he. Many of the large donors are corporations and wealthy people who choose to remain anonymous — 340 of them to date.

Your contribution is as welcome as any of these. Please make it now — and make it as big as your heart.

The enclosed envelope is for your convenience, and your contribution is tax-deductible.

Sincerely,

CHURCHES

In addition to God's blessings, churches, to survive in our era, need cold cash. The most successful solicitation letters include a secular appeal. An appeal made strictly from a religious or Godly or loving or intangible basis will, however, bring forth gifts from certain donors. As with other solicitation letters, the use to which the money will be put should be spelled out. One church letter makes a request for money for two specific, tangible items: seats and an altar rail — both to improve the worship area.

Secular Appeal

Dear Mr. and Mrs. Helverson:

We don't like asking for money any more than you do. But when the cause is just and the Christian spirit is there, the asking is easier.

As we have mentioned in recent Sunday worship services, the Sommersville Community church needs your help in making it a better place to serve you. In particular, we need new pews at the back of the sanctuary and a new altar rail. (It's the rail, not our faith, that has been wobbly.)

The members with whom I have talked agree that these worship area improvements are necessary. The amount needed is $6,500. This money can be raised quickly if each member family contributes $55.

Please join your fellow members in accepting this invitation to make our worship facilities more pleasant. Please use the enclosed envelope which you may mail or place in the collection plate on Sunday.

The entire congregation will appreciate your efforts to continue His work in Sommersville.

Sincerely,

P.S. We hope all contributions will be made within sixty days. Then the improvements will be completed for our Christmas services.

Preparation for Fund-Raising Campaign

Dear Members and Friends:

Is inflation a problem in your finances at home? *Well, of course it is!* And you can be sure it is a challenge to our finances at the Riverside Community Church. To meet this challenge, our church has proposed a 14 percent increase in next year's budget.

Perhaps inflation can provide an opportunity for ALL OF US to prove our loyalty and to demonstrate our devotion to Jesus Christ, Our Lord.

Today's inflation knows no favorites. We who have been charged with our financial planning have looked at the needs that exist and have developed a proposed budget of $138,000 to meet our church's needs for 19___ .

We plead with you to give your church your sincere consideration. Help us make a *unified* effort to provide for the ministry of this church.

Here is how you can help:

Increase your giving to the church to the point of *tithing.* If not a tithe, at least increase your giving in proportion to any gain in income received since last year.

Remember! If all of us maintain the same level of giving as last year, our church's program will suffer greatly.

Please keep in mind that it is only through your continued understanding and related financial support that your church will be able to effectively minister to you and your family and the family of God!

Sincerely,

Dear Mr. and Mrs. Evans,

You will agree, I am sure, that the enclosed Proposal for our church sets forth a program of which we can be proud. We believe we can do this job with the help of the other members and you. Note especially the new local Missions program and the expanded youth activities program.

The Finance Committee of our church, reflecting the mood of our church members and friends, is interested in making this one of our most significant years. Your giving will supply the tools for building the programs that will positively help our community.

A few homes will be visited during the week starting September 7, in advance of our general solicitation. I know you will be giving serious thought to your share in our enlarged program.

Your gift not only brings hope to many others at home and abroad, but it also enriches your own life.

Sincerely,

Dear Church Friend,

After careful study by our church, we have undertaken a greatly increased program of service for the year ahead. Areas of emphasis will be a local Missions program and expanded youth activities.

We need to become stronger in our personal faith. We wish to make our Christian witness more effective. We desire more aggressive action against the conflicts in our country and in the world.

You can help us achieve our goal. It is our sincere hope that you will first pray and then give in proportion to the need and to your ability. Your gift will help us build a more vital program through Jesus Christ.

One of our members will visit each home soon to talk over the needs of our church with you.

For Christ,

P.S. We are asking that each person pledge to support the needy outside our church as well as to support our own church.

Every Member Canvass

Dear Mr. and Mrs. Elender,

On Sunday, September 16, our church will take an important step forward. In a spirit of consecration and worship we will dedicate ourselves to greater service for Christ during the coming year.

We hope you will be present to join with us in this simple service. Although no financial commitments will be taken then, the occasion will start our Every Member Canvass. This year we have two obtainable goals:

1. Every member pledging to local expenses and to help for the less fortunate
2. Every pledge increased

We are enclosing a copy of the proposed budget. It shows you both needs and opportunities.

During the week starting September 16, church visitors will call on all members and friends to discuss our plans for the coming year. We invite you to consider with concerned prayers your part in our enlarged program. Let us face together the challenge that economic need has thrust upon our church.

Plan to be with us on Dedication Sunday, September 16.

Cordially,

Budget Can Be Met

YOU HAVE RESPONSE-ABILITY

To: Members and Friends of Riverside Community Church
From: Bob Barton, Chairman of the Finance Committee

With the knowledge that the work of the church *will* be done and with the knowledge that an informed congregation *will* respond, the financial condition of your church is presented below:

Our budgeted income through 10-31-__	$99,590
Our actual income through 10-31-__	90,746
We are short of our goal by	$ 8,844

At least $7,500 of this shortfall must be collected. Each member MUST prayerfully consider his or her individual responsibility in this crisis situation and respond accordingly.

If 250 members and friends give an extra $30 during the month of December, 19__ , the $7,500 will be raised.

With the knowledge that this request IS possible, we can move on into 19__ with a far greater hope and the assurance that God's work — here and in the larger world — *will* be done.

We appreciate the concern and RESPONSE-ABILITY we know you will share with YOUR church at this time!

Sincerely,

The following letter is a lighthearted reminder to fulfill a pledge to the church. The layout is intended to attract attention and to lead the reader pleasantly to the realization that a pledge is a promise that must be kept.

Delinquent Pledge

Once upon a pledge card . . . Mrs. Arronson,
You promised your support to the Riverside Community Church
Youth Building.
And then,   the architects were called in,
             and a contractor found (we signed);
             the cement arrived one sunny day,
             the foundation was laid, solid and square.
The passers-by observed:
             the floor that was poured
             and troweled so smooth,
             a two-by-four here,
             a rafter truss there:
             the roof was on.
Let's move in!
             an office desk in that corner,
             a class held here,
             a meeting there;
             a pot-luck supper is planned.
And then it happened —
             we found that you were behind
             in meeting your pledge — made
             once upon a pledge card.
Now, what do you think we should do about that?
                                        (Signed by the minister)

Appeal to Faith

Dear Church Friend,

You and I — and the rest of our church members — are joined in
a wonderful fellowship. We have the privilege of worshiping God together, of supporting one another in sorrow and trial, and of aiding
others in our community. To a world enmeshed in conflicts and fears
of war, we present the only hope for peace. An opportunity as well
as a privilege is ours as church members.

We are now facing the future. Being dissatisfied with the past, we
are determined to go out into larger fields of service. With your help —
and the help of our other members — we can realize our proposed
programs. Your time, your prayers, and your gifts are all essential.

I pray that you may give in proportion to the great need and your
ability. Our church aspires to strengthen our witness for Christ in our
community. It all depends upon *your* help.

In His name,

Love Is a Reason for Giving

Dear Church Friend:

Loving, Sharing,
Giving, Caring.
This is what the Lord
Meant Christians to be.

Have you ever given love and not had it returned? Then you know how God must feel much of the time. Love is sharing. Think of the happiest moments of love — moments with your children, with your spouse, with God, at Christmas time — and you realize that giving stands out. God's love was demonstrated by the ultimate gift, "For God so loved the World that he gave his only begotten Son."

Love is sharing.

You have an opportunity now to share your love with your Church. As we enter the period of stewardship emphasis, I appeal to you to show your love by making a financial commitment to God's work for the coming year.

Care deeply for
Christ our Saviour.
Care for the Church as
The Lord cares for you.

Sincerely,

HOSPITALS

Both public and private hospitals feel the need to solicit the public for funds — funds that it is hoped will approach the need. The basic appeal is to the satisfaction the giver receives from helping someone in need. A secondary appeal is the selfish one of helping oneself by giving to a hospital in which one has been or may become a patient.

The first letter from Mount Zion Hospital and Medical Center, San Francisco, is to a prospective donor. The uses to which the donor's money will be put are listed and explained. The last paragraph suggests how much to give and mentions the convenient mailing envelope. A suggested amount and a return envelope are standard techniques — and they are effective; they should be included in all solicitation letters.

Updating Facilities

Dear Friend:

If you made an inspection tour of Mount Zion today, you would see the activity that has already taken place or is getting underway in the hospital's second year program of updating facilities and equipment. For example:

- Renovation of patient rooms.
- Moving of fifty patient beds from "C" Building (which can no longer house patient care facilities because of new earthquake requirements) to the new 7th floor of "A" Building.
- New Courtyard Building under construction to house new lobby, Admitting Office, Dispensing Pharmacy and kitchen.
- Construction of new quarters for Geriatric Day Care.
- Completion of four floors of the Mount Zion Pavilion for the Prenatal Center, including Obstetrics, Intensive Care Nursery, Regular Nursery and Alternative Birth Center.

All of this work and much more has to be done to modernize and renovate our hospital. Space that is today handling a greatly increased volume of patient care programs with new lifesaving technology has not been changed in fifteen years and must be expanded.

We are not adding any new beds, but are seeking to preserve the quality of medical care for which Mount Zion Pioneer, a core group of supporters, has contributed in the historic first two years of our Annual Campaign.

A reply envelope is enclosed for your convenience. I hope to hear from you at an early date and to welcome you as a member of the Pioneers. A gift of $90 would be most appropriate — $1 for each of the ninety years Mount Zion has been serving the community.

Sincerely,

The second letter is to former patients who may appreciate their hospital care enough to contribute to the care of others. The persuasive technique is the use of success stories.

Success Story

Dear Friend:

Do you like success stories? We hope that your stay at Mount Zion was one, and we would like to share with you just two of the many at Mount Zion's Senior Day Health Center:

Mrs. W.S.

65-year-old widow. Residing with employed daughter since husband's death. Adjustment to this living arrangement complicated by a physical condition which worsened, severely limiting mobility and increasing dependency. Since becoming Center patient, occupational therapy with use of adaptive equipment has decreased dependency greatly. Able to assist daughter in meal preparation. Has developed many new interests. Contributes regularly to Center Newsletter. Involved in writing life history and recently has been learning to weave. Only complaint is that days are not long enough.

Mr. C.H.

75-year-old married man. Confined to wheelchair following stroke three years ago. Referred to Center by his disabled wife to whom he has been married 55 years. She attempted to care for him at home but even with maximum allowable homemaker assistance was unable to do so and he had to be admitted to nursing home. Lost interest in life; both he and wife finding separation extremely stressful. Based on availability of Day Health Center services, discharged from nursing home. Motivation increased immediately. Now ambulates short distances with supervision. Enjoys copper enameling and has delighted wife with gifts made for her at Center. Couple now able to give each other emotional support that was integral part of their lives for 55 years.

The Center changes the lives of its patients from hopelessness and despair to happy, fulfilling days of newfound physical activity, new interests and new friends and sociability. This is why we are so anxious to make its new home, about which we told you in my preceding letter, comfortable, cheerful and suited to the needs of its patients. Won't you please help us furnish and equip it by making your gift to the 19__ Annual Campaign today? An envelope is enclosed for your convenience. We suggest $91 — $1 for each year Mount Zion has been serving the community — but any amount is most welcome.

Sincerely,

This next letter is to a previous donor and reminds the reader of the tax-deductibility of a gift. Some uses of the gift are explained.

Equipment for Senior Patients

Dear Friend:

This time of year many people find that they are able to make an end-of-the-year charitable donation. If you are in this position, we hope that you will direct it to our 19___ Annual Campaign.

As you know, gifts to this year's campaign will be used to furnish and equip the new home of the Senior Day Health Center, the Mount Zion facility where senior citizens find a new lease on life through new friends, new interests and new physical capabilities.

The average age of the patients is 75 — the range goes from 52 to 98. Whatever their age, sex, financial ability or living circumstances, they all need the wide range of services the Center provides. Their improvement in physical capabilities and morale, development of new interests or activated pursuit of old ones, enjoyment of new-found friends and response to individualized care are a source of daily inspiration to the dedicated, hard working staff.

Please help us provide the Center with a bright, cheerful new home, equipped to take care of the needs of its patients.

A return envelope is enclosed for your convenience in sending us your tax-deductible 19___ gift today. Whatever the amount, it will be most welcome.

Sincerely,

The tone of the next letter is direct and positive. This candid approach will appeal to many, but the recipients of this frank letter must be carefully chosen.

Need for Continuing Support

Dear Mr. and Mrs. Haliburton,

Clayton Hospital spends a lot of money. For this we are often criticized. But this doesn't bother us because the money is spent to provide the best health and medical care available with the money we have.

Last year, for example, we opened our new Intensive Care Unit to help the critically ill, and modernized our Pediatric floor. The value of lives saved is not measurable but the cost exceeded $3 million. And now a Cardiac Care Unit for patients with heart trouble is being planned, and will be built over the next two years.

Last year we received $500,000 in gifts from our many thoughtful donors. The result of these gifts is better medical care for you. To perpetuate this care, we must be assured of continuous giving.

The money comes from you! And we are asking for more. We need community support, and we need your support. We are asking that you please add Clayton Hospital to your list of tax-deductible annual contributions. A postage-paid envelope is enclosed for your convenience.

Your interest is sincerely appreciated by the staff and especially by the patients.

                                        Most sincerely,

The letter to Mr. and Mrs. Halstrom is similar to the one above and, like it, is straightforward. It is only slightly shorter, but the shorter paragraphs give it a crisper appearance and tone.

Expansion Costs

Dear Mr. and Mrs. Halstrom,

The hospital staff wants to help you!

To provide medical help they must have adequate facilities. Clayton Hospital is expanding to provide you and those you love with better medical care.

Our recent expansion includes a new Intensive Care Unit for the critically ill and a modernized Pediatric floor. During the next two years, a Cardiac Care Unit for patients with heart trouble will be built.

The value of lives saved cannot be measured but the cost will exceed $6 million. Much of this money must come from the community and from donors like you.

How much should you give? That, of course, is up to you, but we suggest a tax-deductible minimum of $25.

This is an opportunity I hope you will take to invest in medical help for your community and for you.

Please send your contribution soon in the enclosed postage-paid envelope.

                                        Sincerely,

P.S. The staff and patients, present and future, are looking forward to
the help your donation will provide.

Maintain Quality Service

Dear Ms. Jamieson:

Our new Medical Center is now open, and with pride we invite
you to take a tour. Just stop by the Pink Lady desk in the lobby.

A large number of people have been pleased with two concepts
we have adopted: mostly single rooms and ramps instead of stairs for
emergency exits.

The use of single occupancy rooms has proved quite successful,
and arrangements have been made with health insurance carriers to
cover patients in single rooms.

The Pacific Northwest Medical Center was built with the support of
numerous private citizens who recognized the need for a modern
medical facility. The Center belongs to all of us, and the Annual Center Campaign requires our dedicated support. Will you do your part
by contributing what you can? The purpose of the Campaign is to
maintain the high quality of medical service we have attained. And
don't we all have a personal interest in that?

Sincerely,

P.S. The enclosed postage-paid envelope is for your convenience in
mailing your tax-deductible gift.

The three following letters are a series mailed to doctors who
work at the hospital that is making the request for contributions. The
mailings were approximately one month apart. The first letter appeals
to our human need to be a part of a group: "because you belong to
the hospital family." The second letter appeals to the doctor's business experience (rare is the doctor who is not well versed in the business aspects of medicine). The third letter is a short review of the
first two. The statement in the first sentence that this is the "last invitation" is both an appeal to give *now* and a relief to the doctor that
no more solicitations will be received.

Doctors Join in Giving

Dear Doctor:

As a member of the Mount Zion family, you benefit from the contributions which the hospital receives in terms of improved facilities

for the care of your patients. Therefore, I am sorry that up until now I have not had the opportunity to share with you what happened last year in one area of support.

For the first time in its history, friends of Mount Zion were asked to participate in an Annual Giving Campaign. Annual campaigns have long been a tradition in many hospitals throughout the country, and they provide a dependable source of support for current pressing needs.

By contributing $1 for each of the 89 years we had been serving the community, a donor could become a Mount Zion Pioneer. The response was so gratifying that we decided to reopen the ranks for the second year. After this, they will be closed.

You were not asked to participate last year, but because you belong to the hospital family I thought that you too might welcome the opportunity to join the Pioneers.

This is my invitation to you to become one by contributing $90 to the 19__ Annual Giving Campaign — $1 for each of the years we have served the community. I hope you will accept. Your support will help your hospital serve you better.

Sincerely,

Doctors as Business Persons

Dear Doctor:

I am writing again to invite you to join the Mount Zion Pioneers by contributing $90 to the Second Annual Giving Campaign — $1 for each of the 90 years the hospital has served the community.

In some ways a hospital is like a business — its facilities and equipment must be improved constantly. As you know, many of Mount Zion's facilities have not been changed in 15 years but are today handling a greatly increased volume of patient care programs with new lifesaving technology. They must be modernized.

The recent Capital Funds Campaign raised a substantial amount to assist with renovation and new equipment, but campaign goals are seldom realized and this one was no exception. Rising costs are another problem.

Notwithstanding, the work in progress must be completed as soon as possible and other phases of the modernization gotten under way (see the enclosed Fact Sheet).

The real Business of Mount Zion is LIFE — helping it to be born; strengthening it; saving it. Please help us provide you with the most

effective medical facility possible in which to do it. Send your gift today and become a Mount Zion Pioneer.

Sincerely,

Last Appeal to Doctors

Dear Doctor:

This is your last invitation to become a Mount Zion Pioneer. The
19__ Annual Giving Campaign is ending soon, and I hope that when
it is over your name will be on this year's list of contributors.

Mount Zion is your hospital and it needs your support in keeping
abreast of advances in medical research and technology.

As you know, your gift will help provide optimum facilities for the
care of your patients, and it is urgently needed to carry on the modernization and renovation program now underway.

As a member of the Mount Zion family, please do become a
Mount Zion Pioneer; give $1 for each of the 90 years this hospital
has served the community, and mail your check in the enclosed envelope today.

Sincerely,

Using a Specific Example

Dear Friend:

A broken arm . . . severed above the elbow in an automobile accident . . . a small incident in our troubled world — but of more than
small importance to Janet Collins.

Two years later she has nearly full use of her arm and hands,
thanks to the expertise of the microsurgery team at Cantebury Hospital.

Janet's severed left arm was picked up by a police officer at the
scene of the accident and packed in ice from a nearby restaurant.
The police sped her to the nearest emergency medical station from
which she was rushed by helicopter to the downtown heliport, then
by ambulance to Cantebury Hospital. The microsurgery team spent
fourteen feverish hours reattaching Janet's arm.

The microsurgery team inserted a steel rod at the elbow, then
brought the rod out at the cut and into the upper part of the arm.
Then an artery and three veins were connected. Major nerves were
tied, and finally the skin was sewn.

Nearly two years were required to get full feeling into the fingers. Therapy and slow progress are Janet's future, but she is happy to have the use of her arm again.

Cantebury Hospital is doing its small part to serve this troubled world. Will you share in the Hospital's efforts? The enclosed envelope is for your convenience in making a gift to Cantebury Hospital. You will receive the gratitude of our many patients.

Sincerely,

Replace Equipment

Dear Friend:

Our medical equipment does not belong in an antique shop — it merely seems that old. The rapid advance of medical technology is the reason for the early obsolescence of much of our medical equipment.

On the other hand, many of our beds have wobbly wheels, and some will crank only halfway up. The floor covering in three rooms is worn through.

Ordinary equipment does wear out, and lives depend on having the latest diagnostic equipment available when needed — when *you* may be the one in need.

Obsolete medical equipment must constantly be replaced, and that is why we appeal to you each year to do what you can to aid the community and yourself through a donation to West Center Hospital.

Contributions last year were generous, and we anticipate that they will be even more generous this year. The enclosed envelope is for your convenience. Whatever you give will be deeply appreciated and will insure continued medical care for all of us.

Sincerely,

Appeal to the Ego

Dear Mrs. Elder:

We recently received a donation of $50,000 toward the purchase of a head scanner for Pleasant Hill Medical Center.

Donations of this size are both encouraging and necessary if we are to continue serving our community with the best medical care possible. The diagnosis of medical problems has advanced remarkably in recent years, and this requires sophisticated — and thus expensive — equipment.

Pleasant Hill Medical Center has doubled the number of its beds in the past five years, and it will continue to improve its services with your contributions.

It is heartening to know that there are people sincere enough about helping their community to contribute substantial sums to back up their feelings. But even if you haven't $50,000 to contribute, we will appreciate your gift. Please give enough to make yourself feel good.

We have patients waiting.

Sincerely,

Join Hospital Foundation

Dear Friend:

Everything in the health care profession is changing — except the need for funds to meet today's demands and be ready for tomorrow's needs.

Today's health care institutions face unprecedented changes. These changes involve new concepts in medical care and treatment, increasing specialization in services and equipment, development of service training programs, government partnership in medical insurance programs, population growth, and changing sociological patterns. A program to develop critically needed supplemental income for our health care institutions is imperative.

The Foundation, an agency through which such a program is to be projected, has been created. The Wheeler Hospital Foundation is a completely autonomous, nonprofit, nongovernmental organization established to support Wheeler Hospital. The Foundation would afford a means for accepting in a legal, orderly manner, the philanthropy of donors who have the spirit and the will to give.

Through a permanent Foundation, the independent financial security of the Wheeler Hospital may be achieved.

Through this Foundation, a fund will be built up year by year that will be available continuously for essential capital and supplemental operational needs. This Foundation, as the responsible agency for a continuing financial program, will embark upon programs that may extend far beyond the life span of any one individual.

The Foundation will involve many influential persons from all walks of life.

The Board of Trustees, consisting of 48 representative citizens of this area who volunteer their time and talents, invites you to regard the Foundation as one of highest priority. It will be both life-giving and lifesaving.

When you join with other leading citizens of this area as a member of this new nonprofit corporation, you will be part of a team dedicated to the development of the finest health care facilities possible. What could be more worthy of your wholehearted support?

Sincerely,

P.S. The enclosed card and envelope are for your convenience in requesting more information about ways you can help.

SCHOOLS

The "old college spirit" often leaves the campus right along with the sheepskin. In an attempt to recapture that spirit, colleges write to alumni with requests for donations to the "dear old alma mater." To be successful, a request for a contribution must be for a specific project or purpose. The first letter requests increased giving to combat inflation and to attract a more competent faculty. The main appeal is to pride.

Give More Than Last Year

Dear Mr. Warner,

Difficult choices must be made during difficult times. Increasing inflation rates coupled with reduced tax revenues make the choices of where and how much to give truly difficult. It is especially difficult for those of us who care deeply about Harcourt College and its 140-year tradition of excellence.

This year you are being asked to increase your annual gift by 20 percent. Last year's gift of $100 was encouraging — and we did manage to balance the budget. But, with __ percent inflation, we need more than that even to think about strengthening our traditional standards of academic excellence, community service, and social responsibility.

Our tradition of excellence and responsibility is ours to improve upon or to let fade away. As president of Harcourt College, I feel a special and personal responsibility to future generations of students. It is through past and continuing efforts of men like you that we can meet the expectations of future students. They too will want to experience the basic qualities of Harcourt College: a sense of honor and decency, a pride in academic proficiency, a feeling of joy and pleasure in both work and play, a love of growing and learning together, and the acceptance by our community. These qualities, although partially intangible, can be realized only in a climate of financial security.

Our strength has been our ability to attract students and faculty of the highest competence. This we must continue if we are to keep Harcourt College what it is today; but the cost will be greater tomorrow.

Viewed this way, perhaps our choices for giving are not too difficult. An increase of 20 percent in annual giving will maintain our tradition of excellence and assure its continuation for the benefit of our students, faculty, and community.

Sincerely,

Dear Miss Lipsky:

How can a private school continue without charging tuition?

Wellington College has done this for 97 years. Our specialized programs require students to work during alternate semesters. This has also been done successfully for 97 years.

Yes, there is a secret to our accomplishments. We have succeeded in convincing a growing number of generous friends that our specialized school fills the educational needs of many of our young people — those who learn best by combining academic study with practical experience. Over the years, our friends have been willing to support their beliefs with their gifts.

This year we are asking for a little more: an increase of 10 percent over last year's gifts. We hope many of you can provide the extra dollars needed to balance our budget.

I am confident that we can meet the needs of the students who need Wellington College.

Sincerely,

The next two letters are similar except that the second is shorter and in outline form. This attracts attention and makes the style more snappy. The appeal is to the satisfaction of helping others. In addition, the postscript offers an ego-boosting suggestion.

Library Needs

Dear Graduate:

A high quality University, Mr. Johnston, depends on current and extensive library materials. We are all aware of how rapidly new information is being discovered and published. However, the University of Washington library is trapped between spiraling inflation and recent budget cutbacks. These problems seriously threaten the library's ability to add to its collections and maintain its high standards of service. There is a gap between the services our library should provide and what it actually can, and unless you and other graduates can help, this gap will widen.

Enclosed is a brochure about the library. It will answer the question, "How will my gift benefit the library and its users?" We can all benefit from the library's strength — library staff, students, faculty, Alumni Association members, Annual Fund donors, and others in the Northwest community.

Large or small, your gift will help improve the quality of the library at the University, Mr. Johnston. Please send your gift today in the enclosed envelope with the reply card.

Sincerely,

P.S. Remember, a gift of $15 or more will qualify you for the library's "Remember the Books" program. If requested, a special bookplate will show your name and the name remembered on a book purchased with your gift.

Dear Mr. Johnston,

As a recent graduate, I believe you would gain much personal satisfaction from strengthening the University of Washington Library by making a donation *this* year.

Because:

- You learned the importance of *current* library resources during your school years.
- You are aware of spiraling inflation and recent budget cuts.

- A strong library benefits students, the library staff, faculty, alumni, Annual Fund donors, and Washington residents who use the library.

Please send your gift in the enclosed envelope today.

Sincerely,

P.S. Remember, with a gift of $15 or more, a bookplate showing your name and the name remembered, upon request, will be placed in a book purchased with your gift.

Alumni Solicitation

Dear Alumnus:

YOU make the difference between mediocrity and excellence.

Think about it.

Your considered gift to the Dartmouth Alumni Fund supports the Campaign for Dartmouth.

Sincerely,

Haven't Given Yet

Dear Fellow Alum:

The Texon University 19__ annual giving campaign ends April 30. Just noticed that your name is missing from the list of this year's donors.

To date, 30,000 alumni and friends have donated nearly $6 million. A gift of only $25 from those who haven't given would add at least $500,000 to this year's total, further enhancing Texon University's position as one of America's leading centers of higher education.

Please mail your check in the postpaid envelope, now! The students will appreciate your help.

Sincerely,

Dear Alumnus:

Have you given your share to Wadsworth University this year? If yes, a hearty thanks, and you deserve the University's congratulations.

The alumni and faculty have consistently led all givers in meeting their goals. Being so close to the University, what else could be expected?

We find, however, that some of you have apparently delayed making your contribution.

The faculty and alumni goal this year is $400,000. I am sure you will help us exceed that amount. We have enclosed a pledge card and a postage-paid envelope for your convenience.

Give as much as you can, and whatever your gift, it will strengthen Wadsworth University and insure an even better education for the students and leaders of the near future.

Sincerely yours,

Dear Ms. Hasland:

I am happy to have been asked to get in touch with you classmates who have not yet responded to the 19___ Fund campaign. Too few of us have given. The Fund this year will provide capital improvements to the Johnson and Guthrie Halls.

In recent years, the prestige of Cleveland Dental School has risen substantially. One indication is the number of articles published in medical and dental journals that are written by our faculty and former students. Another is the increasing number of highly qualified applicants for admission. Also, the number of graduate students choosing Cleveland Dental for research has shown a steady increase in recent years. Your prestige improves right along with that of the School.

Considering your interest in your profession and in your school, I am hopeful that you will use the enclosed card to pledge your support. Several convenient giving programs are suggested on the card. The enclosed envelope is for your convenience.

Working together, we can meet the capital improvement goal and enable Cleveland Dental School to continue its growth in education, service, and prestige.

Sincerely,

Dear Mr. Albert:

I believe you will want to join those who have already contributed to the Granger Graduate School Campaign this year because:

- You have contributed in the past.
- You feel responsible for the continued improvement of your school.
- You have received and continue to receive lifelong benefits from the School and the Alumni Association's work.

Your sincere and immediate consideration will be truly appreciated.

Sincerely,

Minorities Program

Dear Friend:

Today you can take your own giant step for mankind. Let us discuss for a moment how you can do it.

Olin College has a strong program to help Mexican-Americans . . . to give them hope and to break the pattern of impoverishment and hopelessness.

The College is using everything from private consultants to county farm agents.

The Minorities Department is giving assistance to 300 Mexican-American students in Practical English, Everyday Mathematics, and Farming. Other campus programs are helping these minorities in agriculture, drug education, and small business practice. The College is currently looking at other beneficial programs.

As you are well aware, the need is great and it is real. Better education makes better citizens, and better citizens make a better country in which to live.

Your financial help now will benefit all of us in the near future.

Sincerely,

P.S. For making your tax-deductible contribution right now; we have enclosed a postpaid envelope.

Operational Funds

Dear Mr. Mann:

You have kept us going! While many colleges in recent years have been closing, Whittington College has remained open with generous contributions from alumni.

But the crisis of inflationary costs coupled with a declining enrollment has not bypassed Whittington. We have fought the financial crisis by delaying faculty salary increases, reducing service personnel, and putting off needed maintenance.

These can be only temporary solutions. We need your contributions now to keep Whittington from joining the growing number of closed colleges.

Please use the enclosed postage-paid envelope to mail your gift, perhaps larger than the one you gave last year. But gifts of all sizes are needed and appreciated.

Sincerely,

Building Fund

Dear Mr. Cross:

Your gifts to the Computer Science Building Fund of Norfork University are now showing on campus in the form of a new building. We have reached 80 percent of our goal, with contributions coming in daily.

A visit to the building site will let you experience the excitement of dollars being turned into a facility for the advancement of computer knowledge.

We thank you for the gifts that are making the long-time dream of a computer science building an accomplished fact.

Sincerely,

Student Union Building

Dear Humboldt Parent:

As the parent of a student living away at college, how often do you get a phone call from your son or daughter that is for the sole purpose of exchanging pleasantries? Occasionally, we hope. Usually the call is for a little extra cash or transportation home.

This week, however, you will get a phone call from one of our students who is not your son or daughter. Humboldt students will phone each parent, asking for a donation for furnishings for the Student Union Building. The goal is $40,000 to complete the building for use next year.

A Student Union Building can contribute so much to the education of a student. A college education is not limited to classroom academics. Making new friends, sharing new experiences with old friends, trying a new hobby or activity, a lively discussion with one's peers — these are all a vital part of the college experience. A center for social activities encourages participation in this part of college life. A Student Union, run by and for students is an ideal center for college social activities.

When you receive your call from a Humboldt student this week, please respond favorably. It is your son or daughter who will benefit.

Sincerely,

Religious Appeal

Dear Mr. and Mrs. Winton:

Does God love some people more than others? We are taught that this is not true. We are also taught that those who receive more from God should share more of those receipts — be they blessings or money.

If "God so loved the world that he gave his only begotten Son," surely a small financial sacrifice should not be too much for you.

Buchannan University, a private school of higher learning for over 100 years, is one university that emphasizes the human side of learning. Buchannan has schools of Religion, Medicine, Dentistry, Nursing, Law, and Liberal Arts.

The heart, as well as the mind, is nourished here, and this has been going on generation after generation.

We ask for your financial support for the present and future generations at Buchannan, that they in turn may be able to help others.

Most Sincerely,

Financially Disadvantaged Students

Dear Mr. Stone:

This appeal is on behalf of the students of Webster Technical Institute who might not be able to complete their technical training without additional financial aid. Many of our 21,000 students support themselves and members of their families with part-time and temporary jobs. When any emergency occurs, a family illness, a job layoff, or a medical bill — there is no way for them to cope without temporary financial aid.

Many students enter Webster Tech directly from high school and lack the skills necessary for jobs that are available. But they too must buy books and school supplies. We find that many of these students run out of money before the school term ends. Often, $200 or $300 is all it takes to keep a student in school through the end of the year.

We do have a Student Fund Program, supported by donations from concerned groups and individuals. Your help is needed: our Fund is running low, and we don't expect all the money to be returned. All requests for money are thoroughly investigated, and no money is lent or given unless the need is real.

Your contribution is, of course, tax-deductible. Please use the enclosed envelope. We appreciate your consideration of our many needy students as they struggle to learn a trade so they can make their own way in this world.

Sincerely,

Each of the following four letters opens with an interest-arousing sentence. These are good, but the writer must take care not to overdo a good thing and let the sentences get cute.

Every Little Bit Helps

Dear Mr. Allen:

Some alumni have never given to the University of Oregon! Their explanations go something like this:

"Well, I never contributed because, well, because I didn't think my few dollars would be noticed."

I want you to know that the University of Oregon needs *your* financial support, however little. Small gifts have a way of adding up to large sums.

Our immediate needs are two endowed professorial chairs in the social science field and scholarships for Oregon residents.

Please take this opportunity to continue the improvement of your university and your state. Many others are giving. I hope you will too.

Sincerely,

Pledge Not Received

Yes — we are concerned, Mr. Hampton.

We have not recorded your pledged contribution to Ellsworth College. Time is short. The Anniversery Fund closes October 31. The Fund this year will provide new seats for Landon Hall. The need has long been obvious to us and to those attending public performances.

I hope you know that we need *your* help. All donations are needed — and appreciated — however small or large. We depend primarily on gifts from individuals: from you.

Please take a moment now — right now — to send your pledged contribution.

Your consideration and thoughtfulness is appreciated by the Fund committee, the students, the faculty, and the community.

Sincerely,

Request for Small Gift

Dear Barrows Alumnus:

Just a moment of your time, if you can, to talk about a $5 bill. True, it won't buy much today, but we are still interested.

Multiply that $5 by our over 50,000 active alumni and you have $250,000 — not small at all.

We are asking for your $5 to establish an endowment for the science library as part of our struggle to keep it current; not an easy task when new discoveries occur so rapidly.

We will be grateful for your contribution, and I am sure you will feel good about giving. Your check in the enclosed envelope will be greatly appreciated.

Sincerely,

Worthy Projects

Dear Mr. Bronson:

We really don't mind asking for money — when the project is worthy.

At Cornwall College, all projects are worthy — or they don't get started. And we feel this one merits your special attention. A fine arts performing center will bring together our scattered fine arts department. The stage and auditorium will be available to the public, so that they as well as our students will benefit. Our goal is $800,000 to be raised through donations from foundations and the public. This center has long been needed by both our college and our community.

Please take a moment to consider this. Then use the enclosed reply card to make your pledge or contribution.

I know you'll feel glad about helping.

Sincerely,

5

COLLECTION

The primary function of a collection letter is to collect money. To accomplish this, the writer must retain the goodwill of the debtor. This is especially true of personal collection efforts, directed toward individuals or businesses managed by one or two persons. A collection letter to a large business firm, however, need not put as much emphasis on empathy with the reader.

For purposes of comparison, let us for a moment explore the essentials of a business collection letter. The most important thing is to identify exactly what is delinquent. The letter should include:

- the delinquent customer's order number and date,
- the items purchased,
- the seller's invoice number and date,
- the dollar amount that is past due,
- the original due date.

These items are essential to the reader in identifying the delinquent invoice. The letter below was written by a collection agency to a company that receives over a dozen freight bills daily. The bill referred to could be one of several hundred, either paid or unpaid. Imagine the difficulty of tracing this particular bill:

Your past due account in the amount of $12.06 has been brought to our attention by Freight Agencies.

Please mail your check for this amount to Freight Agencies by May 5 so that no future action will be necessary.

The tone of a business collection letter takes second place to the identity of the delinquent item. This is true because in a large business organization a collection letter is delegated to the lowest ranking clerk capable of searching for the bill and determining if and when it was paid. The following letter displays an overly aggressive tone for a first reminder, but the research clerk ignored the letter's harshness and checked the facts stated in the letter.

Gentlemen:

In reviewing our records again, I find that your account is now more than forty-five (45) days past due in the amount of $162.94 for statement dated 7/7/__ .

OUR TERMS! ALL ACCOUNTS ARE DUE AND PAYABLE UPON RECEIPT OF OUR STATEMENT.

Please forward payment immediately.

> Thank you,
> (signed)
> Credit Manager

ALL ACCOUNTS ARE DUE AND PAYABLE UPON RECEIPT OF STATEMENT

For the first three notices to a large business organization, a copy of the delinquent bill or a short reminder is as effective as a letter of persuasion. For the fourth notice, a letter explaining the delinquency, with a copy of the overdue invoice enclosed, will be helpful.

Do not, however, construe this functional approach to the collection of business letters to mean that politeness, fairness, and consideration for the reader can be ignored. The primary difference is that a business collection letter must contain more technical identification of the delinquent items than is usually necessary in a personal collection letter.

The last example above would never do as a personal collection letter, in which the reader's goodwill is of paramount importance. The personal collection letter should excuse the debtor while requesting payment. The delinquent person may have merely overlooked the due date, may be in temporary financial difficulties, or may even be a "professional procrastinator" (one who operates his or her business on money that should have been used to pay the bills). Whatever the reason, let the debtor save face and assume that the delay has not been spiteful.

Continue thinking well of the customer and omit any harsh and abusive language. In addition, omit words and phrases of this nature:

cannot understand	delinquent
remit promptly	ignore
failure on your part	require
we insist	compelled

our demand   wrong
unsatisfactory   cancel

Positive words sound better and bring more favorable results:

respond   your payment
fairness   your check
you   mail today
your credit   please

A personal collection letter must be considerate of the reader. Therefore, give him or her a reason for paying promptly. Rather than saying, "We would appreciate prompt payment so we can clear our books," apply the "you" attitude and write, "Your prompt payment will keep your good credit rating intact," or "Your paying early enough to take the discount will allow us to continue our low prices for you."

Collection letters are a standard part of the collection process. The first notice to the delinquent is usually a copy of the bill with or without a sticker or rubber stamp impression stating "past due" or "have you forgotten" or "second notice." Following this are short and gentle letters, each one successively insistent upon a payment. Phone calls may be interspersed with the letters. The third or fourth letter is often long, making a sincere appeal to sympathy, pride, justice, fairness, or self-interest. The final step is turning the account over to a collection agency or to an attorney for legal action.

How to Receive a Prompt Reply

The surest way to receive a prompt reply is to enclose a post-paid, self-addressed envelope. Mention in the letter that one is enclosed.

An additional device for making the reply easy for the reader is to enclose a card or note showing the amount and date of the next payment. Leave a space for comments. This will be returned to the writer and will save the reader the trouble of writing a letter.

A third technique is to enclose a phone number with the name of a person who can be called.

How to Do It

1. State the purpose of the letter clearly and in an interesting way.

2. Include data relevant to the situation: what the writer is asking for, how the reader can be helped, and reasons for paying now.

3. Restate the request for payment.

Collection letters are a necessary part of managing a business. When asking for a payment, neither apologize nor beg.

Attention-Getting Openings

The opening of a collection letter must attract the attention and arouse the interest of the reader. The techniques for doing this are limited only by the imagination and research efforts of the writer. Opening statements can vary from "Just a reminder that we have not received your last payment" to slapstick comedy in personal letters:

Dear Mr. Wilson:

"Hey, look at this, Bud!"
"Bad news, Joe?"
"Yeah, this guy wants my autograph."
"But, gosh, that's a compliment. Aren't you proud?"
"But this guy wants it on a check."

We, too, would like your autograph on a check — $35.60 for the toaster you bought on February 7th. Please use the enclosed postage-paid envelope.

Sincerely,

Other stories and fables like those listed below can be used as attention getters for readers who will respond favorably to the light hearted and humorous.

An official whose garage delivered his car every day received a card on his windshield one day, "Merry Christmas from the boys at the garage." Two days later he received another card, "Merry Christmas, second notice."

This is a second notice to you about your overdue payment of $99.80 . . .

One mathematician to another, "Now that you have invented *zero,* what do you have: nothing."

Nothing is what we have received from you for your purchase in June . . .

In a similar vein, here are three snappy collection letters:

- Are you holding on to that check for $29.70?
- Might makes right. Right for us is a payment of $52.50. Might for you is a good credit record.
- We think a collection letter should be short and successful. We hope you do too. $32.95.

Just what to include in a collection letter (to be added to or subtracted from the model letter chosen) will depend on various combinations of the following considerations:

- First delinquency
- Continuing delinquency
- New customer
- Long-time customer
- Small debt
- Large debt
- Urgency of need for cash flow
- Value of customer's future business
- Type of approach (humorous, serious, short, long, light, pleasant, or persistent) the writer believes the reader will respond to

A Strong Close

The end of a letter is its most emphatic part; make the last statement or request strong and definite. Be specific about *what* you want, *when* you want it, and *how* you want it done. At the same time, keep in mind consideration for the reader: an offended reader pays slowly. Examples for specific purposes follow:

For Prompt Action

In order to open your account for further purchases, please let us hear from you today.

To avoid additional expenses and unpleasantness, we expect to hear from you within ten days — before August 12.

Because we are anxious to provide fast service, please let us hear from you promptly.

We can help you just as soon as we hear from you.

To Build Goodwill

We are glad to cooperate with you, and look forward to serving you for many more years.

Thank you for bringing the problem to our attention. We are always happy to help.

We appreciate your cooperation.

Thank you for letting us help.

To Soothe

The mistake was obviously ours. We misunderstood your complaint. We have taken steps to correct the situation and hope you will bear with us for a few days.

We cannot disagree with your feelings; we would have felt the same in your situation.

We are sorry we had to take the action we did, but under the circumstances we had no alternative. We hope you understand.

This action may seem unnecessary at this time, but later I am sure you will appreciate what we had to do under the circumstances.

We would sincerely like to grant your request, but we are unable to do so now. We are, however, looking forward to serving you in the near future.

To Apologize

We are sorry for the inconvenience we caused you, and you can be sure we will make every effort to prevent it from happening again.

We feel bad about the trouble we caused you and hope you will accept our sincere apologies.

Thank you for calling the error to our attention so we may correct it. We are sorry for causing you an inconvenience.

Your patience is appreciated, and we thank you for your consideration.

Please accept our apologies. We have corrected the cause of our mistake, and you can be assured it will not occur again.

To Reassure

We appreciate the business you have given us, and we trust you will understand that we cannot be of service to you at this particular time.

Of course we are sorry to have to turn down your request, but we do look forward to serving you in future months.

We dislike, as all business people do, turning away away a sale, but I am sure you understand why we must at this time.

A lost sale leaves us with an empty feeling, but, as you know from the circumstances, it is not possible for us to help you this time. The near future may look more promising.

To Repeat

Again, prompt payment will retain your good credit rating.

To repeat, the sooner we receive payment, the sooner we can help you again.

Which of these two suggestions appeals to you? Please let us hear from you right away.

To prevent these added expenses and the inconvenience to you, please let us hear from you within ten days.

This order cannot be released until we receive your financial statement. Please mail it today!

To forestall bothering you again about this overdue balance, please mail a payment today in the enclosed envelope.

Repeated reminders are a lot of trouble for us and a bother to you. Please help us both by mailing your payment today.

Briefly, a partial payment now will keep your account open.

To Promote the Future

Now that we have your financial data, it will be a pleasure to approve your future orders promptly.

We are available to serve you at any time, so please call at your convenience. We will work hard to make you a happy customer.

We appreciate your prompt payment for your recent order. We look forward to more years of serving your needs.

Now that your account is on a current basis, we look forward to approving your future orders promptly. A continuing business relationship will benefit both of us.

Series of Collection Letters

A delinquent customer or borrower often needs only a reminder that the last payment was not made. Because of this, many firms use a series of from three to six short collection letters. These can be form letters, typed each time as originals, or they can be preprinted — even in booklet form — with spaces for filling in the amount and due date. Each letter is more insistent than the previous one. When these will suffice, the time and effort required for more personal letters can be saved.

Series One, Three Letters: General

Letter One

Just a reminder . . .

of the amount written at the bottom of this note. It hasn't been paid. Will you mail your check today?

<u>$72.90</u>

Sincerely,

Letter Two

Has the mail been delayed again . . .

preventing your check from reaching us? Did you mail a payment on your account recently? If you did, please stop payment and send another check for $72.90. We are anxious to have your account on a current basis.

With hope,

Letter Three

There has to be a reason . . .

why we haven't heard from you after our previous reminders.

Will you let us know why? Or perhaps you would like to spread the balance over a longer period. Please let us know how we can help.

The amount due is $72.90.

Concerned,

Series Two, Three Letters: Business Charge Account

Letter One

Dear Mr. Lemke:

Our records show that the following purchases by you are past due:

April 29, 19__	$761.30
April 30, 19__	92.00
May 4, 19__	76.10

It is to your advantage as well as ours to keep your credit accounts current.

We would appreciate your paying these amounts today.

Sincerely,

Letter Two

Dear Mr. Lemke:

You did not respond to our first reminder of your overdue balance of $929.40. Could you have overlooked our terms of 1 percent 10 days, net 30 days? If there is a reason for the delay, please let us know. Otherwise, a prompt payment will be appreciated.

Sincerely,

Letter Three

Dear Mr. Lemke:

Once again, Mr. Lemke, we ask for your cooperation in paying your past due account.

A prompt receipt of $929.40 will keep your account open so we can be of help when you make future purchases.

Since we don't want to have to take any further action, we will expect a check dated today.

Sincerely,

Series Three, Three Letters: Past Due Freight Bill

Letter One

Gentlemen:

Attached are copies of our freight bills that are past due. Just a reminder that I.C.C. regulations require payment within seven days.

We would appreciate prompt payment.

Sincerely,

Letter Two

Gentlemen:

Although we sent you past due reminder copies of the attached bills three weeks after our original billing date and again after five weeks, the charges remain unpaid and are now seriously past due.

Since we know you wish to pay your bills when due, we expect that these open items are just an oversight on your part.

As you know, I.C.C. regulations prohibit us from extending credit to customers who have past due charges outstanding, and we have no alternative but to withdraw credit privileges in such instances.

We would very much like to continue extending you credit, and you will enable us to do so by sending us your remittance now.

Sincerely,

Letter Three

Gentlemen:

Two weeks ago we wrote to you with copies of the above freight bill numbers advising you that they were seriously past due and in violation of I.C.C. credit regulations, even though we had sent you several past due reminder copies of the bills.

We assumed that failure to pay these open items was an oversight on your part and that our letter would bring a prompt response and enable us to continue extending credit. We regret to see that they are still unpaid and the delinquent status of your account leaves us no alternative but to remove your company from our list of credit customers. Our terminal manager has been instructed to rescind your credit privilege and transact future business on a cash basis.

If the outstanding balance is not paid in ten days, our Collection Department will take whatever action is necessary to accomplish collection.

Sincerely,

Series Four, Four Letters: Make Account Current

Letter One

Dear Mr. Stockton:

We hope that this year has been a pleasant and successful one for you — and that next year will be even better.

To end this year happily, we would like to see you clear your past due balance of $73.20. A check mailed to us today will start your new year with a current account.

An envelope is enclosed for your convenience.

Sincerely,

Letter Two

Dear Mr. Stockton:

I am sure we both agree that a good reputation is essential to a prospering business.

Your past due account, however, does not seem to support your good reputation. We feel it is important for you to get your account on a current basis.

Sincerely,

Letter Three

Dear Mr. Stockton:

Your account is nearly six months beyond our terms of 30 days. I am sure it is not your intention to ignore past due notices at the expense of your credit standing.

We strongly suggest that you make a payment within the next few days.

We are expecting your check.

Sincerely,

Letter Four

Dear Mr. Stockton:

The small balance of $73.20 in your account does not warrant any more of our time and expense to collect. We also feel it should not be placed with a collection agency.

We can write it off as a bad account, but your credit reputation will suffer. Your credit standing can be maintained, however, by a prompt payment — made no later than the end of this month.

Sincerely,

Series Five, Four Letters: Loan Past Due

Letter One

Dear Mr. Ballard:

May we call your attention to your loan payment, that you have no doubt overlooked? It is 30 days past due. The amount is $50.44.

Sincerely,

Letter Two

Dear Mr. Ballard:

Your loan payment is now 45 days past due. Prompt payment of $50.44 will be appreciated.

Respectfully,

Letter Three

Dear Mr. Ballard:

Again we call your attention to your loan payment due March 15. If there is some reason for the delay, please let us know.

We would appreciate receiving your check for $50.44 immediately.

Very truly yours,

Letter Four

Dear Mr. Ballard:

It bothers us more than a little to say this, but we insist on your paying the $50.44 you owe us. If we don't receive your check by December 31, we will be forced to turn your account over to a collection agency. Please save yourself the embarrassment and loss of credit standing this will cause you. The enclosed envelope is for your convenience.

Yours truly,

Series Six, Four Letters: Charge Account

Letter One

Dear Mrs. Cato:

Just a reminder that your account is 15 days past due.

If you have already sent your check for $332.90, we thank you for doing so.

Cordially,

Letter Two

Dear Mrs. Cato:

Patience is a virtue. We may sometimes seem lacking because we get a little impatient, but we try to be considerate of our friends and customers. Therefore, please accept this letter in that spirit.

Your account has become long past due (since February 15). Please send your check for $332.90 today. We are expecting it.

Sincerely,

Letter Three

Dear Mrs. Cato:

You have been a customer of ours since 19__ , a long time. I am sure the reason is not only because we carry merchandise you like but because of our helpful clerks, our easy-pay credit policy, our prompt delivery service (at no extra charge) and our long established reputation for quality.

We do all these things to please our customers and to cooperate with them. But cooperation is a two-way street. To provide for our customers' needs, we need the cooperation of our customers. By paying your bills on time, we have the funds to rebuild our supplies and to continue providing services for our customers.

Your account has remained unpaid for quite a while, since February 15. If you are unable to pay now, please call or write so we can make other arrangements. Otherwise, could you please help us to continue helping you by mailing your check for $332.90 today? A postage-paid envelope is enclosed for your convenience.

Sincerely,

Letter Four

Dear Mrs. Cato:

Your response to our letters about your long overdue account has been completely negative: not one word from you.

We feel, therefore, that we must turn your account over to our attorney for collection. We dislike doing this, and in fairness to you we will postpone any action for ten days, giving you until July 26, 19__ . Please send us your check for $332.90 before that date to avoid the embarrassment of legal action.

                                                                Sincerely yours,

Series Seven, Five Letters: Charge Account

Letter One

Dear Ms. Bronson:

No doubt you have overlooked payment of the enclosed statement. Your prompt remittance will be appreciated.

Account No.   _____
Date Due   _____
Payment Due   _____

                                                                Sincerely,

Letter Two

Dear Ms. Bronson:

Your attention is again invited to your delinquent account. To avoid an unfavorable report of your credit records, we suggest immediate payment of the amount due.

Account No.   _____
Date Due   _____
Payment Due   _____

                                                                Sincerely,

Letter Three

Dear Ms. Bronson:

It is apparent that you have ignored our two previous reminders. Your account is now seriously delinquent.

We must insist that you pay this account immediately, or personally discuss this with us.

Account No.   ——————
Date Due   ——————
Payment Due   ——————

Very sincerely yours,

Letter Four

Dear Ms. Bronson:

There must be a reason for not paying your account. Whatever the reason, we would be happy to discuss it with you. We can make arrangements for smaller payments over a longer period of time if that would help you. We must hear from you or receive a check within the next 15 days.

Account No.   ——————
Date Due   ——————
Payment Due   ——————

Sincerely yours,

Letter Five

Dear Ms. Bronson:

Since you have apparently made no effort to pay the amount due us, we have no alternative to taking legal action. You may prevent this, however, by making payment by August 15, 19__ .

Account No.   ——————
Date Due   ——————
Payment Due   ——————

Very truly yours,

Series Eight, Five Letters: Charge Account

Letter One

Dear Mrs. Watson:

We sincerely hope you have no objection to a reminder that there is a balance due of $999.52 on your monthly account.

If you haven't mailed your check, could you do it now? Then your account will be current.

Cordially,

Letter Two

Dear Mrs. Watson:

You did not respond to our first reminder of your overdue account, but we have confidence that you will send us a check for $999.52 to make your account current.

Please use the enclosed postage-paid envelope.

Sincerely,

Letter Three

Dear Mrs. Watson:

We are interested in our customers and are always looking for ways to improve our customer service. For this reason, we would like to know if there is a reason for your delay in paying your long overdue account. If there is some way we can help — by making your payments smaller or extending our terms or by recommending a loan company — please let us know today.

We would appreciate a word from you — or preferably a check.

Sincerely,

Letter Four

Dear Mrs. Watson:

Several times by letter and phone, we have discussed arrangements for the payment of your account. The following items are still delinquent:

No. 1527	5-4-__	$229.70
No. 1574	6-4-__	320.00
No. 1622	6-7-__	449.82

So far we have received no indication of your cooperation. Thus at this time we must insist on immediate payment. Please use the enclosed postpaid envelope.

Sincerely,

Letter Five

Dear Mrs. Watson:

Is there anything we can do to persuade you to pay your seriously delinquent account? We have tried many friendly suggestions for extending the payment period, for making small monthly payments, for seeking help from lenders, and for at least discussing this matter with us.

We can't give up, but we have about exhausted our own resources. Therefore, we propose to seek aid from outside our own company. Our attorney has been consulted, and he reports that various legal avenues are available for collecting our money.

We dislike even the thought of going to court, and have decided to extend your credit for two weeks — only 14 days. To avoid legal action, we must have your check for $999.52 on or before August 16.

Sincerely,

Series Nine, Six Letters: Slow Pay Business Account

Letter One

Hello Mr. Daws:

Why not start right now to check these invoices that are past due?

No. 1527	5-4-__	$ 229.80
No. 1574	6-4-__	3320.00
No. 1622	6-7-__	429.82

By paying them now, you save the trouble of having to check them again. If there is a reason for their not being paid, please let us know.

Sincerely,

Letter Two

Hello Mr. Daws:

If at first you don't succeed . . . Here is your second opportunity to pay these past due invoices:

No. 1527	5-4-___	$ 229.80
No. 1574	6-4-___	3320.00
No. 1622	6-7-___	429.82

We know you intend to pay them, so why delay? If you have a reason for not paying now, please mail us an explanation or phone us at 000-000-0000.

Sincerely,

Letter Three

Hello Again, Mr. Daws:

Why haven't you paid?
Why haven't you written?
Why haven't you phoned?
Do you intend to ignore your bills?
Surely not, so please mail your check today for $3979.62, covering our invoices 1527, 1574, and 1622.

Sincerely,

Letter Four

Dear Mr. Daws:

With reluctance but apparent necessity, we remind you once more of your open account that is now 60 days beyond our 30-day terms.

Our previous reminders have apparently been ignored, but you can no longer delay payment if you wish to keep your account open.

Please call us now to discuss ways that we can work together to reduce your open balance. We will do what we can to help you.

Don't fail us and your company at this time. At the very least, send us an explanation for your delay. A check sent today will keep your account open.

Sincerely,

Letter Five

Dear Mr. Daws:

Any further delay in paying your balance due cannot be accepted. Your apparent desire to reject our suggestions of working together on getting your account current is having a bad effect on your credit record. We must have a payment at once.

If you cannot send at least a partial payment right now, call us so we can arrive at some workable agreement.

Please respond today!

Sincerely,

Letter Six

Dear Mr. Daws:

Ten days, ten short days, is the amount of time our legal department suggests we extend your open account. After that time — April 28 — our legal staff will take action to collect your overdue account.

This decision should not seem blunt or surprising. We have repeatedly written and phoned your office asking for payment. Your response has been negative. We can no longer be sympathetic. As a businessman yourself, you can understand why we must have your cooperation.

We will expect a payment from you on or before April 28.

Sincerely,

Series Ten, Six Letters: Business Account Delinquent

Letter One

Dear Ms. Bowen:

We all appreciate an occasional reminder of a forgotten invoice. Perhaps you have mislaid the one of February 3. We have enclosed a copy.

Won't you write a check and mail it in the enclosed envelope — today please.

Sincerely,

Letter Two

Dear Ms. Bowen:

We are enclosing another statement of your balance of $401.

Since this amount has remained long past our 30-day terms, we feel an immediate payment should be considered by you.

Sincerely,

Letter Three

Dear Ms. Bowen:

Your account balance of $401 is still unpaid.

Not having heard a word from you, we assume you do not question the amount you owe us.

Now we must ask that you pay without delay.

Sincerely,

Letter Four

Dear Ms. Bowen:

You have received monthly statements from us for February, March, April, and May. You have received phone calls from us March 12, April 14, and May 15. You have received letters from us March 28, April 29, and May 30.

The result: no response.

It is our policy to help our customers as much as possible because we appreciate their business. If you have a problem with the merchandise or with your finances, please let us know what it is so we can help. We must hear from you to understand what the problem is.

Please phone or write today. That will help us both.

Sincerely,

Letter Five

Dear Ms. Bowen:

Should we take drastic action to collect the balance you owe us? Is drastic action necessary?

We hope not, but our letters have been unanswered and our phone calls ignored. A payment by you can no longer be put off. Please send at least a partial payment with a word of explanation about future payments.

We must have your cooperation if we are to work with you in getting your account on a current basis.

Action is required now.

Sincerely,

Letter Six

Dear Ms. Bowen:

Your account is still unpaid in spite of our continual and friendly reminders asking for payment or an explanation for your delay.

It seems that our only recourse now is to take strong measures to collect from you. We will, however, be patient for another 10 days before taking legal action.

We hope to receive your reply promptly.

Sincerely,

The First Collection Letter Is a Reminder

Because the first collection letter is simply a reminder, it should be gentle. The purpose of the letter, however, should be presented in a positive and straightforward way. The reader should have no doubt, after reading the first sentence, that he or she is late in making a payment. A little sales pitch and an offer to discuss extended payments may be included. An enclosed envelope for customer convenience is recommended.

Dear Ms. Orley:

Have you forgotten the last payment on your loan?

The final payment is $65.20. Because your other payments were on time, I thought you would appreciate this reminder. Please use the enclosed envelope to send in your check for $65.20. May we have it today?

Sincerely,

Just a REMINDER, Mr. Egbert,

that you may have overlooked making the last payment on your account. A copy of our bill for $37.98 is enclosed along with an envelope for your convenience.

Regards,

Dear Mr. Moore:

Your check for $54.80 has not arrived.

This may be a small amount, but when multiplied by our several thousand credit customers, the total is a whopper.

Won't you please help out by mailing your check for $54.80?

Cordially,

Dear Mr. Eden:

Just a friendly note to let you know we are still waiting for the next payment on your account. An envelope is enclosed for your convenience.

Remember, too, our new, wide selection of Stanley power tools, designed especially for home workshops.

Cordially yours,

Amount Due: $227.55
Date Due: November 30, 19__

Dear Mr. Hudson:

I am sure there is a reason why you haven't paid your bill for $43.50 at Alex's Men's Wear. It is now 30 days past due.

If you have been ill or out of work or otherwise unable to pay, we are understanding. We can extend your payments. We would, however, appreciate hearing from you so we can work out a mutually agreeable payment schedule.

Please use the enclosed envelope or call us at 000-000-0000.

Cordially,

Gentlemen:

A routine review of your account reveals the following past due balance:

ITEM NUMBER	DATE	AMOUNT	DUE DATE
30.2233	2-4-__	$4355.90	3-4-__

If your remittance is not already en route, your assistance in expediting payment would be appreciated.

Sincerely,

Dear Mr. Davis:

As you requested, we have enclosed a copy of the item listed below that remains open on your account:

Item Number	Date	Amount
33-6632	11/29/__	$411.10

We believe this will enable you to place the above in line for prompt payment. If additional information is needed, please let us hear from you.

Sincerely,

Attn: Accounts Payable Bookkeeper
      Re: No. 14-4438   10/12/__ $914.45

Gentlemen:

Enclosed is a duplicate copy of the above invoice.

We issued credit memo No. 1854 to cancel this invoice. You apparently used the credit to cancel the invoice and also to reduce the amount you paid on one of our later invoices.

It would be appreciated if you could review your records and, if they are in agreement, process the invoice for payment.

Please call us if we can provide additional assistance.

Very truly yours,

Dear Ms. Trimble:

   Re: Invoice No. 99-4568   6/22/___ $3855.70

According to our investigation, this invoice represents a shipment of canvas made against your purchase order No. U-51786 dated 1/4/___ .

As we discussed on May 6, we would appreciate your approving it for payment.

                                                      Sincerely,

Dear Mr. Oxford:

As one of our good customers, there must be a reason why your payments have gotten a little behind.

Is there anything we can do to help or something we should correct? Please let us hear from you.

                                                      Sincerely,

Dear Ms. Penderson:

19___ is almost over; time seems to fly by unnoticed. Perhaps that is why you have not yet paid the $49.99 for your last purchase at Ender's.

Now that you have been reminded, please mail your check right away.

                                                      Sincerely,

Dear Mr. Ashworth:

Your terms, as you know, are net the 10th of the following month.

Right now $239.90 is past due.

We would appreciate a prompt payment.

                                                      Sincerely,

Dear Mr. Maynard:

As I am sure you are aware, the balance due on your account is $329.44. This amount should have been paid by April 23, so you can see it is quite old.

Please let us know when you will pay or at least start by making partial payments. The enclosed envelope requires no postage.

Sincerely,

Gentlemen:

Just a friendly reminder that your account has gone past the discount period and is now past due.

If your check is in the mail, we say, "Thank you." If not, won't you please give this your prompt attention.

Sincerely,

Dear Ms. Watson:

Your attention is directed to the attached list of freight bills, which our records indicate are unpaid beyond the credit period permitted by Interstate Commerce regulations.

You may have already made the payment and it has not reached our accounting department. If these bills have not been paid, however, a prompt remittance will be appreciated. Please mail your check to West Transportation Co., P.O. Box 0000 Arlington, VA 00000.

Sincerely,

Credit Union Loan

Dear Al Sanchez:

We would like to clear up an apparent misunderstanding about your payroll deductions to pay back two Credit Union auto loans.

You signed payroll deduction authorizations for loan No. 05-902, $70 and loan No. 05-993, $55, from each biweekly pay check.

It is approved procedure and standard practice throughout the Corporation to make these deductions mandatory after deductions for payroll taxes, Worker's Compensation, and Union dues. If this leaves you with a negative paycheck, Form A425 can be signed by the plant payroll clerk as explanation for a smaller Credit Union deduction.

We must insist that payroll deductions be started again because your loan payments are now *seriously delinquent.*

Sincerely,

Middle Stages of Collection Letters

Second letters should still be reminders. They need be only variations from first letters, or slightly more irritating first letters.

Third or fourth letters become longer and more persuasive. The delinquent payer has ignored or given little importance to the short early letters, and now a change in tactics is required. An appeal is made to one of several human feelings; for example:

Sympathy: Your small amount due is only one of many accounts.

Pride or Self-Respect: We appreciate your past promptness, but now you are behind.

Justice: We have carried your account too long; be fair and pay now.

Self-Interest: It is in your own best interest to have a good credit rating.

Give the debtor an out by suggesting a longer payment period or at least the opportunity to discuss future payment arrangements.

Dear Mr. Manor:

We expected at least an answer to the last of several letters we sent you. As you know, you still owe us $422.

Truly, we are disappointed. I am sure you are not intentionally trying to make our work difficult, but that's what it amounts to. Is there some reason you have not paid? some difficulty getting the money? too many other bills to pay? Let's make this easier for both of us. Call us, and we can solve any problems together.

We have been fair with you, and now we believe you will be fair with us.

Sincerely yours,

Dear Mr. Reid:

This is somewhat embarrassing — embarrassing to us because you are a good friend, and embarrassing to you because you owe this good friend some money — money that should have been repaid long before now.

Some time ago (April 16, 19___) you purchased a chair from us, and we were happy to accept your promise to pay within 30 days. You seemed pleased with the chair and I am confident it has given you many hours of comfort. Isn't it only fair that you live up to your part of the agreement we made?

Let us be fair with each other. You have a comfortable chair. We would like our money. Since your payment is long past due, please make out your check now for $225.75, and mail it today in the enclosed postpaid envelope.

Sincerely,

Dear Mr. Addams:

We have sent you numerous letters requesting payment of the $302 open on your account since February 23. We have heard nothing from you, not even an excuse, and our patience has just about run out.

We must insist upon prompt payment.

Very sincerely yours,

Dear Mr. Danfield:

You have not made a payment on your account during the past nine months. We realize that financial conditions in your area have not been good recently, and you have not been pressed for payment. By now, however, we feel you should be able to start paying again. We will be glad to work with you in making a reasonable payment arrangement.

Please call or write and let us discuss what can be done to get your payments started again.

Sincerely,

Dear Mrs. Edwards:

I'm sure you are concerned about the $300 you still owe us on the bedroom furniture you purchased last February.

We can understand that problems do arise that prevent prompt payments and possibly that is why you have not kept up. If that is so, we can extend your payment if you will pay $50 before the end of each of the next six months.

We are sure this will be agreeable to you, and we are expecting a payment of $50 by June 30.

An envelope is enclosed for your convenience.

Yours sincerely,

Dear Mr. Nolan:

You have not answered my previous letters asking for payment on your $324 purchase. I doubt that those letters have just been overlooked. More likely you were short of cash. But after so long a period of time — an entire year — we feel that we should be entitled to at least a small portion of the money you do have available.

Could you please make a payment on the $324 you owe us? I am sure the fairness of this will make you feel good.

Sincerely,

Dear Mrs. Allison:

We have several times reminded you of your past due account of $224.76. It is 90 days past due. Why have you not answered?

Simply, we are disappointed that our confidence in you was misplaced.

Not paying your bills on time can hurt your credit standing in the community. You can make time payments if you wish, and we will gladly work with you on a payment schedule you can afford.

Please restore our confidence in you and maintain your good credit rating by sending us a check now — even a partial payment will help.

Respectfully,

Dear Mr. Coughlin:

We have sent you several reminders about the $92.20 you have owed us since March 1. That was nine months ago!

In consideration of your own credit rating in this city, I think you should pay this amount now. Certainly you want to be fair to yourself.

Your check can be mailed in the enclosed postage-paid envelope. Please use it today.

Sincerely,

Dear Ms. Morris:

Your prompt payments on your open account in the past are appreciated by us. We hold customers who maintain current accounts in high esteem.

Now, however, your payments are lagging. If there is some reason for this, please let us know so we can work together updating your account.

We are counting on hearing from you. The amount due is $99.18.

Sincerely,

Dear Mr. Durer:

Dillon Company hates to keep bothering you with delinquency notes and letters, but your long overdue account is damaging your credit record. This is costing both you and me money: you are incurring additional monthly service charges and we are losing interest on uncollected funds. You could help us both by writing your check for $72.99 right now and mailing it in the business reply envelope enclosed.

Sincerely,

Dear Mr. Renquist:

We hate to keep bugging you, but $80.50 on your charge account is still past due.

If you have a reason for not paying, please phone us or use the enclosed postage-paid envelope to explain why.

If you have been merely putting it off, please mail your check today.

Sincerely,

Dear Mr. Sanderson:

You will recall the recent reminder we sent you on May 5 about your overdue account. Is a check on the way?

If not, we are counting on your cooperation in making a prompt payment.

Sincerely,

Gentlemen:

We again call your attention to the following invoices which, according to our records, are still unpaid well beyond our normal terms:

Date	Invoice No.	Amount
7-17-__	78-458	$1444.77
8-25-__	78-789	864.57
		$2309.34

We would greatly appreciate your early remittance or informing us of the reason for further delay.

Sincerely,

Dear Ms. Atherton:

We try hard to be equally fair with all our customers, and I am sure you wish to be fair with us. Your account now shows:

April	30	$ 32.90
May	31	93.40
June	30	56.60
		$182.90

Perhaps you have overlooked these past due amounts. It would be only fair to pay them now. The enclosed envelope is for your convenience.

Sincerely,

Dear Mrs. Solomon:

We provide open accounts for the convenience of our customers — to make your shopping easier.

To continue these open accounts it is necessary that they be paid within 30 days as agreed when they are opened.

As mentioned in our previous letter, your account is long overdue. Prompt payment will be appreciated.

Sincerely,

Dear Mr. Sewell:

Your open account still shows the overdue amount mentioned in our recent letter dated June 27.

Please send us the $99.90 today, or at least let us know your reason for the delay.

Your cooperation will be truly appreciated.

Sincerely,

Dear Mr. Collins:

You have not responded to our previous notices about your open account.

Your balance of $429.90 is considerably past due, and we ask that you give this delinquent amount your immediate attention.

Your cooperation will be appreciated.

Sincerely,

Slow Pay — Terms Explained

Dear Mr. Wharton:

Recent payments of our invoices have been received long after the due date. Invoices appear to be paid in batches rather than individually when due.

Perhaps our terms are not clear, and I would like to take this opportunity to explain them.

Your credit terms are "Net 30 days," meaning that payment is due *here* 30 days after the date of our invoice. If you prefer to pay our invoices several at a time, we can change our terms to "15 Prox.," in which case payment is due here on the 15th day of the month following the date of our invoice. However, if the total amount of these groups of invoices exceeds your credit terms, more frequent payments will be necessary.

If you have any questions about your terms, or wish to change them to "15 Prox.," please call me at 000-000-0000. I will be happy to discuss this with you.

Please remember that continued delays in paying our invoices will result in our suspending shipments to you. We presume this will not be necessary, and look forward to continued business with you.

Sincerely,

Final Collection Letters

The final collection letter is the last step prior to turning the account over to a collection agency (which normally takes 50 percent of anything collected) or to an attorney for whatever legal action he or she thinks will open the delinquent's pocket book.

However exasperated the creditor is, the goodwill of the debtor must be retained. Do not demean the delinquent payer or use any foul language. Care is required to avoid writing anything libelous or even halfway libelous. Tact must be the watchword.

Dear Mr. Evers:

I would like to talk to you in person about your delinquent account. Since this is not feasible, let me talk frankly in this letter.

Your payments were on time until the beginning of this year, but since then we have received no payments. During this time you have continued to buy from us. You have ignored our past reminders.

Something is wrong. Can we help? Please phone or drop in to visit so we can get together on a payment plan.

At this time we must insist on hearing from you within the next ten days. After that, we will have no choice but to cancel your credit and turn your account over to a collection agency. We don't want to do this because it may harm your credit rating. We must hear from you by November 20.

Very truly yours,

Dear Mr. Goodwin:

Although we have sent you a statement, three reminders, and two letters about your unpaid balance of $628.84, we have not heard from you.

If there is a reason for not paying, please phone or write us immediately. After June 14, your account will be turned over to our legal staff for whatever action they believe appropriate. This inconvenience, however, can be avoided by sending us your check for $628.84 before June 14.

Sincerely,

Dear Mr. Danzig:

Do you like taking a beating without fighting back? We don't either. We don't want to fight or take a beating. But you seem to have forced us into a fight.

Your bill for $442.90 is still unpaid — after 12 months. We have tried all the persuasive techniques we know, and now we feel forced to fight for our money.

You will, however, have 10 days in which to pay your bill. If we have not received the money due us by March 20, we will be forced to seek legal advice.

Please let us hear from you before March 20.

Sincerely,

Dear Mr. Addams:

You have not responded in any way to our recent letters about your past due account. Since February 23 you have owed us $302. If you do not reply by December 10, enabling us to arrange for periodic payments, our next step will be to consult our attorney about further action.

                                                    Very truly yours,

Dear Mr. Smythe:

You have not responded at all to our attempts to collect the $492.25 you have owed us since December of 19___ . This leaves us no alternative to seeking legal action.

This step requires unnecessary time and trouble for both of us. Therefore, we will delay any action for ten days from the date of this letter. If we receive your payment by then, we will be happy to continue our business relationship.

Please let us have your check for $495.25 by January 22.

                                                    Sincerely yours,

Dear Ms. Cavell:

We tried,
We are trying now,
We don't want to have to try again . . .
to collect the money you owe us. Your payments used to be prompt, but this last bill is over a year old. You have not responded to our earlier reminders, and now we must have payment by November 30, 19___ . After that we will turn your account over to a collection agency. To avoid this inconvenience, and loss of credit rating, please mail your check today in the enclosed envelope. The amount due is $429.90.

                                                    Very truly yours,

Dear Mr. Atwood:

NOW is the time for action!
Your account is seriously delinquent!

You have not responded to repeated requests for a payment on your past due account. We can no longer stand by and wait. We must have action on your part.

Unless we receive a check from you within ten days — on or before June 17 — we will start legal action to make the collection.

Sincerely,

Dear Mr. Mack:

Because of the extreme slowness of your payments over the past two years, we can no longer extend credit to you. We have discussed this time and time again, but to no avail. Starting today, all sales will be cash-with-order.

We will be happy to continue serving you under these conditions. You can expect the same quality of merchandise and the same fast service — and our super fast emergency service.

We do expect you to make regular payments on your present balance. Appropriate collection or legal action will be taken if your delinquency continues.

Sincerely,

Dear Mr. Edwards:

Our long-time efforts to convince you of the importance of paying your accounts have brought no favorable response. We have offered many varied suggestions to make your payments easier for you, but you have declined even to discuss these. The only course left to us is legal action.

This can be inconvenient and time-consuming for you. It can also jeopardize your credit standing.

If you will make a payment within ten days, we will forget the legal action and consider you a paid-up customer.

We expect a payment within ten days.

Sincerely,

Dear Mr. Wingate:

Because our many letters have remained unanswered, we get the impression that you do not intend to pay the $472 balance in your account.

Therefore, we have taken steps to turn your account over to a collection agency. To forestall this action and its effect on your credit standing in the community, won't you please write or call us this week?

Sincerely,

Dear Mr. Herbert:

You don't want us to call in an attorney to assist in collecting the $1,439.80 you have owed us since April 15, 19___ . We don't want to do that either.

Why not keep both of us happy by settling your account this week? A check from you on or before next Thursday will save us a call to our attorney and you the trouble of defending legal action.

Sincerely,

Dear Mr. Edgeworth:

We have had no response from you in answer to our many phone calls and letters during the past twelve months. Our invoice No. 4447H of March 12, 19___ in the amount of $4,217.90 remains unpaid.

Our next step is to take legal action to collect the money due us. This is unpleasant for both of us and is damaging to your credit rating. However, you may avoid legal action by making payment within ten days: on or before March 30, 19___ .

Whether or not we take legal action is now your decision.

Sincerely,

Dear Mr. Nichols:

Our credit department has recommended that your account be referred to our attorney for legal action. Our numerous attempts to collect from you during the past year and a half have been unsuccessful, but because of our long-term relationship, I am reluctant to accept that recommendation.

I will hold the credit department's suggestion in my desk for ten days in the hope that you will respond favorably by then.

Sincerely,

6

INFORMATION – PROVIDING AND REQUESTING

PROVIDING INFORMATION

The basis of a successful letter providing information is clarity, and the key to clarity is brevity. Too often, adding supposedly clarifying details becomes a distraction to the reader. If you wish to say, "Starting in April, send the FICA Report to J. C. Henning rather than to A. M. Mondale," an explanation of when Henning replaced Mondale, whether this is temporary or permanent, Henning's background and qualifications, whether Mondale has quit, retired, been promoted or shuffled sideways, and your regrets or congratulations are of no importance in getting the report rerouted.

Repetition should be eliminated. To write, "We would appreciate your taking the $188.50 credit we issued so that it can be cleared from our books and your account brought up to date," is stating the purpose twice. Eliminate either "it can be cleared from our books," or "your account brought up to date."

The second paragraph of the following informational letter illustrates the confusion resulting from disorganized thinking:

> General availability of railroad freight cars throughout the country improved slightly during the week as the weather moderated in the Northeast.
>
> We have shortages of high-roof box cars in the Northwest. In addition, the South Bend mill has been short of box cars throughout the week. We expect to clear up the South Bend shortage by Saturday, and we are using standard box cars in lieu of high-roof cars to avoid delays in customer shipments from the Northwest.

What the author has done is to organize the second paragraph this way:

Problem A, Problem B, Solution B, Solution A.

Going from solution B to solution A causes an awkward twist in the reader's thinking because he has to jump backward three steps to relate solution A to problem A.

The second paragraph should be reorganized as follows:

> We have a shortage of high-roof box cars in the Northwest. We are replacing these with standard box cars to avoid delays in customer shipments. In addition, the South Bend mill has been short of box cars throughout the week. We expect to clear up this shortage by Saturday.

The rewritten paragraph is easier to follow and can be outlined as follows:

Problem A, Solution A, Problem B, Solution B.

How to Do It

1. Organize your thinking.
2. Be brief.
3. Be clear.
4. Offer cooperation.

Because the ending of a letter is its most emphatic part, a courteous note that offers additional assistance is helpful in eliciting the reader's cooperation. Below are examples of simple but effective ending paragraphs:

> If you have any questions about this subject, please let me know.
>
> If you require additional information, please let me know.
>
> Any questions should be addressed to me (to this department).
>
> If you have any questions, please do not hesitate to call.
>
> If you have any questions or comments, please let me know.
>
> If you any questions about this information, please do not hesitate to call me at 000-000-0000.
>
> If you wish further details, please call me at 000-000-0000.
>
> If you have any questions, please call me at 000-000-0000.
>
> For further details, please contact me at 000-000-0000.
>
> For further information, please call me at 000-000-0000.
>
> Should you have any questions, or require additional information, please do not hesitate to contact me.
>
> Please let me know if you need additional information.

Shipping Instructions

Dear Mr. Thomas:

When we place orders for aluminum wheels with you, either for our account or to be billed to one of our customers, please be sure they are shipped prepaid and the freight is included on your invoice to us.

We would appreciate your not making any collect shipments.

Sincerely,

Procedural Change

Dear Sales Manager:

Attached are three requests for credits from customers who state that they did not agree to pay for the molds used in making their aluminum castings. They understood that the mold cost was included in our sales price.

This has been a problem, and we will solve it.

We must have a clear understanding with our customers, and a definite commitment if our customer is to pay. The commitment must be obtained before we buy the molds. This is the responsibility of the sales representative.

Until further notice, all purchase orders for molds will be sent to me for approval. The purchase order must state whether we pay or the customer pays.

If you have any questions about this, please let me know.

Sincerely,

Price Increase

Dear Customer:

Due to the rapid rise in labor and operating costs, Ames Fast Maintenance finds it necessary to increase service charges on September 1, 19__ .

Service charge increases will vary, depending upon the type of service your company uses: on call, when needed, or monthly preventative maintenance.

We appreciate your past business and look forward to a continuing friendly relationship.

Should you have any questions, please call us at 000-000-0000.

Sincerely,

Dear Johnson Customer:

Due to an unexpected price increase from our manufacturing plant, the price of all colors of paint, excepting white and black, will increase 11 percent on March 1, 19__ .

At present, there is no increase on paint supplies and equipment, and our selection remains the best in this area.

We appreciate your being a customer and look forward to a continued association with you.

Sincerely,

Purchasing Policy

Dear Mr. Greene:

In order to do the best purchasing job possible, the responsibility for control of major raw materials, process chemicals, maintenance, and capital equipment is vested in the Headquarters Purchasing Department.

We are committed to a policy of buying materials and services at the Division, Mill, Plant, or Office closest to the point of ultimate use, commensurate with sound purchasing practice. This is a system of decentralized buying with centralized control.

Purchasing by Headquarters will be done only in two instances:

1. For those divisions that do not have a purchasing unit
2. In cases where such a procedure will save our company money

Although the purchasing function is decentralized, the basic responsibility for policies and procedures remains the function of Headquarters Purchasing Department. Good two-way communication is essential.

Best regards,

Bid Price

Dear Mr. Crown:

This is to notify you that our bid price is $4,500 for each electric motor, to disassemble, replace worn parts, rewind, and reassemble. These are the six motors we discussed and looked at on April 7, 19__ .

Sincerely,

Complying With Request

Dear Ms. Hollister:

Re: Invoice No. 0000, 12/22/__, $000.00

Enclosed is the copy of the invoice you requested.

Thank you for your cooperation.

Sincerely,

Data No Longer Required

Dear Miss Bell:

The monthly phone call analysis report, 247, and the stationery cost report, 477, are no longer required by this office.

Sincerely,

Dear Mr. Jose:

For the foreseeable future it will not be necessary to submit the quarterly tax information reports to Lawrence & Lawrence as you did in 19__ and 19__ .

You should, however, continue to accumulate the data monthly so that your preparation of the annual tax reports can be done quickly.

Regards,

Lease Instructions

Dear Mr. and Mrs. McLennen:

Regarding the lease at 422 San Carlos Way, Mr. Wells has asked me to send you the enclosed new lease for your house. The lease is for a three-year term beginning the first of July, 19___, with monthly payment of $330 which should be mailed to Mr. Wells at this office.

If the terms are satisfactory to you, please sign both copies where indicated and return them to me with your check for $330, after which I will send you a copy signed by Mr. Wells.

A return envelope is enclosed for your convenience. If you have any questions, please call me.

Sincerely,

Action Taken

Dear Tom:

I received a copy of the letter sent to you by the chief accounting officer of the division of corporate finance of the SEC commenting on one of the financial items on the last 10-K report filed by Ace Manufacturing Co. This is not serious and I think it can be clarified by a short amendment to your 10-K report.

I am sending a copy of this letter to your accountants with a request that they prepare the amendment.

Sincerely,

Confirmation

Dear Mr. and Mrs. Homer:

This is to confirm the closing date of June 30 at 9:00 A.M. in our office.

Mr. Wilson has requested that you bring tax papers, fuel bills, insurance policies, and other papers you have that apply to the house when you come for the closing.

Sincerely yours,

Payment Instructions

Dear Mr. Smith:

Due to our recent computer conversion, our accounts receivable system now requires that each customer location be identified by a customer number.

The customer number located on the above mailing label has been assigned to identify all invoices sent to this location. Your assistance in showing this customer number on all checks is requested.

Invoice numbers being paid must continue to be listed on your check.

This, together with your customer number, will permit us to promptly record the receipt of your payment.

Sincerely,

Continue Procedure

Dear Ms. Michales:

Over the past few months, significant progress has been made in controlling late payments. Your monthly report analyzing the late payments has brought much helpful attention to the problem.

Please continue sending this report to the headquarters Accounts Payable Department.

Sincerely,

Number Code Changes

Dear Mr. Chalbon:

In order to obtain more detailed information from our computer printouts, please make the following changes, effective May 1, 19__:

Old Number	New Number
8000-1200-1722-01	8000-1200-1721
8000-1200-1722-02	8000-1200-1722
8000-1200-1722-03	8000-1200-1723

Because of limited spacing in the computer program, the last two digits of the old number do not show on the printout.

We will appreciate your cooperation in making the changes.

Sincerely,

Repeated Instructions

Gentlemen:

As I have previously requested, all dividends and capital gains for my account should be in cash rather than in shares. I was surprised, therefore, to learn that the gains of December 1, 19__ were being held in shares.

Please forward the capital gain, in the amount of $492.10, in the form of a check.

Sincerely,

Distribution of Reports

Dear Mr. Greene:

The following will be mailed to you in several packages within the next few days for distribution to all salaried employees at your location:

1. A summary description of the new health benefit package and a cover letter from the Chairman of the Board (Please staple the cover letter to the description before distributing.)
2. A blue pamphlet describing medical benefits
3. An orange pamphlet describing dental benefits
4. A report and cover letter from Vice President A. B. Walker on Safety Performance by location for the year 19__ (Please attach the cover letter to the report.)

If any of these is not received by April 30, please call me at 000-0000.

Sincerely,

Confirmation

Dear Mr. Dixon:

Confirming our telephone conversation of May 20, 19__, please cancel our purchase order number 000-0000.

Sincerely,

Claim Against City

Dear Mr. Martin:

It is a pleasure to assist you in your claim against Stewart City for the inadvertent damage to your property. The enclosed form is for your use in filing the claim. It is IMPORTANT that you read and follow the instructions on the back of the form.

My staff will be most willing to provide any assistance. Please feel free to call 000-0000 and ask for Claims Assistance. Your cooperation in returning the claim form as soon as possible will help us to complete the processing with a minimum of error and delay.

Before sealing the envelope, make sure you have filled in your CORRECT street address and phone number.

Sincerely,

Effect of Strike

Dear Customer:

Because of a failure to agree on terms, the Union has called a strike which may effect our operations. Despite this, our company intends to do everything possible to maintain normal shipping operations from our warehouse.

Our priority will be to minimize disruptions that might inconvenience our customers.

Your cooperation during this period is appreciated.

Sincerely,

Insurance Policy Transfer

Dear Mrs. Olsen:

Enclosed is your Original Insurance Policy No. 5107393 on property located in Hayward, California.

This policy should be cancelled as of 4/29/__, or transferred to your new residence.

Regards,

Layoff

Dear Joe Arvella:

This is to notify you that you are being laid off in compliance with Article XX, Section 3 of our current labor agreement. We hope you will be available for recall in the near future.

Please check with the Personnel Department to verify that your current address and phone number are on file.

Sincerely,

Statement of Future Occurrence

Dear Don:

As of March 15, 19__, the metal planer, operation No. 0330, will no longer be available in the Alderwild Machine Shop.

Please note this when scheduling work for this shop.

Sincerely,

Dear Mr. Atwood:

A new 1000 KVA Electric transformer will be installed in the Sitcom Plant during May 19__.

Preparatory to the installation, General Electric requires eight hours of downtime on all existing electrical systems.

The downtime has been scheduled for Saturday, March 13, 19__. There will be *no electrical power* in the Sitcom Plant on that day.

Sincerely,

Test Run Assigned

Dear Mr. Warring:

The test run of XY222 red die has been assigned to your plant. Please schedule the run as soon as possible after you receive the order, which we expect to get from Coddington within the next two weeks.

Please let me know when the test will be run and when it is shipped.

Sincerely,

Policy Change

Dear Mr. Rosen:

The Company announced in a news release on August 15 that certain Divisions will change their fiscal year-end from December 31 to September 30.

This will not change the monthly accounting procedures currently used by the Western manufacturing branches. Adjustments will be made at Headquarters.

Sincerely,

Change in Items Used

H. R. Baker:

As of April 1, 19__, we will discontinue using motor housing numbers 400-500 and use only the substitute numbers 800-900.

Please sell as scrap any remaining housings numbered 400-500.

Best regards,

Address Change

Dear Customer:

Our address for mailing payments is being changed to:

_____
_____
_____

This change is for invoice and statement payments only.

Other correspondence and purchase orders should still be sent to the address shown at the top of this letter.

Your cooperation in changing your records will be appreciated.

Sincerely,

Will Contact You Again

Dear Mr. Franks:

We have received your claim forms for the transit damage sustained in your recent shipment from Watson Co., San Diego.

One of our representatives will phone you within a few days to arrange an appointment to inspect the damage.

Sincerely yours,

REQUESTING INFORMATION

A request for information can be short and direct. For example:

Send me an analysis of steel tubing sales, by customer, for the month of October.

This is brief and functional, but the tone is unnecessarily commanding. The simple addition of the word *please* to start the request would increase the recipient's willingness to help. A word or two of explanation would also improve the reader's willingness by making him or her feel a part of the project. Two examples:

For our annual purchasing department study, please send me a list of the minority vendors from whom you made purchases during the last six months of 19___.

Mr. Holmes has asked that we provide him with an analysis of steel tubing sales, by customer, during October. Please send this data to my attention.

Long requests should be separated into items that can be listed and numbered. This clarifies the request and simplifies the answering. Here is an example:

Please send us quotes on the following:

1. 24,000 B22, 16 oz. cans
2. 5,000 A22, 1-gallon cans
3. 17,000 AA4B, size 14 plastic lids

How to Do It

1. Make the request specific.
2. State or imply a reason.
3. Show appreciation for the expected cooperation.

Because the ending of a letter is the part having strongest emphasis, the last paragraph should be a polite but persuasive punch line in your effort to obtain the information requested. The following are suggested ideas for the closing paragraph:

> We look forward to receiving your reply.
> Your cooperation will be appreciated.
> Your cooperation will be truly (greatly) appreciated.
> Your cooperation and understanding will be appreciated.
> Your prompt reply will be appreciated.
> We will appreciate receiving this information as soon as possible.
> We will appreciate receiving this data by September 25.
> A quote from you would be appreciated.
> Thank you for your anticipated cooperation.
> Your prompt attention will be appreciated.

> Thank you. (This is a common ending for a letter either requesting or providing information. Some authorities object to a thank you in advance because it seemingly implies an end to communication on the subject.) An expression of appreciation is preferable.

A Report

Dear Mr. Willis:

Mr. Marquette asked me to inquire if you could please send him a copy of the report of the last meeting of the Cleveland Realty Board Committee. The subject of the report is Undeveloped Land Acquisitions.

He will appreciate your sending him a copy.

Sincerely yours,

Accounting System

Gentlemen:

Do you recommend a particular system or set of forms for book-keeping for automotive shops? If you do, I would appreciate knowing what the system is and receiving a copy of the forms.

Also, many trade associations collect data related to production and financial activities from members, and summarize these. I would appreciate receiving your latest available data.

Sincerely,

Acknowledgment of Gift

Dear Ansel:

I know this is a busy season for you, but I wanted to ask if the parcel I mailed you on the 12th of last month has arrived. If it hasn't, I'll have the Post Office put a tracer on it.

The parcel is a leather portfolio case, and is a thank-you gift for the time you took from your busy schedule to show Harry Longworth some of the interesting parts of Denver. Both Harry and I appreciate your kind hospitality.

Sincerely,

City Information

Gentlemen:

Auburn, California is one of the locations my wife and I are considering for retirement, which will be in six years.

Please send us general information about Auburn, especially data that would be of interest to a retired couple. We may wish to buy residential property in Auburn before retirement.

Receiving this information would be greatly appreciated.

Sincerely,

Recent Sales Activity

Dear Mr. Rosen:

Once again we are at the time of the year when Mr. Keith Monte of Monte-Atlanta Corp. will wish to discuss can purchases for their Tampa Cannery.

Please let me know what their sales activity has been this past year and what you see for the coming year. This would include prices, quantities, delivery schedules, and other data you think pertinent.

It is Mr. Monte's plan to be in Miami Beach next month from the 15th through the 19th prior to calling on a supplier in Ohio. Could the company boat be available in Miami on the 19th, before his trip to Ohio?

May I hear from you soon?

Sincerely,

Strength Analysis

Dear Rod:

We are sending you samples of our AA21 boat cleats from our first trial run made 8/4/__. Please analyze these for strength under steady and alternating tension conditions.

Please send us a comparison of these test results with previous tests you've conducted for our St. Paul and Elkhart plants.

If you need additional information, please let me know.

Sincerely,

Data for Newsletter

Dear Mr. Robinson:

Our Personnel Manager has requested that we provide statistical data for the monthly Newsletter, as is done at other divisions.

Below is a suggested format. Please discuss this with your Division Manager and provide me with your suggested changes by May 1st.

	June This Year	June Last Year
Bbls produced		
Bbls shipped		
Production Efficiency %		

Your cooperation will be appreciated.

Sincerely,

Review of Claim

Dear Mr. Cote:

In late July, as you know, your Cincinnati Mill shipped a total of 100 three-inch finishing rollers to our Huntington plant against our order JU-0000, whereas the Huntington plant ordered only 10 rollers.

We were able to resolve the disposition problem by having Huntington accept 20, Lexington accept 20, and Charleston accept 20, with the remaining 40 being shipped to your Knoxville plant.

Attached are copies of your tally sheets, our Bill of Lading for the shipment to your Knoxville plant, and the freight bills for the shipments to our Lexington and Charleston plants to substantiate our claim. As outlined on the attached recap sheet, our claim amounts to $00,000, which includes the freight charges to Lexington ($000) and Charleston ($000).

We would appreciate your reviewing this and issuing your credit to our Huntington plant. If you require additional information, please let me know.

Sincerely,

Credit Information

Gentlemen:

We have the name of your organization as a credit reference for

_____

_____

It will be appreciated if you will give us the benefit of your credit experience with this company, as well as any other comments concerning its management and general reputation, which would assist us in extending an appropriate line of credit.

The information you share with us will be held in strict confidence and will be used for credit purposes only. We will welcome an opportunity to reciprocate at any time.

Year of First Sale _____

Highest Credit Last 12 Months _____

Amount Now Owing _____

Amount Past Due _____

Terms of Sale _____

Promptness of Payment _____

Special Comments _____

_____

Enclosed for your convenience is a self-addressed return envelope. Your early reply will be appreciated.

Cordially yours,

Here is a short version of the above letter (it is advisable to enclose a postpaid envelope):

Would you please submit the following credit information on the above-named firm. We appreciate your cooperation and will gladly reciprocate any time.

Then list the information required from the model letter above. Additional facts that could be requested include the following:

Date of last sale	Number of days slow
Average credit extended	Prompt in payment
Recent high extended	Unjust claims
Unearned cash discounts	Referred to collectors
Discount period	Written off to expense

Credit Card

Dear Mr. Henery:

Please arrange to secure a telephone credit card for John Hamilton, who has transferred to our administrative staff. Please forward the credit card to my attention.

Sincerely,

Warranty Questions

Dear Mr. Donaldson:

We are delaying payment of the attached invoice for service work performed by you to make our second cooler operable.

Even though the cooler has been installed for several months, it was not operated until last month. The adjustments you made were adjustments that I feel should be covered by the warranty. Additionally, I was under the impression that when you volunteered your help, it was covered by the warranty.

Please look into this, and let me know what will be done.

Cordially,

Making an Appointment

Dear Harry:

I have looked over the proposed agreement for the sale of your heavy equipment. It meets all the normal requirements, but I do have a few questions and want to go over the payment schedule.

We can discuss the questions over the phone or you can phone for an appointment before May 25, when it will be necessary to sign the final document.

Sincerely,

Dear Clyde:

I will be glad to talk with you concerning your contract with the publishing firm in San Francisco. If you would please call or write me at least two weeks before you plan to come to San Francisco, we can arrange an appointment.

Sincerely,

Old Equipment

Branch Managers:

The Johnson hoists at many branches have fallen into disrepair and many are no longer used for a variety of reasons.

I would like to evaluate the status of this equipment at each branch to determine the cost of repair, how much help you may need from Central Engineering, and what performance and saving opportunities are available.

By Monday, July 7, I would like replies to these questions from each of you:

1. Are the hoists operational? If not, why not?
2. When were attempts last made to repair them?
3. Describe the repair work necessary to make the hoists operational.
4. What savings are possible compared with your present hoisting system?

John Harvey is available at Central Engineering to help you answer the above questions. Feel free to call him at 000-0000.

Sincerely,

Pollution Check

Dear Mr. Watson:

On September 4, 19__, you took samples of our manufacturing plant's smoke stack emissions. Has any testing been done yet?

Our corporate office would like to know the requirements our emissions must meet now and five years from now. We need this data so capital budgeting can be planned if additional filtering or treatment is required.

What information can you give us now?

Sincerely,

Corporate Name

Gentlemen:

Please reserve the name B. C. Manufacturing, Inc. for a corporation that is being formed. The ten dollar reservation fee is enclosed.

Sincerely yours,

Dear Mr. Davidson:

I will proceed to clear the proposed name of your new corporation and arrange to set it up as soon as you notify me to go ahead. When you call me, I will also need the following information:

1. Names and addresses of directors to be elected at the first meeting
2. Names and addresses of officers of the corporation
3. The fiscal year to be selected by the corporation

I enjoyed meeting you yesterday and look forward to meeting the other principals as soon as they are all back in town.

Sincerely,

Please Investigate

Dear Josh:

Thank you for your letter of November 10 about Sanders Company complaints.

Although your letter refers to four complaints from them, we have received only two written complaints as of the first of November. As explained to you over the phone, the complaint on service did not exist. I wonder, therefore, who or what has caused the sudden rash of excuses to cease buying our belting.

I would be interested in hearing if you are able to determine who is really the culprit who is trying to instigate our removal as their supplier.

Sincerely,

Incomplete Files

Dear Ms. Pennington:

In reviewing our major construction project list, the item of sound enclosures for the hammer mill raised a question in my mind. Because of recent changes in office personnel, my files on the noise citation by the State are incomplete.

Would you please review your files and let us know when the sound enclosure should be scheduled for completion.

Sincerely,

Office Furniture

Gentlemen:

Please send us a catalog of your office furniture and supplies. We are planning to purchase new furniture and file cabinets.

Sincerely,

Life Insurance Questions

Dear Mr. Thomas:

Can you help me find the answers to a few questions about my life insurance policy No. 5320116? The questions are these:

1. What is the present death benefit?
2. What is the present cash value?
3. What is the current loan against the cash value?
4. What will the death benefits be at March 30, 19__?

Your reply will be appreciated.

Sincerely,

Correct an Error

Dear Ms. Caldwell:

Account No. 000-0000-00000

The enclosed check No. 0000 was included in our batch of checks paid per your bank statement dated December 30, 19__, copy enclosed.

This check belongs to our Watson Division at Salt Lake City. Please make the necessary corrections.

Sincerely,

Restricting Receiving Hours

Dear Mr. Carter:

In order to meet the shipping schedules required to fill our customer's demands, without increasing the personnel and equipment of our shipping and receiving department, we must restrict the receiving of raw materials to either the day or swing shift. Our primary supplier prefers the swing shift, but this may interfere with our secondary supplier with whom you deal directly.

Please investigate this from the secondary supplier's point of view and let me know your thoughts.

We must act on this soon.

Sincerely,

Using Credit Memo

Attn: Accounts Payable:

Enclosed is a copy of our credit memo No. 1444 dated March 23, 19__ in the amount of $277.77.

This credit is open on your account, and we would like for you to deduct this amount when making your next payment. This will make your account current.

If you have any questions, please call me at 000-0000. Your cooperation is appreciated.

Sincerely,

Procedural Change

Gentlemen:

Your current practice of mailing two copies of your invoices to A. C. Corporation, Milwaukee branch — one marked *original* — and also mailing two copies of the same invoice to the A. C. Corporation headquarters office, Detroit — one marked *original* — is confusing. This has resulted in duplicate payments because two copies are marked *original*.

In the future, please mail your invoices, one *original* and three copies to A. C. Corporation, Milwaukee only.

Your cooperation is appreciated.

Sincerely,

Dear Mr. Hiller:

Last year we received a number of product complaints that could not be tied down to specific dates and crews. I would like to suggest that we stamp or print the factory job number on each item. This would also separate the jobs we have manufactured for us by outside firms.

I would appreciate your comments and any suggestions.

With regards,

Keep Records

Dear Bob:

Because of recent problems with the telephone switchboard, please have your people keep records of problems with incoming calls and complaints about phone service from our customers.

Let me have a report each Friday until the situation has been corrected.

Sincerely,

Reporting Period Changed

Dear Mr. Teller:

In my letter of February 14, 19__, you were requested to prepare Special Fund data as of the end of each quarter in 19__. Please refer to that letter and prepare the data requested for the six months ended June 30, 19__. Do not submit the information for the second quarter only. Please reply by July 22, 19__.

If you have any questions about this request, please call Hal Lorimore at this office.

Sincerely,

Personnel Evaluation

Dear Tom:

Please make a brief written evaluation of each of your fork truck drivers, covering the following points:

1. Description of duties
2. Performance rating for each of the duties
3. Outstanding weaknesses and strengths

Rank performance from a high of 4 to a low of 1. Number 4 is consistent performance above the position's requirements.

Please have these ready for my review by October 14. We will discuss the ratings on October 16, and set up a program for performance improvement.

Sincerely,

Safety News

Dear Martin,

Because of the recent increase in our accident frequency rate, our District Manager suggests a monthly bulletin to publicize our safety activities.

This will be posted on all bulletin boards and will increase safety awareness among our employees.

Let's get it started this month.

Regards,

Price Quote

Gentlemen:

As part of our program for developing vendor sources, a quote from you on the items listed below would be appreciated:

_____

_____

_____

Please return your quote in the enclosed, postpaid envelope.

Sincerely,

(The words *vendor sources* can be changed to *alternate suppliers* if applicable.)

Where Is the Report?

Dear Al,

I am still looking for:

1. Supplies inventory changes you recommended
2. Purchase order study
3. Standard costs for ink usage

Please let me know when you expect to have these ready for my review.

Best regards,

Dear Bob,

What happened to the report comparing manufacturing and purchasing costs of tie-downs?

Sincerely,

Chemical Hazards

Dear Supplier:

In order to insure the safety and health of all our employees, protect the environment, better serve our customers, and comply with current Government regulations, we must identify any hazards associated with the chemicals you supply us.

All of the questions on the enclosed SAFETY ADVICE are important. We would like a response that leaves no spaces blank. Answer each question as completely as possible.

Upon receipt of your response, it will be reviewed in light of our use of the chemical. If further information is required, we will phone or write for the specific data needed.

Any future changes in composition of the chemicals from that currently used should be reported promptly with a revised SAFETY ADVICE.

Your assistance is greatly appreciated, and we look forward to continuing our friendly business relationship.

Sincerely,

Physical Inventory

Gentlemen:

We request that you take a physical inventory on September 30, 19— of all merchandise held by you for the account of A. C. Corporation. This inventory is necessary due to our Fiscal Year Closing on December 31, 19—.

Please prepare your inventory report in triplicate and attach an Inventory Certificate to each copy of your report. Copies of Certificates are enclosed.

Please mail all three copies to my attention.

Please be certain that the cutoff is as of the end of business on September 30 and that all receipts and shipments or deliveries of merchandise up to the time of taking the physical count are properly recorded.

Sincerely,

Opinion Asked

Dear Fred,

Attached is Alex Smith's proposal to simplify our die usage calculations and make them more accurate. I feel that Alex did a fine job improving the procedure.

If you agree with the procedure, Alex will be available to run a short training seminar on the use of the revised system.

Let me know your feelings.

Sincerely,

Survey of Consumption

Gentlemen:

The State of California Department of Water Resources would like to ask your help in an important survey of industrial water use. Our objective is to obtain information on the specific nature, location, and amount of water use that will enable us to develop plans for effective water management and development. Your plant water data will help us estimate future water needs and the need for supplemental water supplies.

Our last survey, in 19___, revealed a total statewide industrial water requirement of about 500,000 acre-feet, or about 20 percent of total urban use. We believe that percentage figure has changed because of increased awareness of the need for water conservation and because of the increased water recycling and reuse by industries such as yours. The 19___ drought emphasized the potential economic threat of a water shortage. Today's demands on our existing supplies emphasize that shortages could occur unless we plan for the future now.

We believe the information we need will be readily available from your 19___ year-end reports. We will of course treat your plant data as confidential, privileged information and will not publish individual plant data.

We would appreciate your returning the enclosed form by May 15, 19___. Please direct any calls you may wish to make regarding this survey to the nearest Department office as indicated on the back of the questionnaire.

Sincerely,

With thanks to Mr. R. B. Robie, Director, California Department of Water Resources.

Claim Follow-Up

Dear Steve:

I am attaching copies of two letters dated January 27, 19___ to which we have had no reply.

The letters pertain to freight claims No. A477 and A479 on shipments to Grand Rapids.

We would appreciate your reviewing these claims and letting us know their current status. If you require copies of the backup material sent with the letters or any other information, please let me know.

Sincerely,

Suggestions

Gentlemen:

To help me update our commodity file index, I need your input in the form of suggestions for items that should be added to or deleted from the present index.

In order for your responses to be incorporated into the revised index, your input is needed by February 27, 19___. If no response is received by that date, I will assume that the present index is satisfactory.

Your suggestions will be appreciated.

Sincerely,

7

COMPLAINTS—
MAKING AND
ANSWERING

MAKING COMPLAINTS

Some people love to complain. Most people don't, but at times writing a complaint letter is necessary. A consumer writing a long, rambling complaint about a product or service can expect a return letter outlining a method of correction that is more troublesome than helpful:

> Please fill in the enclosed form and mail it to us. Under separate cover send the clock to our Central Service Center. After we have received both, we will examine the clock and then send you an estimate of the repair cost if the damage is not covered by our limited warranty. If you accept our estimate, you can notify us by mail. We will then repair the clock, send you the bill, and return the clock when payment has been received.

Perhaps you will receive a form letter that hardly touches the issue:

> Please accept the four boxes of Super Soap we are sending you. Super Soap makes your clothes whiter and brighter.

To get a proper response, the complaint letter must be brief and clear. The items of complaint must be specified or listed. Acceptable solutions to the problem or the requested action must be spelled out or listed.

The complaint letter below is short, direct, positive, and insistent — but still polite. The politeness is emphasized by the use of the phrases "will you please" and "we would appreciate." The most derogatory statement is a mild "so far we have heard nothing from you." The insistence is shown by the phrases "it is imperative" and "your doing this immediately."

The situation has been made easy for the receiver of the letter by enclosing copies of the original request and the original inventory certificate. Both the purpose of the letter and the requested action are stated clearly.

Gentlemen:

On September 12, we mailed you a letter requesting that you take a physical inventory on September 30, 19__. A copy of this letter is enclosed.

So far we have heard nothing from you, and it is imperative that we receive the inventory certificate, copies of which are also enclosed.

Will you please follow through on this request and return the certificates to the locations shown in our letter. We would appreciate your doing this immediately.

Sincerely yours,

How to Do It

1. State specifically what is wrong.

2. Explain your viewpoint in a reasonable manner.

3. Suggest specific adjustments or corrections.

Transit Damage

Dear Mr. Baldwin:

Attached are some photos of a truck shipment of cereal boxes that arrived at Des Moines this morning on our order No. 7771.

As you can see in the pictures, there was a space of about three feet between the last stack of boxes and the truck door. This space was not braced or filled with dunnage, allowing the boxes in the rear of the truck to shift and fall over.

Please call this to the attention of those in charge of loading trucks. Reasonable effort must be made to minimize damage while in transit.

Sincerely,

Cost of Purchases

Dear Jim:

During recent months there has been a substantial increase in the dollar amount of rollers purchased rather than manufactured. This has led to a variety of problems. Internal paper work has left much to be desired. Our controller, working with the Sales Department, has this aspect of the problem under study.

Second, the effect of purchased rollers on profit forecasting has contributed to great variances in two of the last three months. This part of the problem will be brought under control through an improved flow of information from the Sales Department to the Administrative Department. Again, our controller will be calling on the Sales Department to assist him with this part of the problem.

In the future, before a commitment to purchase rollers is made, I want to review the cost, price, and profit relationships. It appears that in some cases we are not breaking even as planned, but are actually losing money.

My review will continue until I have satisfied myself that these outside purchases are contributing to our profits.

Sincerely,

Incorrect Mailings

Dear Ms. Gerald:

The Accounts Payable computer printouts are being processed and mailed on a timely basis. For the past several months, however, mailings have been to the wrong destinations. This delays our accounting closings.

Specifically, there is complete confusion between Portland and Vancouver, possibly because both are supervised by the same controller. But they are not one; they are not the same.

Please try to have the printouts mailed separately and to their separate destinations.

Sincerely,

Inadequate Explanation

Dear Don:

I cannot accept the answers you gave regarding the attached manufacturing complaints. The statement that the valves are not likely to leak does not answer the complaint that the rejected valves are leaking — especially when Ames is asking for a credit of $846.

Please provide a more acceptable answer to these complaints: which crews and persons are responsible; what will be done to prevent future complaints, or preferably, what you have already done.

Please return the complaints with your answers by April 20.

Respectfully,

Messy Work Area

Dear Ms. Warren:

I pointed out three weeks ago that the finish polishing area is a filthy mess. I expect immediate action from everyone to clear the area and to keep it clean on a daily basis.

This is one area that should be as clean as your kitchen.

Sincerely,

Low Sales

Dear Gordon:

As of your March 31 report to Tony Andrews of Willow Pass Co., we are running far behind last year's sales to them.

It was my understanding with our salesman, Bill Boyd, that he and Tony agreed on 4 to 5 million units per month this year. At the rate we are going, it looks like we will average only 3 million units per month.

Being Bill's sales manager, find out how he and Tony explain this.

Sincerely,

Sales Forecast

Dear Gordon:

After reviewing the sales forecast for the next four months, I can see trouble ahead. Each month our salesmen are forecasting a decrease in sales from our budget. When you had the opportunity to change the budget, you elected to stay with the one put together by our previous sales manager.

The real problem will be in March. The salesmen have forecast a reduction from the budget on 190M units, which is less than February, although March has three more working days.

Is your March forecast realistic? If it is, we must cut back from our normal two-shift operation.

Sincerely,

Manufacturing Errors

Dear Jim:

A. J. Token is one of our more profitable accounts. Until recently, we served them 100 percent. During our recent strike and immediately after when we were having printing problems, Token gave a trial order to our competitor, Smith Manufacturing. Now Smith has 30 percent of Token's can business.

Two problems are contributing to this:

1. While it is not economical to run volume orders to precise quantities, Token has repeatedly asked us *not* to underrun orders because they must fill specific orders with our cans. We are consistently shipping both under and overruns.
2. Token picks up most of their own cans from us. Too often they will make an appointment to pick up at a specific hour and then have to wait as long as four hours to be loaded. Idle driver time costs Token as much as on-the-road time.

Although these may seem like minor items, unless they are corrected, they will lose this business for us.

What can you do to correct these problems? What can I do to help you? I would like a reply by July 20.

Sincerely,

Dear Mr. Graham:

Attached is a sample of box board that your plant manufactured with metal particles embossed in the board. Your plant does not appear to be making progress on the elimination of scrap metal.

Metal of this nature, if found in a finished food box, could cause one big suit against our company.

Please let me know what action is being taken to remove this problem.

Sincerely,

Dear Mark:

Our customer, Auto World, is still complaining about our aqua blue paint fading in less than a year. We have been over this problem several times before, and until we can create a new formula, you will have to use the more expensive Z pigment. I understood that you were using it.

Please let me know when you reintroduced the Q pigment and why. Change to Z pigment immediately.

Sincerely,

Dear Mr. Glen:

The front trailer caps made for our last order, No. 78-0000, are too much in variance from the pattern we supplied you.

We can correct the caps we have, but we cannot tolerate such variances in the future.

Regards,

Dear Mr. Watson:

Repeatedly during the last three years, complaints have arisen concerning plastic containers with loose lids manufactured in your plant.

You and I have had many conversations about this matter during these three years. At this time, we have customers indicating that future shipments to them should be made from our Southside plant rather than from your plant.

Considering this, prepare a report covering the conditions that have caused this problem, the steps already taken to correct the condition, and those additional steps you propose to take, using your present manufacturing equipment.

Please send the report to me by March 15.

Regards,

Manufacturing Problem

Dear Mr. Eikart:

We are having a problem with the Boro Air Hammer that your company manufactured, resulting in a drastic decline in our production rate.

Dust is being taken into the lubricating system, causing the machine's emergency cutoff to be activated. After a great deal of investigating, we found that we can operate the hammer if the speed is reduced.

It appears that one of two steps could be taken to correct the problem:

1. Take measures to prevent dust from entering the lubricating system.
2. Install a filtering system sufficient to remove the dust.

I would appreciate having someone from your company take an in-depth look at this problem. May I hear from you soon?

Sincerely,

Shipping Errors

Dear Bob:

We are having a lot of problems with sales to Adam-Sloop Co., and these seem to stem from your shipping department.

Here is a sampling:

1. On 11-12-__, our dray tag 3300 indicated Adam-Sloop's order 1221 "complete" with a quantity of 5000. Adam-Sloop recorded receipts of 15,000. There were probably three units per package, but the quantity should be stated correctly.
2. Dray tag 3322 of 11-15-__ indicated "various" for Adam-Sloop's purchase order number. They had to unravel which orders this shipment applied to.
3. On 12-18-__, a load was received on dray tag 4412, four weeks *after* they received our invoice.

Bob, these are only a few of the current problems. Adam-Sloop has about had it untangling our sloppy shipping procedures. We don't want to lose this customer.

Will you please check into this problem, and let me know if you need more information.

Sincerely,

Billing Error

Dear Mr. Danzig:

In reply to your letter of August 11, 19__, please, please, please! try to get your computer-billing and receivables departments together. We are developing a large correspondence file because of errors on your invoices.

The invoices mentioned in your letter, numbers 8-1-4949, 4950, and 4951, are internally inconsistent: they state "freight allowed" but do not allow the freight that should have been allowed because we paid the freight bills. (See paid copies attached.)

Please correct your records.

Sincerely yours,

Computer Error

Dear Mr. Lucas:

As you requested, this is why we had to rerun your branch's payroll for the week ending August 21:

The payroll card transmission from your terminal for August 19 was dated August 18. The error report we sent to your branch indicated the error, but it was apparently ignored. Thus, the computer automatically paid overtime rates for the hours worked on August 19 but reported as August 18.

We reran the weekly report correctly on August 24 for an additional cost to you of $840.

This situation points out the necessity of checking all input data and any error reports from our center.

If I can be of further help, please call me.

Sincerely,

Catalog Order

Gentlemen:

The enclosed dress was not what the catalog photo made it appear to be, so I am returning it.

Not only was the style different but the color sent to me was not the one I ordered.

I'm enclosing the catalog page. If you can send me the dress pictured in the proper color, please do. If this is not possible, I would like a refund.

Sincerely,

Misrepresentation

Dear Mr. Randall:

It isn't often that I become upset enough with sales personnel in a store to write a letter to the manager. However, a recent incident occurred in your sporting goods department that left me both angry and frustrated — and more than a little disappointed.

As a novice camper, I am far from knowledgeable about the types and quality of equipment required. Because of this, I relied upon your clerk, Harley Stolman, to provide me with accurate information when I needed a lantern. My original intention was to buy a Coleman, a well-known brand, even to me. The department clerk persuaded me that the store brand, on sale at the time, was a better buy in the long run and of equal quality to the Coleman. When I used the lantern this last week, it failed to provide adequate light and was difficult to operate. I am thoroughly dissatisfied with it. I realize now that I should have refused to give in to the clerk's persuasive tactics.

I would like to return the lantern and apply the price to the purchase of a Coleman lantern. The original receipts are enclosed, and the lantern is being returned by parcel post. Please let me know the additional amount of money required. Please ship it to the above address via UPS.

Sincerely,

Parking in Driveway

Dear John Stover:

Our neighborhood has really gotten crowded in the past few years and little space seems to be available. However, I'd like to ask you to no longer park in front of my driveway.

Not only is it illegal, but it has kept me from getting out of my garage on several occasions.

Perhaps you may find parking further down the block.

Sincerely,

Noisy Driver

Dear Mrs. Frames:

I don't like being a wet blanket, but I feel it is necessary to say something about the noise outside my window each morning at 4 A.M.

Everyone's schedule is different but, since I work and your son doesn't, I'm usually sound asleep when he zooms in from a party or whatever. The shouting and screeching of tires have left me bleary-eyed.

I would appreciate it if you'd speak with him and ask him to be a little quieter at that hour of the morning. Some of us need our sleep.

Sincerely,

Meetings Out of Control

Dear Mr. Swanson:

The town meetings need to be better structured if any effective business is to be carried out.

Last week's meeting required over three hours to do what could have been completed in five minutes. Everyone in the audience seemed to be talking and the speakers went unheard.

Perhaps following *Robert's Rules of Orders* would help to organize future meetings better.

Sincerely,

Muddy Newspaper

Dear Mr. Bishop:

Jimmy W. is a good newspaper carrier in most respects, but I cannot convince him to place the paper on my front porch each morning.

He often throws it in the garden, or on the wet lawn, or in the mud, or most often leaves it at the end of the driveway. I like to enjoy my paper with my morning coffee.

Without reprimanding him, or making him uncomfortable, could you instruct him to put the paper on the porch?

Sincerely,

Delivery Person

Dear Ms. Bell:

Having a dry cleaner who still delivers is a luxury for which I am grateful, However, I've had several difficulties with your delivery man recently.

The deliveries sometimes arrive when I'm not home and I've come home to find my clothes hanging on the doorknob or piled carefully on the porch.

Would it be possible, so I can avoid possible loss, for you to notify me in advance approximately what time the clothing will be delivered?

Sincerely,

Barking Dog

Dear Mr. McDowell:

The barking of your dog all night has kept me from sleeping for the past week. I realize that in this part of town a dog is required for protection. However, he seems to be spending half the night howling to get in.

I don't mind when I don't have to work the next day, but getting up at 6 A.M. is hard after losing half a night's sleep.

Is the entrance where the dog scratches and barks to get in at the opposite side of the house from where you sleep, making it hard to hear him? If that's the case, would you mind if I would call you each night just as a reminder that he's out there? I'd appreciate it greatly.

Sincerely,

No Stop Light

Dear Council Members:

The lack of a stoplight or a sign at the corner of East St. and West St. has created a dangerous situation for both motorists and pedestrians.

In the past six months, seven accidents (two of them serious) have occurred. School children must cross East Street at that point to get to school and often have to dodge cars to do so.

In order to prevent further accidents and to save our children's lives, it is absolutely imperative to place a traffic control at that point.

Sincerely,

ANSWERING COMPLAINTS

If we were all perfect, adjustment letters would be unnecessary. But such letters are necessary, and the writer answering a complaint can grasp this opportunity to write what is in reality a sales letter. The writer is selling goodwill.

Answer promptly or the goodwill will melt away as the complainer begins to boil. If no answer is possible immediately, at least let the complainer know you are working on the problem. The problem may seem a slight irritant to you, but to the complainer it is important or it would not have been mentioned. The complainer's viewpoint must be recognized because he or she is your customer or perhaps your neighbor. The friendship of neither should be jeopardized.

There are, however, times when the complainer is out-and-out wrong. Don't say that in your letter, but remain calm and polite and thank the writer for bringing the problem to your attention. Give convincing reasons for your position and, when possible, offer some help or an alternative. End on a friendly note.

Adjustment letters must use positive statements — positive from the complainer's point of view. For example:

Negative – We can't make the adjustment.

Positive – We suggest you talk to your local dealer.

Negative – Your complaint arrived today.

Positive – Thank you for bringing this problem to our attention.

Negative – We don't know what is wrong.

Positive – We are investigating the problem and will let you know as soon as possible.

Remember: you are selling goodwill.

How to Do It

1. Agree with the complainer on some point or thank him or her for bringing the problem to your attention.
2. Tell what action has been taken.
3. End with a goodwill-building statement.

Opening Sentences

Start with this thought in mind: *my customer is the one who keeps me in business.*

We are shipping you a new vase today to replace the broken one you received.

Thank you for your letter of May 23, pointing out a problem with your new washer.

We appreciate the concern you felt when your new vacuum cleaner began to smoke.

Your replacement motor will be shipped tomorrow.

Yes, we certainly will honor our guarantee.

You were absolutely right in feeling cheated.

Thank you for bringing our billing error to our attention.

Closing Sentences

The closing thought for a letter adjusting a complaint is this: *if I am going to keep this customer, I must keep his or her goodwill.*

We shall always appreciate your business and your confidence in us.

We appreciate your telling us this problem and giving us the opportunity to correct it.

We appreciate your business and will continue to do our best to earn your confidence.

We are always ready and willing to help a customer with a problem.

If you ever have problems again, please let us know. We are ready to help.

We service what we sell. Call us at any time.

We are sorry for the inconvenience we caused, and we will make every effort to prevent a recurrence.

Above all, we want our customers happy.

Disturbed Retail Customer

Dear Mrs. Lincoln:

Your letter of May 14 really took us down a few pegs. I will admit that we were partly to blame for the mix-up, but surely our whole organization can't be as bad as you picture it.

We are sorry for the confusion with your order, and we are sending you a new sofa with the pillows and seats upholstered as you requested. Please come in for a visit before deciding to quit us completely. We have served you well in the past and we know we can in the future.

Sincerely,

Our Mistake

Dear Mr. Evers:

You are absolutely right in not liking the way we handled your proposal for extended payments on your account.

Please accept my apologies for our sending you a letter that should never have left our office. It was a form letter to delinquent customers, and was sent because somehow your letter proposing an extended payment plan did not reach our credit department when it should have. Communications between our own departments failed at a crucial time.

As we discussed on the phone, we are happy to cooperate in making your payments easier. If you will sign the enclosed agreement and mail it to us with your first payment, we will again be working together.

We are sorry for the inconvenience this has caused you, and if you wish to discuss any details further, please call me personally.

Sincerely,

Misunderstanding

Dear Barney,

I admit that my letter of April 7 must have confused you. It was dictated and sent to the steno pool before I learned from Mr. Thompson that the two of you had agreed our contract should be changed to include service to the hydro cooler. I agree that this change should be made.

Unfortunately, my original letter did get mailed. I am sorry for the confusion, but am glad that we now agree on all points.

Sincerely,

Incomplete Instructions

Dear Mrs. Wordsworth:

We agree that the blouse you returned shrunk in your washing machine. This particular blouse is not washable although some blouses of similar appearance are. Our sales staff has been instructed to make each customer aware of how each blouse must be cleaned. Sometimes a clerk will forget.

Whether or not this was the case, we are sorry, Mrs. Wordsworth, for the disappointment and inconvenience to you.

Please let me know if you wish a replacement of the blouse or a credit to your account. Above all, we want our customers happy.

Sincerely,

Misdirected Mail

Dear Mr. Fife:

The purpose of this letter is to follow up our phone conversation of July 11, and your letter of June 28.

The problem referred to in your June 28 letter appears to have started earlier this year when some operations were discontinued at San Jose. At that time, we were requested to route *some* reports to San Mateo that previously had gone to San Jose. These instruction changes obviously did not result in proper routing of all reports affected.

We have issued report distribution instructions to correct the problem pointed out in your letter; we believe this will correct the mailing problem.

I would like to mention, however, that members of my group have found it extremely difficult to acquire and verify proper mailing instructions for reports. Letters such as the one you initiated on June 28 are helpful in assuring correct distribution and we appreciate your notification of the problem.

I encourage you to continue calling our attention to any problem of this nature. Please call Linda Arnette at 000-0000, extension 0000, to expedite the notification process.

I am sorry for the inconvenience caused by the erroneous mailing instructions.

Sincerely,

Late Delivery

Dear Mrs. Polk:

Your annoyance at not having received the engraved silver cups you ordered March 4 is understandable.

Orders requiring engraving work require from four to six weeks for delivery. Our salesperson apparently did not make that clear, and we are sorry for the misunderstanding.

Your order will be shipped on Tuesday of next week and should arrive within four days. Please forgive the delay. I am sure you will like the fine workmanship in the engraving.

Sincerely,

Shipping Error

Dear Mrs. Montez:

You are certainly justified in being angry about our blunder in returning the unordered merchandise you had returned to us. Please let me apologize. The error was ours, but it would help us when you return merchandise if you would enclose a note to me or our sales representative stating why it is being returned. This will insure proper credit to you.

You will receive immediate credit for this returned merchandise and all shipping charges.

Again, I am sorry for the inconvenience to you. We do value your business and your friendship.

Cordially,

Delayed Order

Dear Mr. Olin:

We received your order No. 4270 for six dozen lamps No. 4477 on March 17.

We are sorry for the delay, but we no longer make this particular style and ordered it for you from Sunset Lamps. They promised delivery by April 15. If this is not satisfactory, please let us know.

Sincerely,

Delivery Method

Dear Mr. Bruno:

We shipped your order No. 84222 for three air valves air express, special delivery rather than parcel post because we assumed time was a critical factor.

Because our assumption was in error, we are mailing you a credit memo today for the difference in delivery rates.

Sincerely,

Damaged Merchandise

Gentlemen:

Thank you for your letter of July 17 describing damage to the coffee makers you received July 14.

A replacement order was shipped today.

We are sorry about the damage and the inconvenience it is causing you. We have installed a new conveyor loading system and although the product damage problem is nearly licked, we have an occasional setback. We will try harder next time.

Sincerely,

Dear Mr. Shawner:

This is to thank you for your letter of July 7, 19__ and the five dollars for handling expenses.

I am very sorry to learn that the Abrahm lamp shade we sent you arrived damaged.

I am sending you a new shade and am requesting our Accounting Department to issue a refund check for five dollars.

Thank you for bringing this to our attention. If we can be of help at any time, please do not hesitate to call us.

Sincerely,

Dear Ms. Appleton:

We are sorry your table arrived damaged. A replacement will be delivered Thursday, and the driver will pick up the damaged one.

We thank you for your courteous letter explaining the damage. We hope the inconvenience to you was small and that you will enjoy your new table.

Sincerely,

Dear Mr. Guthrie:

We are sending our salesman, James Hatton, to look at the damaged boxes you received on September 27. He will be able to determine if it is a manufacturing error or shipping damage, and he will want to get a count of the damaged boxes. In either case, we will give you credit or rerun the order. Please discuss your preference with Mr. Hatton when he arrives Tuesday afternoon.

We are sorry for the inconvenience to you, but James Hatton will set things straight. We value your business and friendship.

Sincerely,

Auto Defect

Dear _____:

This will acknowledge receipt of your recent letter concerning the problems you have experienced with your __. We regret the circumstances which prompted you to write.

In order to see that these problems receive prompt attention, we have forwarded a copy of your letter to your dealer and our __ District Office for review. A district representative will be contacting you shortly, and will provide you with the name of the individual at the dealership who is best equipped to deal directly with the conditions described in your letter.

The dealership will also review this matter with our district office and the district will advise us when action has been completed.

Sincerely,

With thanks to the Ford Motor Company.

Merchandise Guarantee

Dear Ms. Wells:

Yes, we certainly will honor our guarantee. If you wish, we will refund your money or send you a replacement for your new oven that does not heat properly.

We would like to suggest, however, that our serviceman for your area first check your oven. The problem may be small and could be fixed in your home. Our service representative, Mr. Harold Bentley, will phone you to make an appointment at your convenience.

We are sorry for the trouble the oven has caused you, but we are confident it can be fixed to your complete satisfaction.

Sincerely,

Wrong Style

Dear Mr. Elton:

Please return the lamps (your order No. P2233) to Sunset Lamps and they will replace them with the style you ordered.

We are sorry for the confusion and delays and will work harder in the future to have your orders filled correctly.

Sincerely,

Unsatisfactory Chair

Dear Mr. Brooks:

We were disturbed to learn that the chair you recently purchased from us did not hold up. We want our customers to be happy, and that is why we have a policy of guaranteed satisfaction.

There are three ways we can handle this situation: (1) we can replace the chair, (2) we can give you a full refund, or (3) you can apply the amount to any other merchandise in our store — you may decide that a different chair will suit you better.

Please indicate your preference on the enclosed postcard and also write in the date that we can pick up the chair. Pickups are made in the afternoons.

We are sorry for the inconvenience and do appreciate your calling the problem to our attention.

Sincerely,

Unsatisfactory Recorder

Dear Mr. Abbot:

Thanks for your letter of July 8 calling your dissatisfaction with our Nicord recorder to my attention.

I'm investigating the problem personally and hope to have an explanation for you shortly. I intend to straighten it out — we want our customers to be satisfied customers.

In the meantime, could you please send me a copy of the sales slip. This will help by giving me the model number, serial number, and date of purchase.

You will hear from me immediately after I receive the sales slip.

Sincerely,

Foreign Object in Food

Dear Mr. Dennison:

I was shocked to learn that you found a tack in one of our Krispy Kookies, but we are grateful that you suffered no injury. You can rest assured that we will take every step necessary to insure that no similar incident will ever occur again.

We thank you for bringing this to our attention. Please accept our sincerest apologies for the concern this incident caused you.

Sincerely,

Declining Responsibility — Frozen Food

Dear Mr. Bishop:

We regret that our frozen dinner did not meet your expectations, but we doubt that the problem is in the processing. We carefully control the quality of our products up to the time they leave the processing plant. Sometimes, during their handling in the retail stores, they are allowed to thaw and are then refrozen. This may cause problems when customers prepare them.

Because we feel we cannot accept responsibility for handling damage after the product leaves our plant, we suggest you check with your local store for a possible refund.

We appreciate your interest in Jamieson's frozen foods.

Sincerely,

Pricing Error

Dear Mr. Helverson:

Your check for $12.50 is enclosed. You were right in discovering that our Artic electric blanket was advertised at a price higher than in other stores in this area.

We have built a large volume business on the basis of quality at the lowest price. We are proud of our reputation.

Upon investigation, we found an error in the advertisement. We are happy to send you — and the others who bought a blanket in response to our ad — the difference between our advertised price and our competitor's price.

We are sorry for the inconvenience we caused you and look forward to serving you for many years to come.

Sincerely,

Billing Error

Dear Mr. Mapes:

You are correct. We did make an error on our invoice No. 42772 of January 10. You are entitled to the 7 percent discount that we unintentionally overlooked. We will mail you a corrected invoice today. I am sorry for the trouble this error caused you and thank you for calling it to our attention.

Sincerely,

Dear Mr. Watson:

We are sorry for our error that made it necessary for you to return our last bill.

You are correct that we omitted the normal 10 percent discount. The $32 freight charge, however, is for air express that you requested on the shipment of diaphragms from our Cleveland plant.

A corrected bill will be sent today.

We are sorry for the inconvenience to you and we assure you we will make a special effort to prevent future billing errors.

Sincerely,

Dear Mr. Harding:

Thank you for calling our attention to the error in Mrs. Harding's account. It has been corrected and a revised invoice will be mailed tomorrow.

Please extend our apologies to Mrs. Harding.

Dear Ms. Casey,

It's easy enough to understand your disturbed frame of mind about Sport Center's repeatedly billing you for the baseball shoes you returned on May 29. Our billing department is certainly throwing you a curve. Please accept our apologies.

We finally got the data into our new computer correctly, and you will no longer be bothered with the erroneous charge.

Cordially,

Statement Error

Dear Mr. Mayer:

The error in your October statement showing a charge of $329.99 for a shipment of batteries was due to a billing error.

We are sorry for the inconvenience, and a credit memo to cancel the billing is enclosed.

Sincerely,

Dear Ms. Horner:

Thank you for bringing the errors in your December statement to our attention. The accounting department is now revising your statement, and it will be mailed today.

Thank you for your cooperation and understanding.

Sincerely,

8

TERMINATION
AND RESIGNATION

TERMINATION

A letter announcing termination of employment should be a model of fairness. No matter how angry the writer is with the employee, it should be remembered that a letter is a written record that can come back to plague the writer if it is not reasonable and polite. The company needs complete documentation of the reasons for the dismissal because some dissatisfied employees take their cases to the National Labor Relations Board, the Equal Employment Opportunity Commission, or to their attorneys. The letter should also be brief in order to eliminate a tendency to present the sad news slowly, and thus painfully, to the recipient.

At the same time, the letter must be positive. Leave no doubt in the reader's mind that he or she is being fired. The first question that comes to the reader's mind is, "Why me?" This must be explained in order to make the letter complete. The explanation must sound reasonable and plausible, as well as being true, so the employer's goodwill (as much as possible under the circumstances) is retained. Terminating an employee is an integral part of any business, but it is also a painful experience for both parties. Treat the situation as even-handedly as possible. This can be done by including all the following points in the termination letter:

How to Do It

1. State regrets at having to terminate the employee.
2. State the fact of termination.
3. Explain why the decision to terminate was made.
4. Make a comment that will retain the employer's goodwill.
5. End on a note of encouragement.

Plant Closed

Dear Mr. Perez:

The recent energy crunch and increasing inflation have forced AZE Corporation to close down several of its operations. Your department will cease operation effective January 10, 19__.

I regret having to terminate your association with AZE, as I believe that your work and enthusiasm have made you an asset to the company.

Rest assured that I will recommend you highly to potential employers as a most competent individual.

Sincerely,

Company Cutbacks

Dear Jean:

I regret having to tell you this, but due to a corporate program of cutbacks, your services will have to be terminated. The effective date will be May 31.

This cutback is being made companywide and will affect about 150 salaried employees. Seven or eight will be laid off in this branch. When deciding whom to let go, seniority was the primary factor. However, headquarters management has determined that certain occupations will be affected more than others.

We are sorry to see you leave and will certainly provide a good reference when you need it.

Sincerely,

Dear Mr. Mullen:

As you have become aware during the past six months, economic conditions have hurt us badly, forcing us to eliminate certain positions. This is unfortunate but we see no alternative. Regretfully, your position is one of those to be eliminated. A lot of hard thinking and long discussions with your supervisor, Mr. Thomas, preceded this decision.

We hope that as economic conditions improve we will be able to consider you for another position when one becomes available. We wish you every success in locating a new position and extend our thanks and appreciation for the good work you have done for us.

Sincerely,

Company Merger

Dear Mr. Grossman:

The recent merger of AZE and BFG Shoe Companies has created a large pool of employee talents, many of which duplicate one another.

It is unfortunate, but many faithful employees of AZE will have to be released by the end of fiscal year 19__ in order that a more efficient, cost-effective operation be established.

It is my sad duty to inform you that your position is one which will be terminated.

This unfortunate occurrence is not meant to reflect upon either your competence or productivity, both of which I would personally vouch for.

If there is any way in which I can be of assistance, please let me hear from you.

Sincerely,

Financial Problems

Dear James Calabar:

It is with deep regret that I must inform you of the recent decision to terminate your association with J. Alcove Inc., as of December 30, 19__. Recent financial problems have forced us to scrutinize our manpower resources carefully, and several employees have, unfortunately, suffered in the process.

Your work here has been admirable and I will certainly provide you with the highest of recommendations if called upon to do so.

With your skills and abilities to work with people, I have no doubt that you will soon secure a position with another organization.

Sincerely,

Indiscretions

Dear Mr. Ludding:

The decision has been made to request your resignation effective June 5, 19—.

Recent publicity regarding alleged indiscretions with several of our members has made effective functioning in your position close to impossible.

Although individual board members maintain a belief in your innocence, public opinion has made our decision inevitable.

You are highly competent in your field and we trust that several new positions will open for you.

Sincerely,

Project Completed

Dear Mr. Evans:

You have done a fine job for us this summer. The Emerson project was a masterpiece of thoroughness and provided our top management with just the information needed.

We would be fortunate to have you back with us next season — and, we hope, for longer. We know you will do well wherever you go.

Sincerely,

Personal Friend

Dear Tommy:

We have been good friends for several years now, which makes this the most painful thing I have been asked to do in my business career. After long discussions with Ron Alyn, he has concluded that the best thing for all concerned is that you leave the company.

I know you will be leaving many friends, but conditions are such now that this seems the best thing to do. Your severance pay will allow you time to locate new opportunities, and I'll be glad to help you in any way I can, now and in the future.

Sincerely,

Performance

Dear Allan:

I am sorry to be the one to tell you this, but your service will no longer be required. However, your pay will continue for two full months. The time is based on your years of service.

We have repeatedly asked you to put more effort and willingness into your work. We believe you have the potential to do a competent job, but your last three reports were late, imcomplete, and inaccurate, and therefore useless to our managers who rely on these reports for operating decisions.

Perhaps you should seek a job that is less demanding and has less critical deadlines. I am confident you will soon find work more suited to your abilities.

Sincerely,

Classroom Procedures

Dear Mr. Weeks:

The school board has recently received several strongly voiced complaints regarding your procedures in the classroom. After a thorough investigation into the charges, the board has voted not to renew your contract for the coming academic year.

Admittedly, Miltown is not an avant-garde town, and many unusual approaches to education are not fully appreciated by the parents of the school children.

I trust that you will locate a position in a school system that is more receptive to your techniques, and we wish you well in your endeavor.

Sincerely,

NOTICE OF EMPLOYEE LEAVING

The occasion will arrive when a company terminates an employee but wishes the real reason kept hidden. This wish may be prompted by controversy that would affect employee morale if brought into the open. These notices are brief, noncommittal, and pleasant. All signs of irritation, disgust, or "serves-them-right" feelings are omitted.

In the notice about Mr. Albert Johnson, the company did not wish to reveal that he had been fired. The notice was made because many in the company should be aware of who is holding that position.

Resignation

NOTICE

Mr. Albert Johnson, manager of our Arlington plant, has left the company to pursue other business interests. He will be replaced by Mr. Gerald Norgard, presently manager of the Sutherlund plant. This will be effective July 1st.

(signed)

A company used the opportunity of an office relocation to dismiss Ms. Georgia Hayes, a secretary who was generally inefficient, but not to the degree that she created a reason for being dismissed.

Retirement

NOTICE

Ms. Georgia Hayes has chosen to take early retirement. She preferred not to transfer with us when we move our office to Willows in August. She joined James & James in 19__ as secretary to Mr. Arnold James.

We will miss Georgia, and I am sure all of you join me in wishing her a pleasant retirement.

(signed)

TERMINATION WARNING

Some adults retain the childhood characteristic of needing a superior to restate their limits. A child may extend his limit of walking one block from home to two blocks unless constantly reminded. A teenager will stay out until midnight unless reminded often that the limit is 11:00 P.M. An adult employee will arrive at work later and later unless occasionally reminded that work starts at 8:00 A.M. Coffee breaks increase from 15 minutes to 20 or 25 minutes. Reports will be completed late unless the deadlines are restated each month. Employees overcome by these habits often respond to a less subtle reminder. The direct approach is required.

When these employees reach the line requiring a warning of possible termination, skip over the calm, subtle tones and state directly the reason for the warning letter, the potential consequences of the employee's actions (or lack of actions), and how the employee can avoid termination.

How to Do It

1. State regrets at having to consider termination.
2. Give reasons for considering termination. Mention *specific* reasons or actions or lack of actions or instances or examples.
3. Make clear that the reader is in a probationary situation.
4. End on a note of encouragement.

Personal Problems

Dear Mr. Bowen:

Termination of an employee is never a happy chore, and we make all efforts to avoid the situation. However, unless your work performance shows substantial improvement, AZE will be forced to terminate our association.

Personal problems affect all of us periodically. When these occur, help should be sought so that such problems do not affect work performance to the point that an individual is unable to function effectively.

Unless you seek professional help and make the effort to perform well once again, we will have no choice left but to sever the relationship.

The excellence of your past record cannot be overlooked, and I trust that your future efforts can be equally successful.

Sincerely,

Poor Performance

Dear Ms. Gallo:

We pride ourselves on being a "family store" and regret whenever we have to let an individual go because of poor performance or other difficulties.

Unfortunately, unless several flaws in your performance are eliminated immediately, we will have to terminate your employment with us. Customers have registered dissatisfaction with your rudeness, careless appearance, and reluctance to assist them in obtaining merchandise.

I'm sure that all of this can be worked out without any further complaints occurring, and with no further reminder required.

Sincerely,

Dear Mr. Sorbert:

It is with regret that I inform you that, unless conditions improve measurably, AZE will have to terminate your association with the company.

Personnel performance and productivity rates have shown steady declines in the past twelve-month period. Frankly, unless improvement is observed, the department will have to be revamped and several other employees released in order to make up our losses.

To be realistic, we estimate that such improvement will take a minimum of six months to become visible. Given your excellent performance record in the past, there is no reason to assume anything but success.

Sincerely,

Dear Mr. Phillips:

This is a written record of our discussion following the accounting audit by the Sano Company on May 22, 19__. You have a copy of the 52 errors in accounting procedures and policies noted by the Sano Company auditors.

We discussed with you our concern and disappointment with these errors as well as your performance as an office supervisor. Company management will share this concern, especially because your position as assistant office manager places you in line for promotion to office manager. Your limited experience has been considered, but of more importance is your evident weakness in accounting skills and your lack of ability to organize procedures. In addition, while discussing procedures with members of your staff, we found morale to be unduly low.

At present, you may consider yourself on probation. Your performance will be carefully monitored, and if, in our opinion, a definite improvement is not forthcoming, there is a possibility that steps will be taken to replace you. You have begun to correct some of the problems, but a review of your progress will be made in four months. We expect to determine your permanent status at that time.

Sincerely,

Classroom Performance

Dear Mr. Chaffee:

The school board has received several strongly voiced complaints regarding your practices in the classroom. Unless modifications of such procedures are undertaken, renewal of your contract cannot be a certainty.

In particular, your suspension of all homework assignments and the assignment of comic books as reading material in a senior literature seminar have been cited. Parents also allege that numerous individual class sessions have become no more than verbal free-for-alls, with little direction by you.

Unannounced teacher evaluation will be utilized within the next two weeks in an effort to clear up this matter. I trust that you will make every effort to conform to the standard of education of this school.

Sincerely,

Tardiness

Dear Mr. Torr:

Promptness is important to the management and the customers at Rich Savings and Loan Association. Therefore, while we make allowances for occasional lateness, consistent lateness cannot be tolerated and offenders must be dismissed.

You have reported late to work for 17 out of the last 23 days. Unless this situation is remedied immediately, you will be asked to leave our organization.

Should there be extenuating circumstances, please come in and speak with me. If there is a problem, perhaps we can work it out together. Rich S & L never likes losing a good employee. I'm sure that the problem can be eliminated.

Sincerely,

Absentee Record

Dear Harvey:

Your work has been excellent, but your absentee record is about to overshadow your work record. I don't doubt that your health has been poor, but one requirement of a job is regular attendance. We have difficulty scheduling our operations when we cannot depend on your attendance.

This subject has been discussed several times before, and now your attendance must meet our requirements or termination will result.

Sincerely,

RESIGNATION

A letter of resignation must be fair to both parties involved. Show tact and consideration for the person or parties from whom you are resigning.

Regardless of the reason for resigning — you hate the boss, the work is too hard, the hours are too long, the work is boring, or you *did* get a better offer — tact is always required. A blatant statement of the facts may arouse the ire of the reader and preclude a good recommendation should you ask for one at a later date. The resigner should assume full responsibility and not blame the boss for causing the resignation.

A socially acceptable reason should be given for resigning. It may be because of poor health, someone in your family is being transferred, you wish to change career directions or wish to specialize in your current career, you received an offer of a promotion with another company, or you have served for a number of years. The occasion may arise, however, when a one-sentence statement of resignation with no explanation or comment is all that is required. The recipient of the letter would already know the reason.

Avoid self praise. It is well to mention the pleasant aspects of having worked for the organization, but do so by mentioning how your associates made work pleasant for you, not how you helped them.

Mention the specific date of resignation.

How to Do It

1. State the effective date of resignation.
2. State an acceptable reason for resignation.
3. Briefly mention the good points of having worked there.

New Position

Dear Mr. Larson:

With great reluctance I am submitting my resignation, effective July 31, 19___.

My association with Wiley Company has been a pleasant one, and I will miss the friendship here. However, as I mentioned in our brief discussion last week, the offer I have received cannot be ignored, considering the financial benefits to my family and the future potential of the position.

I appreciate your understanding of my decision to leave Wiley Company.

Sincerely,

Dear Mr. Aurner:

I have been offered a position that includes a wider range of accounting tasks and one that will lead to a supervisory position.

I am eager to accept this new challenge and will be leaving October 1, 19___. Meanwhile, my best efforts will go into training a replacement.

Sincerely,

Seeking New Challenge

Dear Bill,

Harper Clean Air has grown rapidly during the past fifteen years. The problems of growth presented an intriguing challenge. The challenge was met, and I enjoyed my part in meeting it. The future promises more growth, but I have been at my desk handling the same problems over and over for the past five years. I need a fresh challenge.

Thus, with mixed feelings of leaving an old friend and of needing my own "Clean Air," I am offering my resignation, to be effective

November 30. I will join the new firm of Hoskins and Halloid. They manufacture air valves and plan to expand into similar lines.

We have several people here who could take over my position with a minimum of training. Please accept my thanks for the opportunity you gave me to work with you in meeting the challenges of the past fifteen years.

With regards,

College Training

Dear Mr. Carlyle:

To make full use of my college training in business finance, I have accepted a position with the Norcross Development Company, builders of shopping centers. My resignation will be effective March 31, 19__. I will be glad to help in any way possible to train a replacement.

Over the past few years, I have given serious thought to making a change. I sincerely appreciate the opportunity you gave me here at Johnson's Hardware to learn about business and the importance of work, and especially the help this job provided in financing my college education.

I have enjoyed working here and will continue my personal friendship with you and your staff.

Sincerely,

Ill Health

Dear Ms. Willis:

Resigning was the furthest thought from my mind when I worked so vigorously to become director of the City Youth Program. However, I must leave the position at the end of December.

Ill health and growing burdens in other areas have drained me of the energy and enthusiasm needed to conduct such a program.

The young people and those with whom I've worked have added immense meaning to my life. I only wish I could continue to work with them.

Sincerely,

Heart Problem

County Planning Commission:

With much reluctance and regret I ask to be released from the position of County Planning Director.

Because of a heart condition I have developed, my doctor has instructed me to slow my pace of work.

As you may imagine, this is somewhat of a blow to me, but my doctor knows this condition better than I. During the past six years I've enjoyed working with the fine people of our county. It is difficult for me to resign, but I must do so effective August 15.

Let me extend my good wishes to all of you for success on the riverfront project.

Sincerely,

Allergies

Dear Mr. Newell:

Circumstances require that I resign my position as quality control supervisor, effective March 18, 19__.

My unique susceptibility to the materials worked with makes continued employment in this capacity at Jones Company an impossibility. In addition, I have been ordered by my physician to detoxify my system by isolating myself from the substance for several months.

I am appreciative of the patience and kindness shown to me by both co-workers and management as I have sought to deal with this difficulty. Unfortunately, fairness to myself demands that I resign rather than continue.

Sincerely,

Personal Problems

Dear Mrs. Aldridge:

For nine months, I have enjoyed the pleasure and the benefits of being vice president of the Milltown Businesswomen's Club. Thus, it is with great regret that I must resign.

Recent personal difficulties are creating more demands on my non-professional hours. As a result, I cannot give full attention to my responsibility as vice president, and I feel that I am shortchanging the Club.

Working with the other officers has provided pleasure as well as insight into the skills and competence of today's businesswoman. Please accept my regrets.

Sincerely,

Disagree With Goals

Dear Mr. Deihl:

Recent occurrences demand that I resign my position as Vice President for Public Affairs, effective February 9, 19___.

Disagreement with the goals and philosophy of this company has hindered my performance and negated my ability to assist in furthering those goals.

I will miss the challenge and adventure my role offered, as well as the many people with whom I worked.

Sincerely,

Want Less Travel

Dear Mr. Davis:

It is with deep regret that after eight years with Atwater Shoe Company, I must resign my position effective August 6, 19___.

Financial considerations, and the increased needs of a growing family, require that I accept a position that demands less travel and time spent away from home.

The opportunity for growth and the continuing challenges offered by Atwater in these past eight years have been of great personal and professional value to me. I will miss the personal closeness and the consideration shown by all members of the company.

Sincerely,

Credit Union

Board of Directors:

I hereby submit my resignation as chairman of the Credit Union Supervisory Committee effective March 1, 19___.

Sincerely,

RESIGNATION ACCEPTANCE

The acceptance of a resignation should be with sincere regrets. Only ill will can be gained by implying that the resignation was anticipated or that it is eagerly accepted. Say something nice about the person resigning. If nothing else, say that he or she did a fine job. End with an expression of good wishes for the future.

How to Do It

1. Express sincere regrets.
2. Say something complimentary.
3. Express good wishes for the future.

Dear Bill:

We are sorry to see you leave and accept your resignation with regret.

You accomplished a great deal for us during your six years as our mechanical engineer. You deserve much of the credit for our smooth running and profitable operation.

We do, however, understand your desire to be near your family. We know you will do as much for your new employer as you did for us. The best of luck to you.

Sincerely,

Dear Jim,

All the Church School members and teachers will miss you very much. Your eleven years as Church School Superintendent was an uplifting experience for all of us — in our faith and in our attendance.

No one can replace you, but we will find someone to carry on the work.

We wish you well in your retirement and your move "back to the old homestead," as you put it.

With God's blessing,

Dear Bob,

The Board of Directors regretfully accepts your resignation as Chairman of the Supervisory Committee of the Credit Union.

You worked many long, hard hours auditing the books and the operations of the other committees. We got many new insights through your willing efforts. Your judicious handling of the special meetings during our troubled times of changing managers will never be forgotten by the Board.

We want you to know of our deep appreciation of your work during the past five years, and although our acceptance of your resignation is reluctant, our best wishes go with you.

Sincerely,

9

SYMPATHY
AND
CONDOLENCE

The first essential of a letter of sympathy is a feeling of respect for the reader. He or she has lost a loved one or suffered an accident or succumbed to an illness. A respectful mood is called for. The sympathetic situations covered in this chapter are those in which a cheery greeting or humorous get-well card is not appropriate. The letter should be written from the heart, and should be warm, human, and kind. The writer needs a feeling of empathy with and consideration for the reader. All of these feelings, however, need not be put into one letter. In fact, the second essential is brevity. Long eulogies and maudlinism are out. Do not burden the grief-stricken with more grief. The third part of a letter of sympathy is an offer to help. This does not fit into all situations, but if the intent is sincere and follow-up certain, an offer to help at the end of the letter is a real comfort, especially at the time of the death of a loved one.

The use of the word *death*, along with *died* and *killed* in a letter of condolence is objectionable to some people, because these words seem unnecessarily strong. The word *deceased* is also used as a substitute for *dead*, but is hardly an improvement. References to sorrow, grief, tragedy, or loss can be used, and the meaning remains clear to the reader. Some of the examples that follow use the word *death* and some do not. The decision to use it or not will be based upon the writer's understanding of how the reader will react.

Some letters of sympathy include phrases similar to these: "there is nothing anyone can say at a time like this," or "words cannot express our feelings," or "we don't know what to say at this time." Such phrases should be eliminated. They seem to be put in to lengthen a short statement of sorrow, and they express helplessness at a time when the reader needs help.

How to Do It

1. Mention the person about whom the sympathy is being expressed: for example, Henry, Dr. Miller, your boss, or your sister.

2. State your relationship with this person: for example, our friend at work, my acquaintance of many years, or all of us here.

3. Make a complimentary statement: for example, he was loved by all, he was a warm friend, she was always cheerful, she was helpful, or we spent many pleasant hours together.

4. If appropriate, offer to help the reader.

Sentences Expressing Sympathy

A list of sentences appropriate for letters of sympathy follows. In instances where they seem to fit, they can be added to the sample letters. These statements can also be substituted for statements in the sample letters in this chapter or can be the starting point for a self-composed letter.

We hope our caring will make your sorrow easier to bear.

We hope that time will ease the sorrow of your recent loss.

We know that memories will keep your lost one close to you.

May our sympathy help to comfort you.

May you find comfort in knowing that we care.

Our thoughts are with you in this time of sorrow.

We wish to express our deepest sympathy.

May the love you feel for the one you lost lessen your sorrow.

May the love that surrounds you be a source of comfort at this time.

May your memories be a source of comfort.

It may help to know that our thoughts are with you.

May the sympathy of those who care make the sorrow of your heart less difficult to bear.

Some things are hard to understand.

No one is ever ready for death.

We know death is certain, yet it remains hard to accept.

Those who have not experienced the death of a close one cannot comprehend the loneliness.

There is an emptiness that only those who have lost a close relative can understand.

Our sympathy and love go out to you, Mrs. (Mr.) Smith.

We shall miss her (his) smiling presence.

The loss of a son, (daughter, wife, husband) is giving up a part of one's self.

Sentences Thanking the Reader for an Expression of Sympathy

Without you I wouldn't have known where to turn for the endless number of decisions one must make in a time of grief.

You were such a comfort to us following Edward's death.

Jon always thought of you as a real friend, and that you proved to be during my period of grief.

How much I appreciated your kindness and help when Alexander died.

I just couldn't have managed without your help.

The letter you sent at the time of Andy's death continues to be an inspiration to me.

Thank you for your kind words and your understanding heart.

Your kindness overcame the self-pity I was beginning to feel.

Your words of encouragement stayed with me during my bereavement.

Thank you for your understanding sympathy.

Your love and help during my recent difficulty have meant more than words can express.

We wish to thank you for your kind thoughts.

My husband and I wish to thank you for your kind thoughts.

We wish to thank you for your letter. The kind messages sent by friends have been a great comfort to us.

We appreciate your thoughts of us and your sympathetic note.

We appreciate your kindness in writing to us at this time.

We gratefully acknowledge your kind expression of sympathy.

We appreciated your sympathy in our bereavement.

We thank you for your kindness and sympathy.

Your note of sympathy helped me to accept Tom's death more courageously.

Your sharing of your recent sorrow helped me to bear my present bereavement. Thank you.

It is a comfort in a time of sadness to receive such a beautiful expression of sympathy.

Thank you for your kind expression of sympathy.

Your sympathetic note reminded us of the many kindnesses you have extended to our family through the years.

We are grateful to you for helping us bear our grief by your kind letter of sympathy.

I appreciate the kind thoughts that prompted you to send such lovely flowers.

Letters to Hospitalized People

When writing to a person in a hospital, be pleasant and optimistic while expressing an interest in the patient's welfare. Do not refer to the specific illness or injury — that is the doctor's job.

Hospitalized for Illness

Dear Will,

When I called at your office today, I was surprised to hear that you were in the hospital. With your usual spunk I can't see an illness holding you down very long. Take it easy and enjoy the rest while you can. I'll be looking for you to be back at work soon.

With regards,

Dear Al,

Word of your illness just reached me, and I want to wish you a quick return to good health.

Your many friends will be sorry to learn that you will be in the hospital for a few weeks. I am sure it helps to know that you have a large group of well-wishers.

When you return home I'll be over to see you. In the meantime, please ask Mrs. Jacobs what I can do for her here. I'll be glad to help in any way possible.

I hope the next few weeks will pass quickly and you'll be home again soon.

Sincerely,

Dear Eilene,

Gloom hangs over the office since we received news of your sudden illness. We send our wishes for a fast recovery. (We need you here at the office.) We hope the flowers will brighten your room in the hospital and cheer your spirits.

Sincerely,

Hospitalized for Accident or Injury

Dear Margaret,

Your mother called this morning to tell me of your accident Saturday and that you will be in the hospital for three or four weeks. We will miss you but don't concern yourself with your work here. We will take care of it for you.

Rest as much as possible under the circumstances. We all hope for a full recovery.

Sincerely,

Dear Mr. Allison:

I am sorry to learn of your injury. Please accept my best wishes for a quick recovery.

Since you will be confined for a few days, I believe you will enjoy this new book on your hobby of boating.

Cordially,

Other's Illness

Dear Ron,

Your friends at Elton Corporation are sorry to learn of your wife's serious illness. Please accept the flowers we have sent with our sincere wishes that she will have a fast and complete recovery.

Sincerely,

Death of Business Associate

Dear Mrs. Appleton,

All of us here at Sear's Lumber are saddened by the death of your president, Andrew Jennings. You have our most sincere sympathy.

Mr. Jennings was a real community leader and served as an example to all of us. His work with the Boy Scouts will long be remembered.

Sincerely,

Dear Linda,

It is with great sadness that we learned of the death of Thomas. I had worked with him in Denver and then in Atlanta until his transfer last August. We will all feel the loss.

Sincerely,

Death of Business Friend

Dear Mrs. Jader,

It is difficult to tell you how deeply I feel about Mr. Jader's untimely death.

What started many years ago as a business relationship between Harold and me quickly became a warm friendship. It was a privilege to have known him so well, and I will never forget his thoughtfulness and kindness.

With great personal sorrow, I ask to share your loss and to extend my heartfelt sympathy.

Sincerely,

Dear Mrs. Reinhardt,

It was with heartfelt sadness that I learned of William's passing. Bill and I worked so well together on the Bonner Bridge project in the late sixties. We spent many pleasant hours together, off the job as well as on. He was a great companion and a warm friend.

Sincerely,

Death of Spouse

Death of Husband

Dear Jean,

Losing one's husband can cause a loneliness unlike any other, but having your children near will help ease the difficulty of the days ahead.

With your fortitude and courage I am sure you will adjust to your new situation. I know you are grateful for the many happy years you shared with Tom.

Love,

Dear Eldrid,

Your John made friends of everyone he met, even during his last days in the hospital. But this was only a part of his personality. We all will remember him for his generosity. He often involved himself in worthwhile civic projects. The community is richer for his having lived.

I wish we lived closer together so I could be with you at this time. I send my love.

Sincerely,

Dear Mrs. Nunan,

Please accept our heartfelt sympathy in your time of great sorrow. Only those who have lost a husband can know the depths of your feelings. We send you our love to give you strength to bear your sorrow.

Sincerely,

Dear Mrs. Emerson:

Mr. Franklin and I wish to express our deepest sympathy to you and your family.

I came to know Dr. Emerson well these last few years. I had no friend whose wisdom and kindness meant more to me. We shall miss him.

Sincerely,

Dear Mrs. LaCosta,

We wish to express our sympathy on the untimely death of your husband. He was a great asset to our company for many years, and all of us old-timers will miss his steadfastness.

If I can be of any help at all please call me.

Sincerely,

Dear Mrs. Bascomb,

I was stunned yesterday to learn of Fred's untimely passing. I have known Fred since coming to work here nearly twenty years ago, and have enjoyed these many years of friendship with him.

Fred was loved by all his co-workers, and his friendliness cheered us all. He will be greatly missed.

Mrs. Bascomb, our thoughts are with you, and we extend our deepest sympathy.

Sincerely,

Dear Mrs. Sanders,

We were both grieved to hear of your loss. Mr. Sanders was the one person we could always go to in time of trouble, however slight. He was so warm and wise and understanding.

If there is anything at all we can do to help you, please let us know.

Sincerely,

Dear Adele,

When there is love, any life is too short. Fred had a way of making the joys of life contagious. We remember especially his help with our basement — a problem was turned into a pleasant and companionable experience.

We know you are grateful for your life with Fred, and we feel fortunate to have known him.

With sympathy,

Death of Wife

Dear Bob,

Perhaps it will help to lessen the sorrow of Mabel's death to realize that so many of her friends share your grief. We all appreciated the happiness she so willingly shared and inspired in her friends.

I know your courage will help you through this rough time. Our love is with you.

Sincerely,

Dear Mr. Gordon,

I wish to express my deepest sympathy. Mrs. Gordon was one of the loveliest women I have ever known. No one who knew her could ever forget her charm and warmth.

Sincerely,

Dear Mr. Jenkins,

Bereavement is so personal that few of us, unless we have experienced it ourselves, can comprehend its grief. Your wife, Jackie, was loved by all of us who worked with her. Her pleasant vitality was a continuous inspiration. We hope that our caring will lessen the sorrow that you bear.

Sincerely,

Death of Relative

Death of Mother

Dear Mr. Donaldson,

We extend our most sincere sympathy to you upon the loss of your mother. If there is anything at all that we can do to help, please call us.

Sincerely,

Dear Ms. Rutherford,

There is a lonesomeness after the death of one's mother, but I want you to know that your friends are thinking of you and sympathizing with you in this time of your great loss.

I will never forget the friendliness and kindness your mother extended to me. She was loved by all who knew her.

                                        With sympathy,

Dear Robin,

My love for your mother will last as long as my memory of her. During the many years we were neighbors, she shared her smiles, her flowers, her recipes, and most of all her pleasing personality.

No one who knew her will ever forget her. I want to share my sympathy with you.

                                        With love,

Death of Father

Dear Miss Elwood,

May I send you my deepest sympathy at this time and say that my thoughts have been with you since I heard of the death of your father. I admired him greatly. You must be even prouder of his devotion to you. I know you will be brave in your sorrow as he would have wanted you to be.

                                        Sincerely,

Dear Mrs. Lansing,

We were truly sorry to read of your father's death yesterday. We will be over tomorrow to help with whatever we can.

                                        With sincere sympathy,

Death of Daughter

Dear Alice,

No person or experience will ever replace the happy days and love little Lana gave you.

We hope it will be of some comfort to know that you gave her all the love and care possible and that your many friends share your sorrow.

Love to you and Jim,

Dear Mr. Arronson:

It was with sincere regret that I heard this morning of the loss of your daughter. I know what a shock you have suffered. I wish to express my deepest sympathy and the hope that the kind thoughts of your many friends will make your grief a little easier to bear.

Sincerely,

Dear Kevin,

I was surprised and saddened to hear from Mrs. Addison that your daughter succumbed to the injuries from her recent accident.

I want you to know how terrible we feel that you have lost a lovely and talented daughter at such an early age.

Please call me if there is anything I can do to help you.

Sincerely,

Death of Son

Dear Brad,

Please accept my sincere sympathy on the death of your son, Jerry.

Sincerely,

Dear Mr. Welch,

The loss of your son comes as a shock to us at the Boating Club. We all had the greatest respect for him and will miss his cheerfulness and lighthearted humor. We realize our loss is small compared to yours.

We offer our heartfelt sympathy in a time of sorrow.

Sincerely,

Death of Sister

Dear Jane,

I have just learned with sorrow of the death of your sister. Because you and your sister were so close, I realize how deeply this loss will touch you. I know you will be able to adjust, and please accept my sincere sympathy.

Cordially,

Death of Brother

Dear Mr. Mantell,

The death of your brother brought profound sorrow to me as well as to his many friends. During the many years I knew him I often thought of him as my own brother.

May, I extend my deep sympathy to you and your family.

Sincerely,

Death of Others

Dear Mr. and Mrs. Inland,

We were shocked to learn of your recent loss. Louis had such promise and was so well liked that it seems hard to believe he is no longer with us. His passing will be mourned by those of us who loved him so much.

Most sincerely,

Dear Madolyn,

We wish to express our deepest sympathy upon the untimely death of Jim.

He was one of our great managers as well as a personal friend to so many of us who worked with him. The many years he devoted to community services will be long remembered by the people of Little Rock. May your memories be a source of comfort.

Sincerely,

Dear Benny,

I am deeply grieved when I think of your loss. Janice was a wonderful friend who always did more than was expected of her. She made this world a little better for me and for all the others who knew her.

Sincerely,

Dear Mrs. Solons,

It was a distressing shock to learn of Howard's death yesterday. We worked together here for many years. If there is anything I can do to help you, please don't hesitate to give me a call.

Sincerely

Dear Janette,

I just learned in a letter from Dave about Jim's accident and the misfortune you are suffering. It's hard to face the loss of a long-time friend even from far away. If I were closer, perhaps I could be of more help to you at this time to ease your strain. But I do send my deepest sympathy to you and your family.

With sympathy,

Belated Condolences

Dear Mabel,

I was deeply shocked and grieved to hear that Edward passed away last month. I will always remember his pleasant ways and how he made us feel so much at home when we visited with you folks.

I think it is great, and a great help to you these days, that you are spending so much time at the Convelescent Hospital as a volunteer helper.

Sincerely,

Dear Ellie,

I learned only yesterday of your father's death. I always admired the cheerful way he helped your neighbors and his willingness to get involved in the town's activities.

I will always think of him with fondness.

Sincerely,

Death by Suicide

Dear Alice,

Word has just reached us of Jerry's tragic death. As impossible as it must be to understand, Jerry must have felt in his own mind that this was the best alternative.

You have the courage, I know, that you will need to face the days ahead.

We send our love and
sympathy,

Dear Ron,

I am deeply moved by the news of Marie's most shocking death. None of us understand it. I am sure she gave a great deal of thought to her decision to depart at a time of her own choosing.

It will require an untold amount of courage for you to carry on, but I have faith that you can surmount the tragedy.

Bless you,

Death — From a Business Firm

Gentlemen:

I am sure the death of Allen Rogers is almost as great a shock to the entire accounting profession as it is to the members of your organization.

Few men have been held in as high esteem as he was for many years. No man deserved it more.

As a member of our profession, I share with many others this tragic loss.

Sincerely,

Dear Mr. Johnson:

We at Basker Company were saddened to hear of Mr. Condon's death. We extend our deepest sympathy. Mr. Condon's leadership in our business community will be sorely missed by the community as well as by his numerous friends.

Sincerely,

Dear Mrs. Addison,

Just a quiet word to extend our deepest sympathy to you and your family, and to let you know we are thinking of you.

Sincerely,

Dear Mr. Browne:

Your great loss has saddened my staff and me. We wish to express our deepest sympathy to you.

Yours sincerely,

My Dear Mr. Lawrence:

We at Jordan's were very sorry to hear of the death of your daughter. Only one who has lost a lovely, young daughter can know the tragedy of this loss.

All of us here wish to extend our heartfelt sympathy. Please let me know if there is anything that we at Jordan's can do to be of help to you.

Sincerely,

My Dear Mrs. Robertson,

Everyone at our company was surprised and saddened by the sudden death of your husband.

Although sympathy is only a small consolation, even from the hearts of us who share your sorrow, I want you to know how deeply Tom's loss is felt here. He was respected and admired by everyone who worked with him.

We cannot eliminate your sadness, but each individual of our company joins in this expression of our deep sympathy.

Very sincerely,

Dear Mrs. Smith:

No one can take the place of a devoted husband, and only one who has had a like sorrow can understand the grief that you are experiencing.

My words can bring only slight comfort when your grief is so great, but I did want you to know that we at Georgia-Pacific extend our deepest sympathy.

We share your personal grief as we have lost a needed and valued member of our team.

Sincerely,

Dear Mr. Sanders:

We have just heard of the great personal loss suffered by you in the tragic tornado that brought death and destruction to your city.

Buildings and even cities can be restored, but the death of your son is an irreparable loss. We are willing to do what we can by shipping you anything you may need to rebuild your business. We'll gladly extend any length of credit necessary. Will you let us do that much for you?

To hear of a friend and customer losing his store and his son brings home to us the heartaches and sadness from which many people in your city are suffering. May you have the strength and courage to carry on.

Sincerely,

Birth Defect

Dear Anne,

A birth defect seems so terrible now, but since I also have a child with a birth defect, let me assure you that it won't be as bad later on as it seems now.

Some physical defects cannot be changed, but control of expressions, revealing a return of your love, can be learned. With your wisdom and patient understanding, your precious baby can develop so her personality shines right through the handicap.

I'll be glad to share my experiences and learning with you. I'll call you soon.

Cordially,

Divorce

Dear Annabelle,

We were surprised and deeply disturbed to hear that you and Jim are getting a divorce.

We don't know your intimate differences or the deep reasons for your decision, but as long as we have known both of you, we didn't realize there were any serious frictions or problems.

We have written a short note to Jim, also, to let you both know that we are ready to help in any way we can.

With love,

Marriage Separation

Dear Janet,

As a lifelong friend of your mother — and of you, too — I am greatly concerned about your separation from George.

I know you are taking this step after serious consideration, but if it should be because of something that could be ironed out, please give the separation another thought or two. I am concerned that such a promising marriage should not endure. All marriages take a lot of work and compromise, but whatever your decision, I will always remain your close friend.

Love,

Misfortune

Dear Brother,

Misfortune hits each of us at some time or other. Hang in there and don't let this drag you down. You have recovered before from setbacks by driving ahead with the next project. Although right now this may seem worse than before, I know your persistence and stamina will propel you to the top again soon.

We here are all rooting for you and know we can expect the best from you.

Regards,

Personal Reverses

Dear Ben,

A stone wall may be all you see now, but out of your adversity I know your tenacious courage will find a gateway opening once again to the success you have achieved before.

Your friend,

Unnamed Tragedy

Dear Mr. and Mrs. Alder,

I saw the report in the paper about Jim, and want to tell you how sorry I am. Jim was three years younger than I, so we didn't play together often as kids. But when I met him at your daughter's wedding last month, I realized what a fine son you have and how proud you must be of him. You'll just have to take my word for how badly I feel.

Sincerely,

Thank You for Your Sympathy

Dear Mr. Cooly,

We appreciate and thank you for your expression of sympathy upon the death of Mr. Olson.

Sincerely,

Dear Beth,

It was heartwarming to receive your comforting letter of sympathy.

Sincerely,

Dear Ms. Nelson,

Thank you for your warm expression of sympathy upon the death of Hugh. The pain is lessened by your kind offer to help, which I may accept soon.

Sincerely,

Dear Mrs. Coulson,

Thank you for your thoughtfulness upon the death of my sister, Ellen.

Sincerely,

Dear Mrs. Eberly,

We were pleased to receive your letter of sympathy. It was a comfort to us. Eleanor always mentioned you with the greatest respect and admiration.

Sincerely,

Dear Mr. Franklin,

We appreciate your kind expression of sympathy.

Sincerely,

Dear Jane and Roy,

Thank you so much for the gift of your friendship. It is a great comfort to our family to know that Dad had such good friends at work. The spray of pink carnations you sent was just beautiful.

With appreciation,

10

APOLOGY

Writing a letter of apology is an ego-deflating task: one just hates to admit a mistake. Because the other party already knows of the error, the best approach is to take a deep breath and plunge in. To be effective, an apology must be genuine; the regret must be sincere but not overly emotional. To say, "I am sorry," "I am truly sorry," or "I am sincerely sorry for my mistake," is a genuine expression of feeling. But to expound, "I don't know what to say, but I ask your forgiveness for my terrible error of sending the wrong replacement parts. I know this has slowed your production startup and has probably cost you a lot of money. We are extremely sorry," is just too much for any reader.

In most instances, make the statement of apology at the beginning of the letter. It is inconsiderate to the reader to hide the purpose in the middle or at the end. Use the middle of the letter for an explanation of the mistake — if an explanation is deemed necessary. Make the explanation as brief as possible while keeping it clear. Omit long, detailed, or technical explanations. The middle of the letter is also the place to relate what is being done to prevent a recurrence of the mistake, or to thank the reader for being tolerant while a confusing situation is straightened out. If an explanation just isn't feasible, don't ramble on saying nothing. The whole letter can say, in effect, "we're sorry; we'll work to avoid repeating the error."

Close a letter of apology on a forward-looking and positive note. If something has been delayed, state the new delivery, completion, or approval date. Make a promise of future promptness and fewer errors. Relay to the reader your confidence that relations will improve.

How to Do It

The following sequence is suggested for a genuine, goodwill-retaining letter of apology:

1. Apologize at the beginning of the letter.
2. Explain the error and the determination to prevent further errors.

3. Close on a forward-looking, positive note.

Sentences of Apology

Here are some statements that will prove helpful when composing a letter of apology:

> We appreciate your patience in allowing us time to research the information and respond to your complaints.
>
> We are sorry that this is one of the few instances in which we cannot make a refund.
>
> We are sorry for any inconvenience we caused you.
>
> We are proud of our excellent service, and you should expect it at all times. We apologize for our failure and will try not to let this happen again.
>
> We try our best, but occasionally errors do slip by. We will try even harder to prevent future errors.
>
> This is one of a very few areas of loss that Forward Insurance Company does not cover, and we are sorry we are unable to help you in this time of need. We suggest you contact Hanford Insurance of Brooklyn for this type of coverage.
>
> Thank you for your patience while we straightened out the confusion about your order. We are sorry for the inconvenience.
>
> Thanks for staying with us while we contacted all parties involved in this confused situation. Your understanding has helped us clear the many tangled ends.
>
> Again, we are sorry for the inconvenience we caused you.
>
> We appreciate the amount of work you put into your bid, and we are sorry we could not offer you the contract.
>
> For an efficient operation, we have found that our policies must be followed in detail. We are sorry we cannot make an exception for you.
>
> Please accept our apology.

Reasons for an Apology

The following are acceptable reasons for making an apology:

> I am sorry I missed our scheduled dinner meeting yesterday in Kansas City. Because of stormy weather there, the plane did not stop over but went directly to Chicago.
>
> I am sorry to hear about the poor printing on your last order. The printer acknowledges the faded-out appearance and will credit you for the full amount.

There was a delay in shipping because the demand exceeded our expectations, and we had to order a second printing.

The delay in shipping was due to a local trucker's strike and alternate carriers were busy beyond their capacity.

The delay was due to our error, for which we have no excuses. If you cannot use the belts sent, please return them for a full refund.

Please accept our apology. We have no explanation for our obvious error.

Mr. Johnson has been ill for the past week.

An unexpected field trip kept me away from the office.

The Chicago trip required two days more than I anticipated.

Unfortunately, due to my oversight this notice did not go out sooner, and I must apologize.

Mr. Sanders is away for two weeks but Ms. Lawson will do the report and have it for you as soon as possible, probably by next Wednesday.

We regret the delay in getting copies to you, but our copying machine broke and we had to send your work to another printer.

We are sorry we omitted the samples when we sent your package yesterday. We made the mistake, but the samples are on the way now.

Unexpected developments prevented my being there.

Bad Behavior

Dear Mr. Hall:

I am sincerely sorry for what happened Wednesday, and especially for my actions. I hope you will accept my apology, and rest assured that nothing similar will occur again.

Regretfully,

Dear Mr. Hallen:

My behavior at the party following our recent dinner meeting was deplorable. I assure you it will not happen again. I was wrong, I have no excuses, and I am sorry.

Regretfully,

Billing Error

Dear Mr. Rodgers:

You are right and we are wrong. We apologize for the error and thank you for calling this to our attention. A corrected bill is enclosed.

Sincerely,

Sorry for the error . . .

We're enclosing for you, Mr. Silva, one invoice not included with your February statement. We are sorry this invoice was omitted. The total of the invoices will now equal the statement amount of $150.65.

We appreciate your being a customer since 1957.

Customer Service Division

Company Procedure

Dear Ms. Arthur:

I am sorry we cannot write you a check from our local plant for your past due freight bill No. 278-089789 as you requested.

We received the copy of the bill on Wednesday, November 21. We have matched it with our purchase order and will mail it today to our headquarters in Detroit for payment.

Although the bill is overdue, because we have not received the original bill, our corporate procedure requires that our headquarters office pay the bill. This procedure speeds payment in practically all instances and includes an audit of all paid freight bills.

You should have your money in less than a week.

Sincerely,

Confusing Word Usage

Dear Mr. Dunbar:

I want to apologize for not helping to sponsor the TV program on containers and the environment that we discussed last Wednesday. We were favorably inclined until we realized that the word *contain-*

ers as you used it meant beer cans, pop bottles, and plastic bottles used to contain thousands of varied products.

In the paper and forest products industry, the word *containers* means corrugated boxes (often called cardboard boxes).

I hope you understand our confusion and appreciate that we do not wish to help sponsor a program not related to this association's industry.

Sincerely,

Declining Dinner Invitation

Dear Mr. Hamilton:

Julie and I appreciate your invitation to dinner on July 10, and it is with regret that we find we have another engagement on that date.

Thank you for thinking of us.

Sincerely,

Dear Mr. Peters:

We are sorry we can't accept your invitation for dinner and the Snappers show on May 3. I have a budget meeting scheduled for that night, and there is no way I can skip that meeting.

With regret,

Dear Mr. Jones:

Since accepting your kind invitation to dinner and the theater on March 2, I have learned of the serious illness of my mother and I will be leaving for Chicago tomorrow.

I am sorry to have to forego a delightful evening with you.

Sincerely,

Delayed Answer

Dear Ms. Gaines:

I deferred writing to you until I had all the facts, and I am glad that I did. New developments show that you were correct in stating that you have not missed the deadline for submitting the manuscript for the article. I was surprised to learn that your arrangements with Mr. Anderson were not communicated to me. I was, therefore, under the impression that you and Mr. Anderson had also agreed on the original date of May 1, rather than the revised date of August 1.

I apologize for the inconvenience I caused you. I am looking forward to seeing your manuscript by August 1.

Cordially,

Dear Ms. Ralston:

Please excuse my delay in answering your letter of February 13, but this has been one of those busy, hectic periods beset with all kinds of deadlines.

I am glad you found some of my survey data useful, and look forward to seeing your report on condominium growth in San Diego.

Sincerely,

Dear Mr. Wilson:

I hope you will forgive the long delay in answering your letter of June 9. We are temporarily understaffed, but we *are* getting inquiries answered — although admittedly somewhat slowly.

The information you requested will be mailed early next week. We are happy to send you records of our experience with the Anhold starch maker, which we find exceptionally efficient.

Thank you for your patience.

Sincerely,

Dear Mr. Appleton:

Please excuse the delay in answering your letter of June 7 in which you requested a current report on the cost of operating our number 0501 converter. Mr. Judson has been assigned to Phoenix for a two-month period and I was out with the flu until today. I will get right to work on the report and expect to have it in the mail tomorrow.

I hope this won't be too late to be of help to you.

Sincerely,

Dear Ms. Herlock:

I apologize for not writing sooner about the letter you objected to receiving, which pertains to an unpaid bill for $239.79. I was away from the office for almost two weeks with a severe cold and have just returned. I checked your account with our bookkeeper, and I am happy to say that you are correct: you don't owe us any money.

The error was caused because we have another customer whose name is Jan Herlock. We are correcting our records.

We apologize for any unpleasantness and concern this may have caused you. We value your goodwill.

Sincerely,

Delayed Credit

Dear Mrs. Sanders:

I am sorry you had to wait so long for your credit of $51.20. We had some difficulty tracing the sale and the return of part of the merchandise. The refund check to you is now in the mail. Again, please excuse the delay.

Sincerely,

Postponed Dinner

Dear Mr. and Mrs. Rulless:

Mr. Webb and I regret that, due to the illness of our daughter, the dinner arranged for Friday, September 28 must be postponed.

Regretfully,

Delayed Order

Dear Bill:

I don't have any excuse for the delay, and I am truly sorry.

The booklets you ordered are being mailed today, and I'm sure you will find them worth waiting for. I enjoyed working on them for you, but they did take a little more time than I had anticipated.

I would appreciate hearing how well they are received by your clients.

Sincerely,

Delayed Paper Work

Dear Ms. Sampson:

Thank you for reminding us of the credit due you. We ran into unexpected delays, but the accounting department has notified me that your check for $51.20 will be in the mail today.

Thank you for your understanding.

Sincerely,

Dear Mr. Childress:

My apologies for not getting the Ward Company freight claim information to you earlier. I was sent to Chicago to work on a machine installation for six weeks and got back just yesterday.

I called Ward Company this morning and Mr. Andrews said he had a detailed listing of the expenses for your claim. He will mail a copy to you. If you don't get it by Tuesday of next week, call me and I will follow up with Mr. Andrews.

Again, sorry for the delay.

Sincerely,

Delayed Return of Borrowed Item

Dear Ms. Sanders:

Let me apologize for not returning your folder and two pamphlets on the collection of delinquent accounts.

I have found the information of great benefit but was slower in getting through it than I had promised.

It is really helpful when two credit unions can exchange information.

I hope you haven't been inconvenienced by my delayed return of the data. I thank you so much for your generosity.

Sincerely,

Dear Mrs. Stone:

I'm really sorry I didn't return your book sooner. I put it in the bookcase when I returned home from the hospital and completely forgot about it. The book was just lively enough to keep me in good spirits while spending so much time flat on my back.

I appreciate your lending me this interesting book, and I apologize for keeping it so long.

Sincerely,

Dear Mr. Parker:

Last year's issues of *Business* magazine that you lent me are being returned. I owe you an apology, as well as a thank-you, for not returning them sooner as intended.

I found the articles I was looking for and got much useful information from them.

It was kind of you to lend me these magazines, and I hope the delay has not been an inconvenience to you.

Sincerely,

Delayed Thank You

Dear Mr. Carswell:

Please excuse my delay in thanking you for the interesting visit with you and your staff on June 16 and 17.

I found our contract discussions helpful: we now have a better understanding of your needs. I know we are a little behind schedule, but we are working on the proposed contract for your approval and expect to have it ready by the end of next week.

Again, thank you for the information tour.

Sincerely,

Dear Mr. Simon:

Please let me apologize for not writing sooner to thank you for your assistance with the Bradford Associates account while I was in Phoenix. Your previous experience with them proved a great help in putting across my proposal.

Don't hesitate to call me when I can be of some help to you. As they say, I owe you one.

Sincerely,

Indiscretion

Dear Mr. Stamm:

Please forgive us for the indiscreet inquiries we made. After I explain the reasons for the questions we asked, I hope you will accept our apologies.

For open credit of $100,000 that you requested, we investigate our customer's credit potential thoroughly, often following seemingly insignificant leads. Our forty-seven years of experience have proven this to be beneficial to both us and our customers. A customer suffers as much as we do from overextended credit.

We apologize for any inconvenience and hurt we have caused you. You will be glad to learn that your open line of credit for $100,000 has been approved.

Sincerely,

Dear Mr. Tunney:

I am sorry that we seemed indiscreet in making inquiries about you. Let me explain the reasons and then I hope you will forgive us.

For a life insurance policy as large as $250,000 we investigate our clients rather closely. Issuing such a policy is a risk to us. To lessen our risk and to insure our financial stability, we sometimes check references two or three people removed from the references given by you. We have found this to be a sound business policy, and we are sorry for the concern we unintentionally caused you.

You will be pleased to learn that your policy has been approved.

Sincerely,

Ignoring a Customer

Dear Mr. Avery:

I was surprised when I heard that you feel you haven't been getting the same attention you received when we were a smaller company. I was wondering why we hadn't seen you lately.

I am truly sorry if anyone in our organization has been giving you less service than you deserve, since you have been one of our most loyal customers for many years. If this is the case, I offer my personal apology, and trust you will give us another chance.

I look forward to seeing you personally the next time you stop in. I would enjoy discussing our business relationship, and I will see to it that you are taken care of to your satisfaction — and incidentally to mine as well. Our relationship has been very pleasant and profitable for both of us, and I would feel hurt — less for business than personal reasons — if through some fault of ours that relationship were changed in any way. See you soon.

Sincerely,

Incomplete Instructions

Dear Mrs. Wordsworth:

We agree that the blouse you returned shrunk in your washing machine. This particular blouse is not washable although some blouses of similar appearance are. Our sales staff has been instructed to make each customer aware of how each blouse must be cleaned. Sometimes a clerk will forget.

Whether or not this was the case, we are sorry, Mrs. Wordsworth, for the disappointment and inconvenience to you.

Please let me know if you wish a replacement of the blouse or a credit to your account. Above all we want our customers happy.

Sincerely,

Incomplete Project

Dear Mr. McGuire:

We have just discovered that it will be impossible to complete the project for you as we promised.

My colleagues and I spent many hours collecting the data you requested. Most of it was in a car that was stolen, and to date the local police haven't recovered it.

Please accept our sincerest apologies for any inconvenience to you. Enclosed is a refund of your $100 retainer fee.

If our property is recovered soon, we will send the data to you without charge.

Sincerely,

Late Report

Dear Opal:

You're absolutely right; my project report is due this Wednesday, the 7th. I'm embarrassed to say I haven't finished it. In error, I had noted on my calendar that it was due next Wednesday, the 14th. I just confused the dates.

I'll start working on the rest of the report today, and it will be on your desk Monday. In the meantime, is there something I could do to alleviate any problem my lateness may have caused you?

I appreciate your patience.

Sincerely,

Missed Appointment

Dear Mr. Fowler:

Please accept my apology for not meeting you for lunch Tuesday. At 11:30 our press had a breakdown and I had to be there to help locate the reason for the breakdown.

Could you have lunch with me on Friday? I don't anticipate any maintenance problems then, and we should be able to enjoy a leisurely lunch.

Sincerely,

Missed Meeting

Dear Mr. Denton:

Mr. Anderson was called to Houston unexpectedly and asked me to express his regret at not being able to attend your demonstration of the Hasting-Allison process. He was looking forward to an interesting afternoon.

Sincerely,

Dear Mr. Donaldson:

There is no excuse for my not meeting you for lunch yesterday or at least getting word to you. I had the appointment written on my calendar, and was looking forward to the occasion, but somehow I thought our date was for next Thursday. It was just one of those days.

Please forgive me. I am anxious to talk with you, and will phone you Tuesday to see if we can arrange a meeting before you leave town. I won't let you down this time.

Cordially,

Dear Miss Sampler:

This is an apology I feel embarrassed to have to make. I have no excuse for not checking my appointments calendar before dashing off to Denver — even if it was an emergency call.

After looking forward for six weeks to meeting you and discussing your latest research results of the Matson project over lunch, I feel bad about forgetting to even notify you of my absence.

I will call you next week when I return and perhaps we can get together in San Francisco at your convenience.

Please accept my apology.

Sincerely,

Missing a Caller

Dear Ms. Englund:

I am sorry I was out of the office when you called Tuesday. I had told you I would be available any time during the week, but a labor problem at the Northside plant required my presence Tuesday afternoon.

Please phone and let me know when you will be in town again. I'll try to forestall any emergencies that day.

Sincerely,

Project Failure

Dear Mr. Anwar:

I have never before experienced the failure of a project like the Atchison project. I assure you it will not occur again. All our people feel bad about it and have reviewed in detail with me the reasons for failure, and, more important, ways of preventing mistakes in the future.

My apology at this time cannot undo past damage, but my regret is sincere, and my efforts in the future will be guided by this experience.

Sincerely,

Quote Error

Hello Mr. and Mrs. Watson:

I am sorry to report this, but I made a mistake on your homeowner's policy. The policy will cost you $428 per year rather than the $379 I told you.

I confused the policies issued by two of the several insurance carriers we write for.

I am sorry for the mistake. You have the option of canceling the policy if you wish, or having us rewrite the policy for coverage that will cost you only $379 per year. Please let me know which you decide.

Kindest regards,

Shipping Error

Dear Mr. Banter:

Will you accept our apology? We made an error in putting your shipment of May 22 together. Thank you for calling this to our attention. We work hard to please our customers, but obviously we must work even harder.

The chair you ordered is being shipped today. You may return the other chair, collect, at your convenience.

Sincerely,

Dear Mrs. Montez:

You are certainly justified in being angry about our blunder in returning the unordered merchandise you had returned to us. Please let me apologize. The error was ours, but it would help us when you return merchandise if you would enclose a note to me or our sales representative stating why it is being returned. This will insure proper credit to you.

You will receive immediate credit for this returned merchandise and all shipping charges.

Again, I am sorry for the inconvenience to you. We do value your business and your friendship.

Cordially,

Slow Payment

Dear Mr. Allison:

We are sorry to have caused you a financial inconvenience by not paying a group of your invoices sooner. We have had internal problems, but these are resolved now. We will start paying your invoices tomorrow.

You could insure quicker payment in the future by extending us terms of 1 percent, 10 days. Invoices marked this way are paid as soon as received. Invoices with no payment terms are paid in 30 days.

Again, we are sorry for the past inconvenience, and future payments will be on time.

Very truly yours,

Small Reward

Dear Frank:

It was an exciting year, struggling to overcome our many difficulties. You are given much of the credit for the turnaround toward profitability.

I realize that a thank-you is small reward for your diligent work, but next year we expect to make our thank-you more tangible. Meanwhile it's great having you on our team. We are running strong and in the right direction.

Sincerely,

Statement Error

Dear Mr. Wendell:

A corrected statement of your account is enclosed. We are sorry about the error and hope that it didn't cause any great inconvenience. We check every step in our processing of accounts, but even then clerical errors occur at times. Please accept our apologies. And we do appreciate your giving us the opportunity to be of service to you.

Sincerely,

Our Apologies . . .

The finance charge information for 19___ is not printed on this statement, but will appear on your statement next month. Please use your February, 19___ statement for income tax preparation.

Thank you for being our customer.

Sincerely,

Dear Customer:

Hello! Here we are again. We recently mailed you the Statement of Account for your mortgage loan for 19___ .

Our face is red because that Statement of Account appeared to have had some errors.

The Revised Statement of Mortgage Account, enclosed, is current and the errors are eliminated. Please review the amounts under Taxes and Interest.

Again, we wish to apologize for any inconvenience our error may have caused you.

Sincerely yours,

Wrong Information

Dear Customer:

OOPS! WE GOOFED!
Our order blank states: "All offers expire April 30, 19___ ."
It should read: ALL OFFERS EXPIRE JULY 31, 19___ .

Sincerely,

11

CONGRATULATIONS

We enjoy sharing our enthusiasm and delight with friends who have won awards or have been recognized for outstanding work. This special accomplishment is an occasion for a letter of congratulations, a time to send good wishes. Your friend will appreciate a little boost to his or her ego. If you are writing to a business acquaintance or associate, a letter of congratulation can do much to stimulate cooperation between the two of you or to strengthen an existing good relationship. Goodwill should be nurtured at every opportunity.

Many occasions are appropriate for a letter of congratulation: winning a hole-in-one golf tournament, winning a skating championship, receiving a superior rating in a music contest, earning an appointment to an office, doing the best selling job last month, receiving a job promotion, or winning a bride.

Write a letter of congratulation as soon as possible after the event. Six months later, your friend may feel let down that it took you so long to recognize his or her promotion.

Along with your bubbling enthusiasm, sincerity must come through to the reader. Use expressions that would be natural in a conversation with the reader; don't overblow the occasion or smother it with flowery phrases. The tone of the letter, however, will depend on your relationship with the reader. To a staid business acquaintance, straightforward and conservative statements may be appropriate, while to a sorority sister or fraternity brother, jocular informality may be just the thing.

Now for the easy part: make the congratulatory letter brief; from three to six sentences is sufficient.

How to Do It

1. State the occasion for the congratulation in the first sentence.
2. Make a comment that links the person and the occasion.
3. Write or imply your expectation of continued success.

Sales Volume

Dear Bob,

Your successful sales efforts have secured an annual sales volume of $1 million from Amsterdam, Inc.

My congratulations to you for this fine job. As you know, business conditions being what they are, the Amsterdam account is doubly important. Keep up the good work!

With best regards,

Dear Tom,

Congratulations on estblishing a new sales volume record in the month of March. I recognize that this is the result of work done during the past year by your sales staff, but it looks great on our financial records, and I know you played a big part by inspiring your sales staff.

Sincerely,

New Customer

Congratulations, Jim —

on securing this new account!

I know you worked hard on this one and it is great that you were able to close the deal before being transferred out of the territory.

Again, let me say, "a job well done."

Regards,

Good Job

Dear John:

About the Baker's Dozen Bakery account:

G R E A T!

Sincerely,

Dear Mr. Mullen:

I would like to congratulate you and your people for the fine job that has been done in reducing our raw materials inventory in the recent months.

This result, so effectively presented by the graphs that were prepared, turned out to be a high point during the recent manager's meeting.

I would appreciate receiving these graphs each month.

Sincerely,

Dear Joe:

Please note the attached copy of Mr. Robinson's letter of congratulation.

To it I wish to add my own congratulations for the outstanding achievement in inventory reduction.

Keep up the good work.

Sincerely,

Top Salesperson

Dear Janet,

Congratulations on being the #1 salesperson in the Northwest sales group last month. Your volume and the gross margin dollars were the highest for any November in the Company's history.

Good luck in December,

Exceeding Goal

Dear Joe,

My congratulations to you and the sales force for having surpassed our 19__ goal on scrap recovered from our customers. During the month of October we collected 485 tons which amounts to 5,800 tons on an annualized basis. This is well in excess of our 4,000 ton goal.

Regards,

Graduation

Dear Jack,

Congratulations! and an extra hurrah for making the top ten! Our family is proud of you.

We regret, Jack, that earlier commitments prevent our attending your graduation ceremonies.

Best wishes for continued success as you start your new career.

Sincerely,

Dear Mrs. Long,

We just heard that Patricia graduated from the University of California at Berkeley with honors. You must be extremely proud of her accomplishments, and I am happy right along with you.

Please give Patricia our best wishes for continued success as she enters law school. (. . . pursues her career.)

Sincerely,

Dear Lynn,

I was delighted to receive the announcement of your graduation from Stanford. Congratulations on your well-earned degree.

My blessings go with you as you face a new career and new challenges.

Cordially,

College Degree

Music

Dear Howard,

Your long years of study, practice, playing, and teaching have finally won you a coveted Master of Arts degree in music from Mills College. My hearty congratulations on an honor that does not come easily. The degree will certainly enhance your opportunities for teaching; you are already widely recognized as one of the best.

Keep up the good work; we are all proud of you.

Sincerely,

Specialized Teacher

Dear Jean,

Congratulations on your graduation! I understand you already have a position teaching blind children. It is most encouraging to you, I am sure, having the opportunity to apply your specialized training so soon. With your interest in children, you and they will surely have a pleasant learning experience.

I am confident you are equal to the unusual challenge.

With best wishes,

Handicapped

Dear Kathy,

You'd be the last one to want special recognition for graduating from college, but with your handicap you deserve the highest praise for your accomplishment.

Your hard work and courage will carry you far in this world. You are a heartening example to many others.

Sincerely,

Promotion

Dear Arlene:

Congratulations on your promotion. It has always been a pleasure working with one as competent as you.

We look forward to more of the same fine work in the future.

Sincerely,

Dear Bud:

It was great to hear of your recent promotion. There is no doubt you have earned this promotion, and I am confident it will not be the last.

I have always felt you handled the problems we sent you exceptionally well.

We look forward to working with you in the future.

Sincerely,

Dear Mr. Rosen:

Congratulations on your promotion to Manager of the Converting operations. I know you worked hard for that promotion and no one is more deserving of the position you have attained. We are all proud of you.

Sincerely,

Dear Ben,

Congratulations to the new Manager! You are certainly deserving of the promotion.

I look forward to congratulating you in person in two weeks.

With regards,

Dear Mr. Mosk:

Our entire family cheered when we learned of your advancement to Regional Manager. Congratulations! It is an elating feeling when a former neighbor — and such a friendly one — is given a big promotion.

Sincerely,

Dear Jim,

I'm glad to hear that you have been promoted to Production Manager — a real step up. Perhaps I should congratulate Lenkurt Co. for recognizing a good man.

Regards,

Dear Frank:

The good news of your appointment as president of Saxxon Company came to me today from our friend Bob Anslow. Hearty congratulations, and may I wish you every success. I agree that you are the best one to keep the company on its profitable course. The work, I am sure, will be hard enough to be interesting and let's hope light enough not to be a burden.

It is with true friendly pleasure that I congratulate you and wish you continued success.

Sincerely,

Dear Tom,

Our family cheered in unison when we heard of your promotion. Congratulations! We hope the added responsibility will not keep you too tied down. When you are more settled, please call us, so we can congratulate you in person.

Sincerely,

Dear Henry,

I was more than pleased this morning to hear that you are now a vice president. It couldn't happen to a nicer or more deserving person.

We both wish you continued success.

Sincerely,

New Position

Dear Mike:

Congratulations on your new position as an aeronautical design engineer. You must be glad to get back to a familiar line of work. Around here, we will miss your cheerful personality and most sorely miss your willingness to help in any problem areas.

Please stop by any time you are in town: we don't want to forget you.

Again, congratulations,

Service Award

Dear Marge,

I quite agreed with the members of the Golden Years Club when they honored you with this year's Special Service Award.

You have made many contributions to the club and to this community with your long hours of dedicated work — a beautiful example of unselfish love.

We are all proud of you.

Sincerely,

Five Years

Dear Andy Colfax:

Five years of service with Jacobs Company deserves recognition. The continued success of our company depends on loyal employees who pull together. Your work and loyalty are appreciated.

Your five-year pin will be presented at the general office meeting on February 26 when several others will join you in receiving service awards.

In another five years, I hope to see you receive your ten-year pin.

Sincerely,

Twenty Years

Dear Donald,

Congratulations on your twentieth anniversary with Fibre Containers.

Your steady progress is a result of your many accomplishments, but the one that stands out is your success in getting cooperation from co-workers as well as subordinates.

We would find it difficult, Don, to get along without you. Best wishes for many more rewarding years with us.

Sincerely,

Retirement

Dear Ms. Landers:

It will seem strange here without your cheery "good morning" each day. Our customers will miss you too (but I hope not enough to forget us).

Let me say once again how much you have done to give our store its reputation for friendly service. After thirty years of being so helpful, I doubt that anyone can replace you.

Please accept my personal gratitude for your devoted service and my best wishes for an enjoyable retirement. Come to visit us as often as you can; we think of you as one of our family.

Sincerely,

Dear Tony,

I want to congratulate you and to extend my best wishes for your retirement next month. You are to be commended for forty-seven years of productive and innovative work. Many of the procedures you established will continue for years to come.

You should have all the time you want now to play golf with your buddy Charlie; no more waiting for the weekend.

We will miss your smiling presence, but do enjoy your leisure.

Sincerely,

Dear Employees:

Alfred Parton, general manager of the Western Core Division, will retire June 30 after a long and distinguished career with Antelope Machine Corporation.

I know you will join me in extending to Alfred our appreciation for the leadership he has provided in developing the Western Core Division into the strong organization it is today. Out best wishes go with him in his retirement.

Sincerely,

Dear Tim:

Your approaching retirement, I am sure, will not mean loafing and relaxing. You have been active in too many projects for that, and I believe that is the only way to retire: stay as active as ever, but restrict the activity to pleasurable things.

I am sure you will enjoy yourself, and let me add my congratulations to the many others you receive. You deserve them all.

Sincerely,

Dear Frances,

When you started your career, retirement seemed an endless distance away, but here it is. It seems to me that anyone who devotes that many years to public service deserves the most hearty congratulations!

You probably won't stay retired long. I can see you becoming deeply involved in public volunteer work and working harder than when you were working.

Best wishes to you for a long-deserved change.

Sincerely,

Golf Tournament

Dear Tony,

Congratulations on winning the company golf tournament. A champion manager can also be a champion golfer. Keep up the good work.

Sincerely,

Industry Award

Dear Mr. Miles:

Let me congratulate you on winning the Hartford Award! Your leadership in our industry has long been known to many of us, and I am happy to see you receive the nationwide recognition you have earned by your years of diligent work.

Best regards,

President of Rotary

Dear Mr. Briney:

It was a pleasure to read in last night's *City Ledger* of your election as president of Rotary.

Let me offer my most sincere congratulations upon your receiving this honor. I wish you success in your new office.

Sincerely,

Anniversary

Dear Mary and Joe,

Congratulations on your anniversary!
May the past happy memories be a prelude to future memories.

Happy Anniversary,

Honorary Sorority

Dear Joan,

So you made the Honorary Sorority! Congratulations to a hard working (as well as bright) girl. I know your pleasing personality played a large part too.

Best wishes for the continuing scholastic achievements I know you will earn.

Cordially,

President of Association

Dear Mr. Ramsey:

My hearty congratulations to you on your election to the presidency of the Western Management Association. Your election is earned tribute from your colleagues, and is recognition of the outstanding work you have done for the Association and for your profession.

The Association chose the right man in my opinion. Best wishes for success in your new position.

Sincerely,

Opening Store

Dear Andy,

Congratulations on the opening of your own hardware store! I know it has been a dream of yours for many years. With your know-how and willingness to work, there is no reason why you shouldn't have a booming business in a short time.

We are happy to see you make the big step.

Good luck,

City Councilman

Dear Ray,

Congratulations on your election to the Concord City Council. I am pleased that we now have a financial expert in our city government. We can look forward to a closer scrutiny of fiscal matters, something we have needed for a long time.

Sincerely,

Loan Paid

Dear Mr. Crown:

Congratulations!

We are pleased to notify you that you have fully paid the enclosed loan.

Now — why not continue making regular payments into one of our savings accounts? You have already discovered a convenient, safe place to save money — and be paid for saving it — and a friendly place to borrow money at a low interest rate.

Sincerely,

Marriage

Dear Andrew,

Congratulations on your marriage.

Let me wish you and your bride your full share of happiness as the years go on.

Sincerely,

Dear Alice,

It is somehow hard to believe you are no longer the pretty little girl down the street, but have already grown up to become a happy bride.

Please congratulate your husband for me, and tell him I think he is most lucky.

You both have my best wishes for a long and happy life together.

Affectionately,

12

THANK YOU
AND
APPRECIATION

A thank-you letter should be sincere, expressing appreciation without excessive flattery. The tone should be pleasant. Clearly state what the thank-you is for and, if appropriate, offer something in return.

Business people appreciate receiving a thank-you letter because it adds a touch of warmth to the cold world of business. The letter reveals consideration and appreciation. Large manufacturers often receive letters from students asking about products, processes, or procedures. These are usually answered with pamphlets, brochures, and letters from production managers or administrative executives. One corporate executive complained that after sending out large quantities of printed material and innumerable letters, no thank-you letters were received. He lamented that even a post card saying, "Thank you for the materials," would have shown consideration for his company's efforts. The goodwill of your company, and also of yourself, can be enhanced by a letter of thanks.

A thank-you letter should be short. The sincerity of the thank you is emphasized by brevity. Basically, all that need be said is, "Thank you for this," or "Thank you for that." A long thank-you letter may be a sales letter in disguise, or it may be loaded with unnecessary flattery, lowering the reader's opinion of the party sending the letter.

Pleasantness is another requirement of a good thank-you letter. One way to accomplish this is with an informal opening, for instance:

> Enjoyed meeting with you and appreciate the time given to Don and me.

> Just a "thank you" for being a customer this past year.

Any harsh thoughts or words should be eliminated because their inclusion will completely destroy the purpose of the letter, which is to show gratitude for help that has been given.

While thanking a person for something he or she has done, it is often possible to return more than just words of thanks. This will emphasize the writer's gratitude. When a person has spent time showing you his or her company's operation or the sites of the city, offer to do the same when that person visits your company or city. When giving thanks for information received, it would be appropriate to relay how the information is being used; for example:

> The sketch fits so well in our den.
>
> I would never have heard of the exhibit otherwise.
>
> Your suggestion led to this fabulous job.
>
> Your recent payment clears your longstanding debt.
>
> Your work made it possible for us to catch up.
>
> The information is exactly what I need for my report.
>
> Your suggestions enabled us to increase our machine speed 20 percent.

When an organization has helped your group in some way, volunteer your group's help as a return favor.

Thanking someone for a favor indicates polite manners — and is good business practice. But thanking in advance is considered, by some authorities in the use of the English language, an objectionable habit. For example, it is common to write:

> Send the completed project to Mr. A. B. Andrews at Headquarters by September 15.
>
> Thank you.

This seems to imply to the reader that the project was of so little importance that a thank-you for an excellent and timely submission will not be worth the effort of writing again. To overcome this possible adverse reaction by the reader, start the letter with, "Will you please" or "I will appreciate your sending . . . " or "Please." An alternative is to end the letter with a paragraph stating appreciation, for example:

> Your sending this project to Headquarters by the 15th of September will be greatly appreciated.
>
> Your sending this freight bill to Friedman, Inc. is greatly appreciated.
>
> Sending me the samples will be truly appreciated.
>
> Your cooperation and hard work on this project is really appreciated by us.

When a letter expressing thankfulness is appropriate, a prompt answer will make the reader aware of your thoughtfulness. Three months later, the reader shouldn't be reminded that he or she had been piqued by not having received a deserved note of thanks.

While writing the letter, assume an attitude of polite sincerity.

How to Do It

1. State what the thank-you is for.
2. Mention the appropriateness of what was received.
3. Be sincere, brief, and pleasant.
4. When appropriate, offer something in return.

Gift

Dear Friends in Albany,

My heartfelt thanks (no pun intended) for the beautiful terrarium you sent while I was in the hospital for heart bypass surgery. It will remind me for years how nice friends can be.

Sincerely,

An alternate last sentence might be:

It will remind me for years of my many friends in Albany.

Dear Mrs. Patterson,

The sketch of a cowboy is a beautiful gift and it fits so well in the den. A special gift from a special friend is always appreciated. Thank you for your generous thoughts.

Sincerely,

Dear John,

You have that rare ability to select just the right gift. The puzzle you sent kept me up half the night — I'll get it yet.

Sincerely,

Pamphlet

Gentlemen:

Thank you for the illustrated pamphlet on personnel forms. We are considering changes in our personnel reporting and will find the samples useful.

Sincerely,

Information

Dear Mr. Arronson:

Thank you for your prompt reply to my inquiry about scheduled tours of U. S. Steel's Pittsburgh plant.

Because of our commitment to the Martinez Boy's Club as volunteers, we are unable to schedule a tour as a group.

Sincerely,

Dear Marge,

Thank you for your letter and the announcement of an antique dealers' convention in New England. I would not have learned of the meeting otherwise. It was nice of you to take the time to send it when you knew I would be interested.

I'll see you there.

Cordially,

Materials Received

Dear Mr. Benson:

Thank you for the materials you sent with your letter of September 25. The samples will be helpful.

Sincerely,

Dear Mr. Latter:

Thank you for the brochure *Trees are Forever.* It contains exactly what I need for a speech I am preparing.

Sincerely,

Thank you . . .

For your interest in our Plain English Multicover Policy. I am pleased to enclose an information kit for your review.

Cordially,

Career Help

Dear Ms. Allen,

I really want to thank you for all you did for me in your legal secretary class. I followed your suggestion and registered with Temporary Service. With the help of your recommendations, I was employed by the District Attorney's office for five weeks, by the trust officer of Bank of California for two weeks, and by Marsh and Marsh for four weeks. The experience as a background for law could not have been better. I am off to school next week to start my pre-law studies.

I can't thank you enough for the help you gave.

Sincerely,

Advice

Dear Mr. Manning:

You helped me a great deal with my future plans only six years ago as we sat in your office working to eliminate my frustrating uncertainty.

I took your advice — probably the best thing I ever did. Since then I have advanced several times with this company. The cooperation of the people here is better than I should really expect. I am sure my future is here.

I want to express my sincere gratitude for your consultation and help and to wish you and your family a happy holiday season.

Cordially,

Recommendation

Dear Ellis:

Just a short thank-you for the recommendation you gave me yesterday. Your well-chosen words were a big boost in getting me the transfer I wanted.

I sincerely appreciate your help.

Regards,

Dinner Invitation

Dear Tim,

It was certainly a privilege to be with you and your friends at the excellent Service Club dinner last night. Tom Powers had a message to give and he gave it superbly.

Thanks ever so much for inviting me!

Sincerely,

Recognition

Dear Jan,

Thank you for mentioning my Music Teacher's Conference award. It is a great feeling to receive recognition for work covering a period of years, and I appreciate your mentioning it in your daily column.

Sincerely,

Dear Jan,

Thank you for mentioning my Music Teacher's award in your column. The award means a great deal to teachers and I appreciate your giving it public recognition.

Sincerely,

Going Away Party

Dear Lois,

Frank and I are most appreciative of the dinner party given for us last Saturday. We really enjoyed your efforts, the good drinks, the good food, the friendly chats — and the bridge cards.

Leaving a group of such good neighbors and friends after 15 years fills us with a puzzling mixture of nostalgia and appreciation.

We will try to get back from time to time, but meanwhile, our phone number is 000-000-0000.

Sincerely,

Companionship

Dear Katy,

This gift is only a token of how much your friendly companionship this summer has meant to me.

There will always be love in my thoughts of you.

With affection,

Friendship

Dear Don,

This gift is just a small thank-you for the friendship you showed me this summer.

I will always think of you as a kind friend who took a real interest in both my work and play.

Sincerely,

Dear Sandy,

You have that rare knack of making strangers feel right at home. Sharing your friends with me yesterday certainly made a newcomer feel like a comfortable old-timer. I know I will like this friendly city, and I hope Ron and I will be here for a long time.

Thank you so much for all you have done for me.

Sincerely,

Appreciation

Dear Tommy,

It was thoughtful of you to write me and let me know how much you enjoy working at Exxon. It really doesn't surprise me, because I well remember your enthusiasm as well as your record here at the University — and also your popularity among the students. I was glad to be of help in setting your career course.

Kindest regards and best wishes for your continued success.

Cordially,

Dear Mr. Watson:

Your letter of appreciation for my work on the recent project was warmly received. It was a time of struggle for both of us. If you need any data from me during my short absence, please call and leave a message. I will be able to pick it up in the evenings.

See you in November.

Sincerely,

Dear Dave,

Thank you for your letter of appreciation for my work during the past year. It was generous of you to give me so much credit for the company's operating improvements.

Our struggles and difficulties certainly did add interest to the year's activities. I do enjoy working with and for you, and am sure next year will be economically better for the company.

Sincerely,

Sympathy

Dear Mrs. Franklin:

We appreciate your kind expression of sympathy.

Sincerely,

Dear Mrs. Coulson,

Thank you for your thoughtfulness upon the death of my sister Ellen.

Sincerely,

Dear Beth,

It was heartwarming to receive your comforting letter of sympathy.

Sincerely,

Dear Mr. Cooley:

We appreciate and thank you for your expression of sympathy upon the death of Mr. Olson.

Sincerely,

Dear Ms. Nelson,

Thank you for your warm expression of sympathy upon the death of Howard. The pain is lessened by your kind offer to help.

Sincerely,

The Sanford Office Group:

I wish to thank all of you for remembering me in my time of need. The plant you sent is beautiful.

Sincerely,

Dear Beth,

Thank you so much for your thoughtfulness in sending me the beautiful dwarf pine. I appreciate your caring.

                                        Sincerely,

Dear Mrs. Eberly,

We were pleased to receive your letter of sympathy. It was a comfort to us. Eleanor always mentioned you with the greatest respect and admiration.

                                        Sincerely,

Gentlemen:

On behalf of all of us at Morton, Martin, and Grove, I wish to thank you for your kind expression of sympathy upon the death of our Mr. Allen Rogers.

It is true that we have sustained a shock and great loss by his sudden passing. We believe the greatest tribute to him will be maintaining the high professional standards he represented and so strongly encouraged.

                                        Very Sincerely,

Illness

Dear Fred:

Thank you for the letter you wrote to me while I was in the hospital. It really helped to brighten my days.

I am now back at work on a half-day schedule, but will be working full-time next week. The operation went well and the recovery period gave me a chance to relax. I was a little disappointed though that the office got along so well without me.

When you are in Los Angeles again, please stop by and we can share a couple of hours over lunch.

                                        Sincerely,

Dear Nadine,

No one but you would have thought of having a comic card delivered each Sunday during my convalescence. What a terrific morale booster. You are so thoughtful.

With love,

Job Well Done

We would like to thank you, Mark,

and all the other people there at Tomkin's for a job well done this past year, especially during the Christmas rush when we were adjusting our orders so frequently.

Your interest in Samuelson Company and the courtesy and cooperation you have extended is sincerely appreciated.

Best regards,

Dear Andy,

Just a note to let you know that your hard work during the past year has been sincerely appreciated.

I hope that you and Theresa enjoy a happy holiday season and vacation in the West. You both deserve a good rest and I trust the weatherman will cooperate to make your stay in Phoenix truly relaxing.

Cordially,

Dear Jim,

We know you will be pleased to hear that your June sales broke all previous records. It's great to have you on our team.

Sincerely,

Dear Mr. Ludwig:

Your decision to retire as director of Ableson Corporation has been received with deep regret by the directors and officers of the Corporation.

Leaving after nearly half a century is not easy, but during your tenure you played an important part in doubling our market coverage. Your annual market survey trips endeared you to many throughout the corporation.

I look upon your retirement as a real personal loss. Your example and counsel has been most beneficial to my work as officer and director. For that I thank you.

I sincerely hope your retirement from many years of cares and tensions will be a pleasant experience for you.

Cordially,

Dear Mr. Walton:

I have just read of your retirement from the Alameda Real Estate Board. I would like to express my appreciation for the work you have done, especially in acquainting the public with the variety of ways a real estate agent can be of help to a buyer, seller, or investor in real estate.

Your contributions have been great, and although you will be missed, you deserve an enjoyable retirement.

Sincerely,

Dear Mr. and Mrs. Hancock:

Your daughter, Jo Ann, has worked for us for six months now. I thought you would like to know that she is doing a remarkable job, and we are extremely pleased with her work attitude.

Jo Ann is a credit to you, her parents. We are proud of her and we know you are too.

Sincerely,

Dear Frank:

It was an exciting year, struggling to overcome our many difficulties. You are given much of the credit for the turnaround toward profitability.

I realize that a thank you is small reward for your diligent work, but next year we expect to make our thank you more tangible. Meanwhile it's great having you on our team. We are running strong and in the right direction.

Sincerely,

Being Our Customer

Dear Mr. Smith:

Just a "thank you" for being a customer this past year.

We want you to know we appreciate the business you have given us, and we hope to continue serving you during the coming year.

With regards from Hamilton's Heavy Hardware.

Thank You

I want to let you know how much we value your business. The prompt manner in which you maintain your account makes it a pleasure to do business with you.

I hope Ralph's can continue to serve your motoring needs for many years to come.

Sincerely,

Charge Account Request

Dear Mrs. Warner:

Thank you for the opportunity to add you to the growing number of satisfied charge account customers of Long's Department Store.

The privileges of a charge account are many. You have 25 days to enjoy your purchases before paying for them. You are notified of special sales before a general announcement is made; and often, by presenting the mailed announcement, you may purchase sale items a day or two before the sale officially begins. Special delivery and lay-away services are open to charge account customers. When you wish to place an order by phone, or want a special favor, please mention your charge card and just ask. We are always pleased to do a little extra for the convenience of Long's customers.

Sincerely,

Dear Mrs. Wilson:

Thank you for requesting a charge account at Ansell's. Your credit has been approved and you may use the enclosed charge card at any time. It will add convenience and enjoyment to your shopping.

You will be pleased with the fine quality merchandise and pleasant service always available at Ansell's.

Sincerely,

Sales Presentation

Dear Mr. Wyley:

The "shoe box size" package you lost and inquired about in your letter of June 7 was found behind a chair in the lobby.

We are happy to return it to you via United Parcel, and wish to thank you again for your informative presentation of your computer line.

Sincerely,

Accounting Help

Dear John:

Thank you for coming to San Jose Wednesday to help us straighten out our accounts with you. We have been short-handed for several months and just couldn't seem to get our payables accounts right. Your help in reconciling the differences got us on top of the work and I believe we can keep our records in agreement with yours from now on.

Again, thank you for your help.

Sincerely,

Payment

Dear Mr. Evers:

Thank you for your payment of $327.80. This clears your delinquent account.

We appreciate your cooperation and look forward to serving you again.

Sincerely,

Dear Mr. Jones:

Thank you for your partial payment of $200. This leaves only $92.40, which will be due in 30 days. By making this payment on time, your account will be open again.

We look forward to having you as an open-account customer again.

Sincerely,

Referral

Dear Mrs. Mayer:

Thank you for referring Peter Seller to me for an eye examination. I certainly appreciate your thoughtfulness and want to assure you that your confidence in me will be justified.

If at any time in the future I may again be of service to you, please feel free to call me.

Once again, thank you for referring Mr. Seller.

Sincerely,

Attending

Dear Mr. Ronald:

Thank you for attending our meeting last Thursday and for sharing your suggestions based on your long years of experience. Being new, our group found your suggestions and recommendations extremely helpful.

We hope we can return the favor by doing something for your group. Please call when we can assist in any way.

Sincerely,

Dear Mr. Alberts:

The Business Elders group wishes to thank you for your inspiring remarks at our dinner last Wednesday. You gave us some good ideas that we will discuss at our next regular meeting, and I believe we can successfully act on some of them.

We will let you know the outcome of your ideas. The dinner committee is already planning to ask you to speak again.

Cordially,

Visiting

Dear Mr. Hanson:

I wish to thank you for giving me the opportunity to visit your plant and to have discussions with you and with your friendly staff.

The visit to your plant was one of the highlights of my visit to your country and I hope to see some of the Fibreboard people in Australia at some future date.

Yours sincerely,

Dear Mr. and Mrs. Lyons:

Thank you for visiting Highland Estates.
If I may be of any help, please call me.
My home phone is 000-0000 and my office phone is 000-0000.

Sincerely,

Dear Bill:

Enjoyed meeting with you and appreciate the time given to Don Allen and me on such a short notice.

As we discussed, we are going to pursue the problems you are encountering with various materials you purchase from us. We anticipate that when you visit our mill in the near future, our technical people will have some answers.

Thanks again for the time and courtesies shown to Don and me.

Sincerely,

Dear Bob:

It was a pleasure meeting with you last Friday and having the opportunity to visit the Centrex production facility. Your operation looked quite good. The volume produced in that one location is surprising.

When you are in Washington this fall, I hope a tour can be set up for you to see a fully integrated paper mill operation.

Thanks again for your time and hospitality.

With regards,

Dear Mr. Greenland:

I really enjoyed my visit with you during my recent trip west. You were more than considerate to rearrange your schedule on such short notice and to spend the afternoon with me.

When you come to Chicago next time be sure to call me and we can have another pleasant visit.

With regards,

Departing Employee

Dear Kathy:

It is always with mixed feelings that I write "goodbye" letters. We never like seeing one of our members leave, but at the same time, we want you to know our best wishes go with you.

I am sure you are looking forward to your new surroundings. Changes are usually exciting, but we are sorry that your husband's transfer will take you away from Highland Hospital.

Thank you for your valuable contribution and the many faithful years of loyal service to the hospital. Our sincere good wishes to you, and if you are ever in the area, please be sure to stop in and say "hello."

Sincerely,

13

OTHER
BUSINESS
LETTERS

Only the imagination of the reader can limit the number of categories for business and personal letters. It is hoped that the variety this book presents and suggests is enough to fulfill your needs. Many letters fit neatly into more than one category; a little thumbing through related areas may turn up just what you need. Perhaps parts of different letters can be combined to provide one better suited to your need.

Regardless of how the letter is classified, remember that it is the reader who must play the starring role. Forget I and me and we: think *you*. Give full consideration to the feelings of the reader. Be pleasant and sincere. Revealing an attitude of sincerity is the art of writing a letter that accomplishes its purpose. Along with attitude, correct technical aspects of word usage will help the reader respond positively to your letter.

GOODWILL

A letter of goodwill is basically a low-pressure sales letter — low-pressure because no particular product or service is being pushed, only a friendly relationship. The letter can also be thought of as a public relations gesture — something that is often neglected with good, steady customers — or as a reaching out for a kindly feeling of approval and support. If we express kindly thoughts towards our customers or friends, we hope to receive consideration (and increased business) in return. The expressions or impressions of goodwill may be combined with a thank you, appreciation, request, apology, regrets, or just pleasant thoughts.

The letter can vary in length from a short statement of appreciation to the several paragraphs appropriate for a year-end holiday season letter. A combination of the occasion and the mood of the letter writer will determine the length — but don't overburden the reader.

Goodwill is not a one-time thing, but a continuing relationship. With this in mind, do not make the letter a conclusive statement, but indicate a desire to continue the friendship. For example, the model letter headed "Sales Agreement Ended" expresses regrets that a customer has ended a sales agreement, but the writer is not ready to admit that this is a lasting decision. He ends the letter with the upbeat, "I know our paths will continue to cross in the future."

How to Do It

1. Begin with a complimentary or pleasant statement.
2. Make a comment that relates to or expands upon the first statement.
3. Express anticipation of continued good relations or of a future meeting.

Season's Greetings

Dear Mr. Anderson:

Do you remember those exhilarating childhood fantasies? I do. They are a part of that wonderful voyage of growing up. They provide the thrill of imagined experience and almost always the rewards of success and victory.

Not many weeks ago, I was walking through an apple orchard in upper New York State with our granddaughter, Rebecca. We had driven there to see the annual red and gold turning of the autumn leaves for which that part of the country is so well known. We were not disappointed. We were picking apples, and Rebecca, who is 3½, was telling me with great enthusiasm one of her wonderful tales of fantasy.

It occurred to me that among the glows and warmth of the holiday season are the fantasies with which we associate these days. Children take to them particularly. Whether it is the tree trimming, the heralding of the coming of Santa Claus down the chimney, or the glow of the Hanukkah candles, it all spells the gathering of families to celebrate love and being together. This is no fantasy.

I hope this year, as the fantasies dance all about your home, that not only will you enjoy them with your families, but that you will gain the real reward of experiencing their love.

Sincerely,

Thanks to Mr. Mitchel Flaum, President, S&S Corrugated Paper Machinery Co., Inc., Brooklyn, New York.

Good Work

Dear Frank:

It was an exciting year, struggling to overcome our many difficulties. You are given much of the credit for the turnaround toward profitability.

I realize that a thank-you is small reward for your diligent work, but next year we expect to make our thank-you more tangible. Meanwhile, it's great having you on our team. We are running strong and in the right direction.

Sincerely,

Free Bulletin

Dear Miss Conrad:

Here's a copy of our latest news bulletin. I think this one will keep you completely informed about our industry. Other publications lack many of the special features that we include.

If you'd like to receive it monthly, just drop me a note and I'll put your name on our mailing list — no charge to you.

Sincerely,

Golf Invitation

Dear Bart,

We enjoyed having you with us Saturday.

Since I know you will forgive the photography, I am enclosing some pictures of you and Ray at the Yacht Club.

If you happen to be in the Bay Area and have time for a game of golf, please let me know and maybe we can get together at the Westlake Course.

Sincerely,

To a Salesman's Wife

Dear Ann,

Rick is a great guy. I'm sure you have known that for a long time, and now we know it too. His sales volume is rocketing. We planned on some increase when he took over the Salinas area, but his sales have far exceeded our expectation.

I just want you to know that we appreciate the encouragement you have given Rick. Your interest in his work has meant a great deal to us. Thanks again.

Sincerely,

Sales Agreement Ended

Dear Ben:

We are sorry to learn of your desire to terminate our sales agreement, which has been in effect for nine years. We can understand your position and appreciate the reasons.

Although nothing was said in your letter, I assume you wish this agreement to terminate as of October 22, 19__ without the ninety-day cancellation notice mentioned in the contract.

It has been a pleasure to work with you, Ben, and although our formal arrangement is terminated, I know our paths will continue to cross in the future.

Sincerely,

To Parents of Young Employee

Dear Mr. and Mrs. MacMahon:

Your daughter, Lynn, has worked for us six months now. I thought you would like to know that she is doing a remarkable job, and we are extremely pleased with her work attitude.

Lynn is a credit to you, her parents. We are proud of her and we know you are too.

Sincerely,

Enjoyed Meeting You

A candidate for an elective office made a personal visit. The candidate follows up with a goodwill note.

Dear John:

I enjoyed meeting you this past weekend.

Sincerely,

Real Estate Service

Dear Mr. Robinson:

Just a note to say thank you for thinking of me for real estate service.

I look forward to working with you in the future if your move to Denver works out.

I'll be seeing you Saturday.

Sincerely,

Fishing Trip Invitation

Dear Rick:

Glad to hear you are all fine and that the trip was uneventful. There is nothing worse than car trouble when you are out in the middle of nowhere.

Yes, I know Elvis Waters. He is in charge of our printing sales and annually fishes in Canada for salmon. Maybe the next time I get up there we can both do some fishing.

Please give my best to Cheryl and let us hear from you if you plan another trip to Detroit.

Regards,

Gift Received

Dear Danny:

Just received your "volume of songs" and want to thank you for the many hours of pleasure and elbow bending they will provide for me. Cheers.

Hope you are beginning to make plans for a trip to the East Coast after the first of the year. We should again visit our Southern and possibly our Northern mills.

Hope all the family is well, and give my regards to Alice.

Kindest personal regards,

Requested Information

Dear Dan:

It was a pleasure meeting you on my recent visit to San Diego. My wife and I always enjoy ourselves on a return visit. The changes in the city leave us in awe as we remember the "old home town" of the 1940s.

I will look forward to receiving your mailings on scuba diving trips to Mexico. It is a certainty that some members of our household will be participating in this activity.

My family anticipates spending two weeks in San Diego during Easter. If you are about, I will be happy to share a pitcher of Margaritas.

Best Regards,

Sending Information

Dear Walt:

Please forgive me for not answering your letter sooner, but both my travel and my secretary's being on vacation have postponed most of my correspondence.

I am glad to hear that things are going well with you and that you are busy with new packaging developments. You may find the attached reprint of interest, although it is more appropriate for more expensive equipment than you use in your particular manufacturing operation. Should I come across anything else, I will send it along to you.

Please give my best to Jill and everyone in Denver.

Sincerely,

INTRODUCTION

The purpose of an introductory letter is solely to introduce one person to another. It is not a reference letter, which can be used to sell the qualifications of one person to another, so get right to the point with a letter that is brief.

The tone of the letter will depend on the relationship between the writer and the reader, and the anticipated relationship between the person being introduced and the reader. This will usually be a friendly and informal relationship, requiring a letter with a touch of warmth.

Provide at least the first and last names of the person being introduced, and, when possible, background, or at least some interest common to both parties. An explanation that is reasonable to the reader should be given for the introduction. This is often really asking for a favor; therefore give full consideration to the feelings and probable reaction of the reader.

In commenting about the person being introduced, make the reader *want* to meet him or her. Without overdoing a good thing, make the person sound interesting.

How to Do It

1. Provide the full name of the person being introduced.
2. Give a reasonable explanation for what is really a request for a favor.
3. Make the reader *want* to meet the other person.

New Sales Representative

Dear Jack:

Our new sales representative, Andy Watson, will be calling on you soon.

Andy has a wealth of background in bag-making machinery, including manufacturing, assembling, and repairing, as well as supervising machine operators and scheduling orders — and even sales. Not many people have such thoroughgoing experience with a machine they are selling and servicing.

You will find Andy as pleasant and helpful as he is knowledgeable. We are proud to have him represent us, and I know you will soon think as highly of him as we do.

Sincerely,

Friend for Sales Position

Dear Mr. Gibson:

Mr. Jack Stanton is a long-time acquaintance of mine. He has been a successful salesman for many years in the industrial equipment field.

I believe he would fit well into your organization and cover the needs you described to me last month.

Please give him your consideration. You will find him worth it.

With regards,

A Friend

Dear Mr. Blackman,

Marvin Melville is a good friend of ours. He will be in Minneapolis about the middle of next month for a few days, and I would like him to meet you. You both have a strong interest in juvenile runaways. Marv is doing research in San Francisco now, and I told him about the study you did on juveniles in Chicago last year. I'm sure you both would have a lot to talk over. You'll find Marv extremely pleasant.

May I give him your phone number? Please write and let me know.

Best regards,

Dear Charlie,

My good friend Jim Hoskins will be in Atlanta the week of February 10. Jim is director of marketing for a large folding carton manufacturer. I told him you are doing research for a textbook on the use of graphics designs in advertising. Jim was more than a little interested in your project and how it might apply to the sales of folding cartons, which his company makes and prints.

If you have the time, give him a call at 000-0000, room 000. I told Jim you might be tied up that week, so he will understand if he doesn't hear from you.

I know you would enjoy each other's company.

Regards,

Academic Assistance

Gentlemen:

This will introduce Mr. Joe Phillips, who is studying for his master's degree at the University of Washington. We believe you can help him in the area of foreign trade. Your help would be greatly appreciated by him and by us.

Sincerely,

For a Job

Dear Mr. Allen:

Mrs. Lee Andry has been with us as secretary for three engineering managers for five years. For personal reasons she has found it necessary to move to Atlanta. Because she is a highly qualified secretary and administrative assistant, I thought you might be able to use her in your company. If not, perhaps you could offer her some suggestions for continuing her career in the Atlanta area.

If you or any of your staff should be coming to the Northwest, please call me; we can set up a business dinner.

Cordially,

INVITATIONS

A letter of invitation is one of goodwill. It is a friendly letter (even if solely for a business purpose) because you wish to retain the reader's good thoughts about you. It is also a personal letter because you are writing to one person who will feel praise in being singled out. To attain this good feeling, the letter must be warm and express an honest wish for acceptance, as in these sentences:

We will be waiting to hear from you.

Please let us hear from you soon.

We are anxious to get together with you again.

Please confirm by May 4 that you can attend.

It will be so good to see you again.

The degree of formality to use in the writing depends on the relationship between the writer and the reader. It can vary from "old buddy" jocularity to third person formality, from "Hi Skip, I hear you'll be back in town next week. How about pouring a few with Don and me at Morland's," to "The Onward Civic Club cordially invites you to attend . . ."

As well as being specific about when and where you will meet the recipient of the invitation, it may be appropriate to mention why you have invited the reader. This is primarily true in business invitations: you wish to discuss a specific aspect of your business relationship, or you have a particular reason for inviting this person to speak or to join an organization.

How to Do It

1. Mention the purpose of the invitation.

2. State when and where and, if appropriate, why.

3. Request confirmation or express anticipated acceptance.

Luncheon for Old Friend

Dear John:

Tom Hardy, "dear old Tom," will be in town next week. I am getting several of his friends together for a luncheon at the Aztec Hotel Fireside Room on Friday, November 23 at noon.

I sure hope you can join the old gang; there will be an empty spot without you. I look forward to seeing you there.

Cordially,

To Do Advertising

Dear Mr. Callby:

We have a new line of coated stainless steel cookware ready to market. Would you be interested in discussing the product and the possibility of advertising it for us?

Please phone me before Friday to arrange a date for further discussion. I will be waiting for your call.

Sincerely,

Use Company Hotel Room

Dear Mr. May:

When you come to Minneapolis for your sales meeting next month, perhaps you would enjoy staying at our company hotel room. I can reserve it for you for March 17, 18, and 19.

I think you would enjoy the location (as well as the room) because it is only three blocks from your meeting place.

It will be a pleasure to reserve the room for you. I must have your decision by the 15th of this month.

Please let me hear from you.

Most sincerely,

Ball Game

Dear Barbara and Bob,

Jan and I would like to have you attend the Cal-Stanford Big Game with us. (I just happen to have two spare tickets.) It would be a great reunion for us after your many years in the South.

You could meet us at our house in the morning of __ , 19__ for a snack before leaving for the game.

We are looking forward to hearing from you.

Your old buddy,

Dinner Guest

Dear Jim,

The East Bay Accounting Society is having an exciting guest at its dinner meeting next Thursday. The guest is Ben Stoddard, who has won fame as a tax avoidance authority — not tax *evasion*, he will point out.

I thought you would be interested in attending as my guest. The meeting is at 7:00 P.M., Thursday, the 24th, and will be over by 10:30 P.M.

Please let me hear from you. I can pick you up on my way there, and I know you will enjoy the evening.

Best Regards,

Accepting Invitations

A letter accepting an invitation should emphasize warm gratitude and anticipated enjoyment. It was really nice of the person to invite *you*, and in return you can say you are grateful by writing:

I shall be happy to accept . . .

It was thoughtful of you to invite me to . . .

Thank you so much for thinking of me.

Thank you for your invitation to . . .

An invitation is written only to those who are expected to enjoy the occasion, and it is appropriate for the acceptor to concur with the writer's statement of impression that a good time will be had by all. For example:

We look forward to seeing you again.

We always enjoy the Michigan State games.

It will be a pleasure to meet your club members.

You can count on my being there.

The degree of formality or informality in the acceptance letter would normally follow closely the tone of the invitation.

How to Do It

1. Express thanks for the invitation.
2. State acceptance.
3. Confirm time and place.
4. Express pleasant anticipation.

To Speak

Dear Mr. Lawson:

Thank you for the invitation to speak at your fund-raising committee meeting. You suggested reviewing last year's successful campaign. I think that is a great idea. I plan to emphasize the positive aspects and suggest how you can build upon the successful techniques to strengthen this coming year's campaign.

I will be at your meeting place a little before 7:00 P.M. on Friday, May 17.

I am happy to do what I can to help your campaign.

Sincerely,

Football Celebration

Dear Dave,

Thank you for the invitation to celebrate the A's victory at your home.

Doris and I will be there about 4:00 P.M., Saturday, the 24th. We always enjoy visiting with you, and it seems like a long time since our last get-together.

See you Saturday,

Retirement Dinner

Dear Sharon,

Thank you for inviting Cheryl and me to attend a retirement dinner at the Aztec Restaurant on May 4 at 7:30 P.M.

We will be there.

I think it is nice of you to add something special to our standard retirement activities.

Cordially,

Dinner Invitation

Dear Mr. Sheridan:

In reply to your mailgram invitation of May 24, 19___ , I would be pleased to meet with you and Mr. Hanson on Wednesday, June 6th at 7:00 P.M. at the Marboro Hotel Dining Room.

Sincerely,

Join a Group

Dear Alice,

Thank you for inviting me to join the Women's Hospital Auxiliary. I do have many years of enjoyable experience in this line of work and am sure I can be of much help to your organization as well as to the patients we serve.

I will be able to attend your meeting on August 4 at 4:00 P.M.

Sincerely,

Declining Invitations

See Chapter Two, **Declining Requests.**

ACCEPTING JOB OR POSITION

Although accepting a job is usually done orally and the acceptance consummated when personnel records are completed, it is a polite gesture to mail a letter of acceptance. When accepting an office or position with a social organization, the acceptance letter will probably be the only written record of either the offer or acceptance.

The first sentence should include an acknowledgment of the acceptance and an expression of appreciation; having accepted the job, you should have no trouble feeling appreciative. Here are some examples:

> I am happy to accept your offer to join your purchasing department.
>
> I am pleased to accept the position of assistant sales manager.
>
> Your acceptance of my bid for the position of head nurse is greatly appreciated.

An expression of thanks for being considered can enhance the employer's confidence in you and in his or her judgment in selecting you.

> Your confidence in selecting me will be well founded.
>
> I appreciate your selecting me from the large number who applied.
>
> I am happy that you found a way to utilize my varied experience in this field.

In some acceptances of a position, you may be able to include what you hope to accomplish. This lets the employer know you are looking ahead, but be general and cautious; many unknowns await the new employee. You may, however, be able to include statements similar to these:

> Your decision to grant me full control will enable me to give first priority to improving merchandise quality.
>
> I have some procedures in mind for improving control of the accounting data.
>
> There are effective sales promotion programs that can be implemented with a miniumum of change in your current procedures.
>
> I am aware that long hours will be required to accomplish your immediate goals.
>
> Although this is a part-time job, I will involve myself fully.

How to Do It

1. State with appreciation what is being accepted.
2. Express thanks for being considered.
3. Indicate what you hope to accomplish.

City Clerk

Dear Ms. Brown:

Your eagerly awaited letter stating that I have been selected for the position of City Clerk arrived today. Your confidence in me is appreciated and I heartily accept your offer.

As soon as it is appropriate, I would appreciate discussing the function and duties of the position with the outgoing clerk.

Please let me know when I can start.

Sincerely,

Lions Club

Dear Mr. Samuelson:

Thanks for passing on the word that I've been selected as the next president of the Lions. With so many good men in the running, I hardly expected to make it to the top five, let alone the presidency itself.

A training period will be necessary, however, to familiarize myself with not only the official duties but also with the ceremonial aspects of the position.

My efforts are aimed toward making this year the most successful one in a long while by promoting unity as well as service among members.

Sincerely,

Purchasing Agent

Dear Mr. Williams:

I was pleased to receive your letter offering me the position of purchasing agent with S&A Parts. The offer is particularly enhanced by the fact that a large number of applicants vied for the position.

Your confidence in me will prove well founded. Experience and judgment gained in past years will guide me in conducting an efficient operation.

I look forward to working with you.

Sincerely,

Store Manager

Dear Miss Wilson:

Thank you for offering me the position of branch manager of the Regan Department Store in Markette. Your confidence in my ability is gratifying.

The decision to grant me full control of all facets of the store operations will provide the means of initiating needed changes in both merchandising and advertising. These two areas will become my first priorities in improving the image of the store.

I am eager to begin work as soon as possible.

Sincerely,

Part-Time Job

Dear Ms. Walters:

How can I thank you for the joy that your letter gave me? I checked the mail daily for the last month, eager to know if you had found a way of utilizing my talents and experience. Your response justified every moment of anticipation.

Although employment with *Bank* magazine will be only part-time, I intend to involve myself fully in the operation of the magazine. As I revealed in the interview, the position is of great value to me as a means of reentering the job market after taking time out to raise my children. Therefore, you will find me eager to accept all manner of assignments.

I look forward to beginning work.

Sincerely,

ACCEPTING JOB APPLICANT

A written record of being accepted for a job is appreciated by the applicant. The letter eliminates doubt and confusion and clarifies details such as where and when to report. Information about lodging availability and what to expect the first day will be of help in some situations.

This type of letter affords a great opportunity for a sentence or two (no more) of good impression building. Make the new employee glad to have accepted a position with this particular employer. Include a congratulatory statement.

How to Do It

1. Make a congratulatory statement.
2. State or imply that selection was made from many applicants.
3. Present a low-key sales pitch for the employer.
4. List any special conditions: when, where, and to whom to report; temporary lodging; first assignment; or other.

Junior Accountant

Dear Ms. Wallen:

It is with great pleasure that I inform you of our decision to offer you the position of junior accountant with A. Simm and Co.

The great number of applicants made the selection process rather lengthy. However, in order to maintain our fine reputation in the business community, such careful selection is necessary.

Please report to the senior accountant's office on Monday, July 8, 19__ . Mr. Samuels will familiarize you with your duties and get you off to a good start.

Congratulations on being selected.

Sincerely,

Office Clerk

Dear Miss Garcia:

Your recent application for office clerk has been reviewed and approved by the Personnel Department. Your abilities appear suitable to the needs of J.P. Sundstrom and we can offer you a position beginning immediately at the pay discussed.

At J.P. Sundstrom, every employee is an important member of the firm. All employees have the opportunity to rise according to their abilities. Thus, even entry-level employees are selected with great care.

Congratulations on your selection. If you choose to accept our offer, please report to the Personnel Office on Wednesday, September 17, 19__ , at 8 A.M.

Sincerely,

Foreman

Dear Mr. Smith:

I am pleased to offer you the position of foreman at A. C. Diesel Company. You were selected from among many applicants who eagerly sought employment with A. C. Diesel because of our low turnover.

We hope you will accept our offer.

You may report to the Personnel Office on Thursday, September 18, 19__ , for your assignment.

I look forward to having you join our company.

　　　　　　　　　　　　　　　　　　　　　　Sincerely,

School Teacher

Dear Ms. Rhymer:

I am happy to inform you that Burns school can offer you the position of instructor for the 19__ - 19__ school year. Selection from among so many qualified applicants was difficult. However, the results of your interview, coupled with the fine recommendation we received, made us decide in your favor.

You should arrive the Saturday before classes resume. Temporary lodging will be available at Beogan Hall. Just call ahead or ask at the gate. We can also help you to locate an apartment in the area. Our classes begin September 7 and the first few days will be rather hectic. Be prepared.

I will assume that you accept our offer unless I hear from you in the next week. Once again, congratulations on your selection.

　　　　　　　　　　　　　　　　　　　　　　Sincerely,

Store Manager

Dear Mr. Sawyer:

Congratulations on being selected as our new Pareson store manager. I hope that you will accept our offer and that the salary offer is commensurate with your expectations.

The decision was a tough one since many qualified people were being considered. However, your creativity and enthusiasm won out over the others. I personally feel that the right choice was made.

We're a difficult store to work for since the public eye is always on the image projected by both our fashions and our employees, but you should have no problems in this area.

Try to arrive in town by September 2, so you can get settled before the big season really begins and your duties multiply by the hundreds. Call when you're ready to begin work. My best to you in this new undertaking.

Sincerely,

COVER LETTER

The purpose of a cover letter is to help the recipient save time and effort. Rather than having to read the first part of a written document or a group of papers, then having to decide what they are and what they are for, the reader can read a cover letter and know immediately what is enclosed.

A cover letter should be brief. For example:

Four copies of the May 1 revision of the 19__ Budget are enclosed.

That statement tells what is enclosed and how many. In this case the reader was expecting the budget revisions, but some cover letters must include a little more information. If several different items are enclosed, a listing is helpful. It may be appropriate to mention who requested the enclosures or who instructed the sender to mail them. If the receiver is not expecting the item, an explanation of its purpose may be required.

A job resumé cover letter should also be brief, but long enough to mention what job you are applying for and one or two of your strongest selling points.

People given the task of reading resumés usually do this infrequently; it is an added-on task. They are still busy with their regular work. The cover letter, therefore, should be brief, to the point, include an applicable selling point, and, of absolute importance, make the reader anxious to turn to the resumé itself.

How to Do It

1. State what is enclosed or attached; if in answer to a request, name the person who made the request.
2. If applicable, mention the quantity enclosed or make a brief listing.
3. The purpose of the enclosure may be mentioned.

Expenditures Request

Dear Mr. Wade:

Attached for your consideration is our Capital Expenditure Request No. 400-32, covering installation of cooling units ahead of the roof ventilators. At present, the ventilating air picks up a large amount of heat from the tar-covered roof.

Regards,

Lists

Dear Mr. Holmes:

Enclosed are three (3) copies of lists showing miscellaneous items in Warehouse Inventories.

These lists have been revised to October 31, 19__ .

Sincerely,

Dear Mr. Erwin:

Enclosed is our Division's list of items normally expensed that could be carried as inventory, as requested in J. P. Connor's letter of February 28, 19__ .

Regards,

Agreement for Signature

Dear Mr. and Mrs. Custom:

Enclosed is the Modification Agreement as proposed in our letter of April 30, 19__ .

If you agree to the change, please sign the agreement, have your signatures notarized, and return the document to this office.

Sincerely,

Warehouse Report

Dear Ms. Anwan:

Enclosed is Ashton Warehouse Co. Commodity Report covering the inventory for Ren Bearing Co.

Will you please reconcile this report to your records.

Sincerely yours,

Certificate of Incorporation

Gentlemen:

Enclosed for filing is the certificate of incorporation of H.H.H. Associates, Inc., together with our check for $60 to cover the filing fee, ($50) and two certified copies of the charter ($10).

Sincerely,

Statement Requested

Dear Ken:

Attached is the signed Compliance Statement requested in your letter of December 14.

Sincerely,

Commodity Codes

Dear Mr. Sanders:

The attached copy of the Master Commodity Code carries an effective date of January 1, 19___. Will you please cross-index your working files with these codes so that your purchase invoices will be properly classified.

Sincerely,

Savings Statement

Dear Miss Donner:

Enclosed are sealed envelopes containing individual Savings Account statements as of December 31, 19— for:

C. O. Sanders
A. T. Younts
B. B. Wankel

Please mail the statements to these individuals.

Sincerely,

Insurance Renewal

Dear Mr. Matson:

Your insurance renewal is enclosed, continuing this important protection for you over the coming months. This renewal protects you against lapse of coverage and is in force from the expiration date of your present policy. After looking over the coverage, should you have any question or if any corrections are necessary, please call or write our office promptly.

Our sincerest appreciation for your continuance of this business. Do not hesitate to contact our office if there is any way we can be of further service.

Once again, thank you,

Price Increase

Dear Ms. Waterford:

The Abel Paint Company has announced a price increase of approximately 6 percent effective July 1, 19— . Attached is their National Account Price List No. 17.

Two changes have been made in this latest price list:

1. Chemical Coatings have been added.
2. All products are now listed alphabetically by name, making them easier to find in the list.

Sincerely,

Job Resumé

Gentlemen: (To a corrugated box manufacturer.)

In answer to your advertisement in the Los Angeles Times on February 26, 19— for a sales representative, I have three years of experience as a sales representative for a corrugated box manufacturer. With the same company, I have two years of experience in the plant and three years in the purchasing department.

I am prepared for the long hours and travel required of an effective salesperson.

My resumé is enclosed.

Sincerely,

Gentlemen: (To a truck manufacturer.)

In answer to your advertisement for a Regional Chief Accountant, I am currently a plant accountant with full responsibility for the monthly profit and loss statement and the accompanying details and analyses.

I have over twenty years of varied industrial accounting experience, the last fifteen with a truck manufacturer.

My resumé is attached.

Very sincerely yours,

FOLLOW-UP

A follow-up letter can be a reminder, a progress report, a request for an explanation, or even a sales letter. Examples of these are in this section, along with letters to follow-up job interviews.

Start right off with a statement of the event or situation you are writing about. State the topic in the first sentence. This is followed by facts, figures, or a description of what has occurred between now and your prior contact with the reader. End with a statement of what action you will take or specifically what you are now requesting.

If the time interval between contacts is short, the facts and descriptions in the second step may be omitted, assuming there is no doubt in the reader's mind about what has occurred, as in this introductory sentence:

Is my face red! I just read your letter of January 17. How we could make a mistake like that I don't know, but we did, and here's what we are going to do about it.

A follow-up letter after a job interview can often be the extra push that gets you the job. A letter received two or three days after the interview will keep your name in front of the employer. The letter also provides an opportunity to add what you wish you had thought of during the interview.

A short thank-you for the interview is sufficient for the introductory pleasantries. Then mention the main topic of the interview — the main topic from the *interviewer's* point of view — and what you can contribute to that situation. Follow this with helpful information that you may not have included in the first discussion. You can then add reminders of your strong qualifications and abilities. End with a statement of when you will contact the company to discuss a second interview.

Keep in mind throughout the letter that you are selling your ability to help the company you wish to work for.

How to Do It

1. State the situation or event that is being followed up.
2. Describe what has been learned or has happened since prior contact with the reader.
3. Stipulate what action you will take or what you are requesting.

Correct an Error

Dear Ed:

As a follow up, I am attaching copies of two letters dated April 19 and May 27, 19— to which we have had no reply.

The letters relate to incorrect shipments to our Charleston and Richmond offices.

We would appreciate your looking into this and letting us know what you find.

If you require copies of the backup material sent with the letters, or any other information, please let me know.

Sincerely,

Additional Information Requested

Dear Mr. Naughton:

Stanley Company's quote on the cost of relocating two presses appears to be more general than specific. Working with our local engineers, you will have to take the information supplied by Stanley, get what information you can from sources within our company, and come up with some hard dollar figures on the cost of this project.

I think it's important that we give this immediate attention.

Sincerely,

Additional Information Provided

Dear Mr. Dearborn:

Following up on the problem of building a stacker behind the Wallington machine, which I discussed in my letter of January 15, we have reviewed the situation and have a plan. The problem now is getting maintenance time to get the job done.

We will move this job up on our priority list and see if we can't come up with the solution within the next month.

Sincerely,

Inactive Charge Account

Dear Ms. Walters:

Have we disappointed you?

We hope not, but we are disappointed . . . that you have not been using your open credit account recently. When an account is active, we know you are pleased with our merchandise, our service, and the convenience of charging your purchases.

If there is something in particular we can do to make your shopping more convenient, please let us know on the postage-paid card enclosed.

Our goal is to have happy customers.

Sincerely,

Power Lawn Mower Purchase

Dear Mr. Morton:

Your Huston Power Lawn Mower dealer, J & J Warner Bros. of St. Louis, has written us of your recent purchase of a Huston mower. We at Huston headquarters, as well as J & J Warner, appreciate your decision to buy a Huston. We are sure you will become a satisfied owner.

We are proud of our dealers: they are responsible business people, they operate sound businesses, and they participate in community activities. They help make your city a better place in which to live and grow.

Your Huston dealer is trained and qualified to assist you with any maintenance problems or operating questions. J & J Warner stands ready to help you.

We are enclosing three Western prints for your enjoyment. Every three months for a year we will send you a small gift to show our appreciation and continued interest in you, our customer.

Sincerely,

Purchasing Position

Dear Mr. Arlington:

Thank you for the interview on the 22nd. I am confident I can fill the position of purchasing assistant. I agree that with your expanded activities, you need someone who can devote time to comparing prices and researching alternate sources of supply, and I have a program in mind that has been used successfully by other firms. Because it could easily be adapted to your operation, I would like to present this procedure for your consideration.

In my previous job we purchased from several of the same suppliers that you use. I believe I can adapt quickly to your purchasing procedures.

I will phone your office on the 30th to see if we can set a time to continue our discussion.

Sincerely,

Retail Selling

Dear Mr. Edwards:

Thank you for explaining the opening in your hardware department. The position sounds interesting, and I believe I can help you. My experience with Baker and Hamilton is directly related to the work you require. Also, my school background and my work with Jones Simpson Company provide a strong base in retail marketing.

I am enclosing the completed application. My school transcript will be sent directly from San Jose State University.

I enjoyed our talk yesterday, and will call you next Friday morning.

Sincerely,

Accounting Position

Dear Mr. Becker:

Thank you for the interesting interview on Monday, April 14. We did find an amazing number of similarities between the accounting operations of your company and the one I am now involved in, although the two industries are shipbuilding and paper finishing.

You mentioned several difficulties in getting data necessary for accurate cost controls. Most of the same difficulties were experienced where I work. Several problems were solved and others are being solved. I would like to present these solutions in more detail when we meet again. I am sure that many can be adapted without any changes in your accounting procedures, merely changes in details.

I will phone you Wednesdsay, the 30th to see what we can arrange.

Sincerely,

14

OTHER PERSONAL LETTERS

Because they contain elements of both, some letters are hard to classify as personal or business. A business letter should have a touch of personal friendliness. Even a letter containing only straightforward, cold facts can be presented in a way that is more friendly and warm than cool. See Chapter 6, **Information — Providing and Requesting**, for some suggestions. Going further, even a business letter of criticism or reprimand must show personal consideration for the reader or the reader will become disturbed, with the result that the letter does not accomplish its purpose. Should the person to whom you are writing a business letter be a personal friend, both your personal and business relationships can be enhanced with a sentence or two referring to some mutual, personal interest such as, "Give my regards to Alice," "How do you like your new city by now?" or "I'll call you next week about the Bowling Club dance."

On the other hand, a personal letter has some aspects of a business letter. When you wish to give information to a personal aquaintance, the same techniques of organizing and presenting facts will be used as in business letters. Again, the introductory remarks in Chapter 6 will help. If you are writing a get-well note to a co-worker, it may be a personal expression, but the fact that you work together keeps your business relationship from being completely excluded.

Whether you believe you are writing a business or a personal letter, keep the reader uppermost in your mind. Write what will interest the reader, what you want the reader to know and believe, what will appeal to the reader, and foremost, what will get the reader to react the way you want him to. A letter, even a friendly note, is written to accomplish a purpose, and the key to this accomplishment is to think the way the reader does. Put yourself in his or her place and ask, "How would I react to this letter if I were the reader?"

WELCOME

"Glad to have you here! You will find us friendly." This is the congenial mood that a letter of welcome should reveal to the reader. It is a gesture of courtesy and consideration.

Since a welcome letter is also a second cousin to a sales letter, you can mention something nice about your organization, place of work, or group. Let the reader know that you are proud to belong, hoping that he or she will be too.

Include some suggestion as to how the person can fit into your group, or how he or she can learn what is available, or what you will do to help orient the reader.

End the letter with a note of encouragement or a suggestion of how the reader can take the initial step.

How to Do It

1. Express pleasure at making the welcome.
2. Make complimentary remarks about your organization or place.
3. Draw a relationship between the person and the organization.
4. End with an encouraging comment.

To New Resident

Dear Mr. and Mrs. Webster:

Welcome to Seattle, the heart of the Evergreen State!

Coming from the East, you will especially enjoy our temperate climate, but you will not be leaving behind the thrill of the changing seasons. Most of all, you will enjoy the friendly, down-to-earth people here.

To help you get acquainted, please phone the New Residents Club at 000-0000. We will be happy to answer any questions you have, and we will suggest that someone call on you for a more personal discussion of how you can find your niche in this wonderful city.

Sincerely,

Dear Mr. and Mrs. Conrad:

Welcome to Sacramento!

We understand that you and your family plan to reside here, and we know you will find Sacramento a pleasant and friendly place in which to live and work.

If there is anything we can do to help you, come in and let us know. Our business requires us to keep completely informed about local conditions, and we may be able to help you in a number of ways, such as providing a street map, list of civic clubs, list of social clubs, bus routes and schedules, and answering questions about Sacramento.

If you can use our services, we will welcome the opportunity to include you among our clients.

Sincerely,

To New Member

Dear Ms. Wallace,

As president of the East Side Bridge Club, I want to extend a welcome to you.

I am sure you will be a great help to us in our annual, friendly competition with the West Side Bridge Club.

I also want to explain that our Club is involved in social activities as well as in playing bridge. We have parties, see stage plays, go on picnics, and have other activities that get families, and their friends, joining in a pleasant fellowship.

Welcome to our group, and I am sure you will enjoy the friendship.

Sincerely,

To New Business

Dear Mr. Hancock:

Welcome to Cupertino!

As our city grows, we welcome new business people who have already shown success. Your past experience indicates that you will make a definite contribution to the development and growth of our retail trade by meeting the needs of our shoppers.

The Retail Trade Association is prepared and happy to help you in any way to get established here.

Sincerely,

To New Customer

Dear Mrs. Albertson:

Bardahl's wishes to welcome you to our growing number of new customers, and to thank you for your recent purchase of a washing machine. You can depend on years of service from a Wells washer. (If any trouble should develop, please call our service department immediately.)

We carry a wide selection of name brand appliances and will be most happy to welcome your visit to our store and to answer any questions you may have.

Sincerely,

To New Employee

Dear Mr. Larson:

We at Aatel are glad to welcome you to our financial staff. We admire the work you did for Pierce Tractor and believe you can do as much for us. You will find a professional and cooperative staff here, and I am sure you will enjoy working with them.

I will arrange to have lunch with you soon to discuss some aspects of your work. In the meantime you will find Mr. Bond most willing to answer your questions.

Welcome aboard,

Dear Miss Ellis:

It is a pleasure to welcome you to Farnsworth, Inc. We are sure that you will find working here a pleasant and rewarding experience because we work especially hard to insure that our employees and their jobs are compatible.

Our progress and growth are the result of each person's taking responsibility for a share of the work that needs to be done. As responsibility increases, so do the rewards. We take pride in our accomplishments, and I am sure you will too.

Best wishes for success at Farnsworth.

Dear Mr. Rush:

With great pleasure we welcome you to A and S Associates. You will soon feel the sense of pride we share in belonging to this growing organization.

Our personnel policies and benefits — among the best in this area — will be explained to you as part of your first day's orientation. A visit to the manufacturing plant will be arranged.

You were selected from a large number of applicants. We have confidence in your ability to contribute to our continuing growth and profitability.

Welcome to A and S Associates.

                 Sincerely,

Dear Mr. Greene:

My first position with Lambert Company was as storeroom clerk. True, I had an engineering degree from the University of Washington, and later took a series of courses in Management Supervision, but becoming president of our corporation did not occur to me then. What did come to mind was that I could become the best storeroom clerk Lambert Company ever had.

The next step up was assistant purchasing agent. I studied that job and eventually got it. I then studied the job of cutting foreman and eventually got that position. In every position I had, I learned the job thoroughly and then prepared myself for the next step forward.

Only one person can hold the position of president at one time, but, as is true in every successful organization, each position in this organization is worth one's best efforts.

I send you my best wishes for a successful career with Lambert Company.

                 Cordially,

To Wife of Salesman

Dear Mrs. Wentling:

Welcome to the Sun Ray Distributors family.

As the wife of one of our new salespersons, you become a part of our growing family. We are pleased to welcome you.

We are a new company, but the selling and installation of solar heating systems is expanding rapidly, making the potential for growth almost unlimited. We know Ted Wentling will play a large part in our growth. He was carefully selected as one who will dig in now to get us going and continue his enthusiasm as he participates in our growth.

We have a quality product to sell; our engineering consultants made sure of that, and our growing list of satisfied customers points to the truth of their findings.

As with all salespersons in a new position, Ted Wentling will find a few tough spots and discouragements at first, but we have found that wives are a real source of understanding, encouragement, and cheer during the initial period of adjustment to a new job.

Ted will also find you a help in entertaining an occasional customer and in recognizing that selling is not a straight 8-to-5 job. Some late hours will be required as well as a small amount of traveling.

We are sure that these few inconveniences will be worked into your time schedule and you will derive pride and satisfaction from contributing to Ted's success with Sun Ray.

Sincerely,

GOOD WISHES

A letter of good wishes is appropriate for a business friend who is also a personal friend, one to whom you can express your feelings in a friendly and natural way. It is a letter of sincerity combined with informality.

One special occasion for a letter of good wishes is the year-end holiday season. You can use this annual time of goodwill and good feeling to thank a customer for being *your* customer, to wish him or her well in the coming year, and to express pleasant thoughts to acquaintances and cheerful thoughts to friends.

Another occasion for sending good wishes is the convalescence of someone who has been ill or in an accident. A cheerful thought is great therapy, and all it takes is a short letter.

Whatever the occasion — even if there is no occasion — being remembered is always appreciated.

How to Do It

1. Mention the occasion for the good wishes.

2. Describe briefly some common topic or feeling or idea that is appropriate for the occasion.

Season's Greetings

Dear Mr. Allen:

As the magic of the holiday season approaches, our thoughts turn to those who have made our progress possible. We wish to express our appreciation for your goodwill — the very foundation of business success. In the spirit of friendship, we send you our hope for a continuing business relationship and best wishes for a pleasant holiday season.

Sincerely,

Dear Mr. Evans:

At this time of the year, many of us like to reminisce, and that led me back to our especially pleasant visit when you were here in September.

In the future, I hope we can have more of these interesting and stimulating meetings.

Have a relaxing holiday season — you have earned it — and we'll plan another get-together early next year.

Cordially,

Dear Mr. Elmers:

As the end of the year approaches, we like to take a moment or two from the usual rush of business to thank you for the fine relationship we have enjoyed this year and to extend our best wishes for a happy holiday season and a good year ahead.

Sincerely,

Dear Mr. Cunard:

With the holiday season close at hand, let me say that all during the year I think of you more as a personal friend than as a business acquaintance. Your friendship is valued, and I hope we can continue it during the many years ahead.

Sincerely,

Convalescing

Dear Ethel,

How good it is to send a note to your home for a change. You must feel by now that you own the South Wing of the hospital.

I'm glad to hear that you are better and will be back to work soon.

Sincerely,

Dear Robert,

Being out of the action can't be much fun these sunny autumn days, but for sure it's only temporary.

Remember our coach saying that being on the bench gave you a chance to see the whole field? Hang in there and make the most of it.

I'll keep in touch and come to see you soon.

Regards,

Dear Tim,

Now that your operation is over it is great to have you on the convalescent list.

A forced pause in a busy person's life can sometimes be a blessing. I am hoping this pause will turn into a blessing for you.

I know you like historical fiction, so I am sending you one of the latest books.

Happy hours of reading, resting, and pausing.

Your pal,

Dear Jean,

It's been a long, hard pull, but you made it! Your doctor tells me you're now on the way to recovery. All your friends are cheering for you. Believe me, we are full of admiration for your spirited determination to get well.

Sincerely,

ENCOURAGEMENT

Baseball players are not alone with their batting slumps. The rest of us have "batting slumps" too. That is when we need encouragement to try harder, to take a deep breath and hold on, to blink our eyes and take a new look. When you see a person feeling low or in a state of depression, a letter of encouragement may be just the needed stimulant.

Whatever (or whoever) the cause, admit that an adverse condition exists. Trying to offer help while avoiding mention of the problem that necessitates the help requires the type of thinking best left to politicians. If, however, a problem does not exist, and you wish to make your letter more of a compliment than an encouragement, please refer to the section on Compliments in this chapter.

Admit that a problem exists, and mention what it is so that you and your reader are thinking together, but don't dwell on the problem.

If you are offering encouragement, you must be convinced that the adverse condition can be overcome. With this conviction in your mind, it will almost automatically show in the words and phrases you use.

The really helpful part of an encouragement letter is your suggestion of *how* an improvement can be made. Strong, forceful language or ideas are likely to create resistance or even discouragement. A more successful way is to make a clear and simple statement. For example:

Encourage your staff to be more aggressive.

Please reconsider, then I would appreciate discussing your decision.

Consult your advisor about reorganizing your format.

We will rework the equipment to provide you with better working conditions.

You love challenges, and have met them before.

Abe Lincoln found himself a defeated candidate for eight offices before being elected President.

When you feel your rope is nearly played out, tie a big knot at the end; it will help you hold on.

How to Do It

1. Admit that an adverse condition exists.
2. Mention the condition or problem.
3. Indicate conviction that the condition can be overcome.
4. Suggest how to overcome the condition.

Sales Contest

Dear Ed,

You were second in our sales contest last year, and you had Sam working so hard to stay ahead that he was glad retirement came before this year's contest. I'm rooting for you to win this year.

Right now, you are neck and neck with Don. To keep ahead, it may take just a little more push on your part. I am sure you can make the special effort to become number one this year.

Sincerely,

Low Productivity

Dear Mr. Prescon:

Recent figures indicate that changes in the ventilation system have not resulted in the expected increase in productivity.

Work crews will be sent in to revamp the ductwork and other equipment on Tuesday.

We are fully confident that once the difficulties have been resolved, your production levels will meet and even exceed previous figures.

Sincerely,

Dear Mr. Waterman:

Recent reports indicate that productivity has dropped to an all-time low in your department. It appears that the new computer system is slowing the output of your daily reports.

Our estimate that installation of the system would result in improved efficiency was inaccurate. We will, therefore, remove the computer and make a study of alternate computer systems.

Your operation has been hampered for a time but I am certain that, in light of past performance, your department will not only resume normal promptness but get even more reports in ahead of the deadlines.

Sincerely,

Promotion

Dear Mr. Phillips:

The main office empowered me to offer you the position of CEO of its Wagner facility, with all of the accompanying difficulties the position entails. As you know, several recent strikes have literally crippled the plant and the Board has several times suggested shutting down the facility entirely.

Your continued strong growth with the company, and the abilities you have exhibited here in the last two years, recommend you as the ideal person to return the plant to a profitable operation.

Please consider the offer and let me know as soon as you have reached your decision.

Sincerely,

Research Paper

Dear Ms. Roback:

The committee did not approve your dissertation on Fulani mating habits. The manuscript was somewhat carelessly written and researched and the approach echoes Powder's view of the subject too closely.

Stop in and discuss the problem with me. Let's see where we can tighten up some of the writing and pull in a few more sources on the subject. It might be good for you to review both the style manual and the handbook of research before coming to see me.

With all the research you've already done and the recent papers you've presented, the corrections should pose no real problems. The committee should approve your efforts at their next review.

Sincerely,

Fund Drive

Dear Miss St. George:

Time is closing in on us and, with the end of the fund drive only two weeks away, the goal seems awfully hard to reach.

The early mix-ups in planning and scheduling delayed our moving ahead with much of the publicity and soliciting, but we still haven't picked up the proper momentum for getting people interested. A little more publicity in the area and some strong staff support should do it. But, we have to really begin moving to meet that goal.

The past few fund drives have been pulled through by your special talents, and we hope that this one will be the same. You just have to get your people moving.

Sincerely,

Teaching

Dear Ms. Silva:

Teaching at P.S. 24 is a difficult assignment for any teacher and even the most seasoned instructors often find that the integration process takes time. Therefore, it comes as no surprise that you have spoken of submitting your resignation at the end of the school year.

Discipline remains a problem for many new teachers here, as you have discovered. Students tend to "test" a teacher. However, once the test is passed, teachers often find themselves responding with enthusiasm to the challenge.

Take a little time to reconsider your decision, then please see me to discuss the matter at your earliest convenience.

Sincerely,

Dear Mr. Skiles:

Word has reached me that you are ready to hand in your resignation and to leave P.S. 24 at the end of the school year. I can't say that I blame you. A teacher can only take so much of the testing and of disciplining instead of teaching before throwing in the towel. P.S. 24 is the ultimate test.

Maybe, though, you're being a little hasty. The past months have been rough but this was what you wanted. You always spoke of the challenge of teaching in the inner city. Your face would glow as you anticipated giving children the thrill that you've found in learning.

The school was difficult to face but you've really brought out the talents of several students whose previous teachers had never given them a chance. These children may be difficult, often trying human beings, but they are also very grateful to you. You're a fine teacher and they've truly learned something from you.

Sincerely,

COMPLIMENTS

What is nicer to receive than a compliment? Not too many things, because everyone appreciates praise. A pat on the back can make new friends, cement old relationships, win admiration, and, furthermore, can be a powerful influence in making day-to-day relationships more pleasant and rewarding.

Sincerity must be at the heart of every compliment to make it acceptable to the other person as truth. Beware of flattery which can destroy an intended congratulatory remark and lower the esteem of the writer.

Above all, a compliment is an effective stimulant to those who are thus recognized for a job well done.

How to Do It

1. State what the compliment is for.
2. Comment on the action that led to the compliment.
3. Encourage continuance of that action.

Staff Help

Dear Allen:

Efficiency accompanied by courtesy is a rare combination in today's work world. The courtesy extended to me by your staff during the recent week of meetings and planning sessions was impressive because of its rarity.

Both office personnel and executive planners provided detailed explanations and personal assistance when needed.

Such concern is refreshing and should become more widespread.

Sincerely,

rt Assistance

Dear Ted,

Just a note to express my sincere appreciation for the job both Pete and Tom performed while here in Baltimore. Between them they saved us untold thousands of dollars in material costs.

Tom just left after having spent most of the last twenty-four hours helping our people run tubing with a system that does not yet have sufficient power to maintain proper temperatures. Without his help, it is doubtful that we would ever have identified the true magnitude of the problem.

Please let Pete and Tom know how much we appreciate their help.

Sincerely,

Orientation Help

Dear Ellen:

You've got quite an operation going, and your people are even more to rave about. They seem to love their work and carry out their duties both competently and enthusiastically. Certainly, productivity is high as the monthly report shows. Morale appears to be equally high.

During that round of meetings and brainstorming sessions last week, your people worked to fill me in on unfamiliar material. Without being asked, they pulled files, reports, and memos to justify items and to increase my knowledge of vagaries. They even supplied me with advice regarding several good restaurants and entertainment in town.

With your production rates and the quality of your people, you must be doing something right. Keep it up.

Sincerely,

Better Truck Loading

Dear Calvin:

The average weight of 28,297 pounds for each truckload shipped in July makes it a record month.

The increased business has helped, I'm sure, but most of the credit goes to you and your loading crews. Keep up the good work.

Regards,

Unusual Help

Dear Jerome,

Many thanks for the long hours, weekends away from home, and all the other inconveniences you've endured during the past months. The help you gave is much appreciated.

I have a fishing trip out of San Francisco scheduled for May 27. I'd like to invite you to join us if you can. Please let me know.

Best of everything to you in the future.

Sincerely,

Finding Error

Dear Mr. McAbee:

Tim Andrews, during his routine posting of energy usage for the month of July, noted an unusual increase and questioned me about this increased cost.

I investigated the procedure for recording electric power usage and found that an error in calculating the kilowatt hours used during July raised our costs by more than $4,000. An adjustment will be given to us next month.

I would like to compliment Tim for his alertness and thank him for the added $4,000 bottom-line profit.

Sincerely,

Getting the Facts

Dear Mr. Emory:

The city of Fairfield has just awarded us the contract for construction of the Municipal Plaza due to begin early next year.

Your involvement in gathering the data and presenting the proposal proved vital to our success.

Your expert approach made a formerly difficult task manageable. Such talent is indeed an asset to our firm.

Sincerely,

Construction Bid

Dear Tom,

Your proposal passed with flying colors and Fairfield has given us the Municipal Plaza job. Construction should start next fall, but we'll be needing your talents in the meantime for a few other bids we're working on.

Our specifications needed that extra polish that your way with words gave them. The Council looked at the proposals of a half-dozen other firms and accepted our offer faster than we'd anticipated.

Don't get too tied up in other work for a while. We'll be in touch in a week or two. Once again, we appreciate the great job.

Sincerely

Good Salesman

Dear Torry,

The order from Easton arrived today and it alone raised our sales volume for the month by several points. Allen managed not only to sell a new account, but one that eluded us for several years despite serious work by several of our best people.

Allen's perseverance paid off. He spent several days trying to see Easton's president and finally caught him in the evening. Thanks to Allen's refusal to limit his working hours, the biggest account on the West Coast is ours.

You've got an eye for talent, and Allen is one man who's going far in this company.

Sincerely,

Sales Volume

Dear Bob,

John Harvey from our headquarters office reports that your sales volume for August was more than double July's volume.

We offer a good product to consumers, and equally important are the aggressive and competent employees like you who take our product before the public.

Continue the good work.

Sincerely,

Sales Increase

Dear Dave,

The latest issue of ACE had a circulation of over one million, a figure that no one thought we'd reach after the setbacks of the last three years.

A large part of the credit goes to you and the people you've chosen to rework what was once a dying publication. It looks like you've chosen a new format. Eliminating the "cute" departments and mindless quizzes has had its beneficial effect. You, Tom, Jean, and Dale have something to really gloat about in the industry. And ACE can look forward to increased profits in the months to come.

Please pass my appreciation on to your staff. Continue the good work.

Sincerely,

Dear Mr. Byran:

Circulation of ACE magazine has just passed the one million mark after a three-year lag in subscription sales. Although exposure has increased, your complete overhaul of the format and staff assignments have been key factors in this new success.

Keep up the good work.

Sincerely,

Vote Getter

Dear Wendell:

Rarely has a city experienced so high a percentage of voter turnout as in this last election. Well-planned publicity and careful scheduling brought out 72 percent of the registered voters who made their voices heard and their choice known.

Although the opposition often echoed the platform presented by our candidate, your work behind the scenes in managing the campaign made a major difference in voter reaction.

Local politics needs more dedicated workers like you.

Sincerely,

RECOMMENDATION

In a letter recommending one person to another, mention two or three points of strength. The person you are recommending should have more than one good quality, but if too many are listed, the authority of the letter is diminished.

Statements should be specific. Rather than saying, "Joan has a good attendance record," say, "Joan was absent only four days during the three years she worked here." Rather than saying, "Kathy is a good worker," say, "Kathy turns in her reports on time."

Assume a pleasant state of mind when writing the letter, because a cool or standoffish attitude will only harm the person you are trying to help. A feeling of warmth and enthusiasm should be felt by the reader.

Of course, mention the full name of the person you are recommending. Also state your relationship: employer, teacher, friend, and how long you have known him or her.

Usually the last sentence can be an affirmation that the person of your letter will fulfill the needs of the reader:

I recommend her highly as a statistical clerk.

I wish I had her back.

She will rise to the top, whatever she tries.

Tom was always a great help to me.

He is one I can recommend with complete confidence.

I know he will measure up to your expectations.

He did so much to increase our sales, and I know he can do the same for you.

She earned the confidence of all her customers.

His enthusiastic hard work will be sorely missed here.

Her efficiency may surprise you.

How to Do It

1. Mention the person's name and his or her most favorable trait.
2. State your association with the person — use specifics, not generalizations.
3. Reaffirm your recommendation.

Recent Graduate

Dear George,

Harry Watson recently graduated from Stanford Law School. I have known him for over seven years and can honestly say that he is one of the few intelligent, ambitious, and likeable young men available. Had he studied engineering, I would take him in without a moment's hesitation.

I hope you can find room for Watson in your office. Someone will start him on his certain, brilliant career in law.

At the least, he will appreciate a visit with you because he has greatly admired your work.

If you learn of any bright and ambitious engineers, send them to me. I'll be happy to return your favor.

Cordially,

Job Promotion

Dear Mr. Andrews:

Robert Winslow has developed at an accelerated pace during the past two years. In his capacity as Sales Service Manager, he has displayed much decision-making ability. Leadership is one of his stronger qualities.

Although the youngest person in the Sales Service Department, both in age and seniority, Robert was able to assume command upon promotion to his present position. He is rated as a No. 1 performer.

Robert has indicated a desire for line management and is willing to relocate. He is capable at this time of functioning as a Field Sales Manager.

Regards,

Personal Referral

Dear Mr. Archer:

This is in response to your letter March 4, 19__ requesting a personal letter of referral on Robert R. Riley.

I have personally known Robert for a number of years. He is a good friend of my son. I also know his family well because his father is my wife's doctor.

Robert is a tenacious young man and seems to be a determined, straightforward individual who knows where he is headed.

If you need further information, please write or phone.

Sincerely,

Customer

Gentlemen:

This is to inform you that we have done business with our customer, Seymour Port Company, for more than five years. We are pleased to report that all business has been conducted by Mr. Seymour and his company in a highly satisfactory manner.

Mr. Seymour and his staff have always been most helpful in providing information and advice about both domestic and overseas packaging and packaging materials. In the specialized field of overseas shipments, we have found that he has a broad range of information that has been helpful to us.

If you wish further information, please write or phone.

Sincerely,

Secretary

Dear Mr. Faulkner:

Ms. Eleanor Scott is highly recommended as a secretary. She worked for me for six years as secretary and statistical clerk. Not many will surpass her as a take-charge confidential secretary, and her statistical work is accurate. Her attendance is above average, she is on time, and she willingly works late when I ask her. Her handling of telephone calls and personal callers is most efficient and pleasant.

Sincerely,

Dear Mr. Langston:

Marcia Reddy was my secretary during my seven years with Lord and Taylor in Seattle. I was certainly sorry to lose her when I moved to Portland.

Ms. Reddy is an excellent secretary. She is conscientious, efficient, well-organized, bright, and tactful with all people.

I make no hesitation in recommending her; you will find her a big help.

Sincerely,

Accounts Payable Clerk

Dear Ms. Wiles:

Theresa Anderson receives my hearty recommendation as an accounts payable clerk. She did excellent and accurate work under my supervision during the last six years. She got the bills paid on time, was cooperative and willing to do other assignments — mostly in the area of accounting reports. She has no accounting background but was extremely helpful with routine reports. Her typing is top quality. She was on time and had a better than average attendance record.

I wish I had her back.

Sincerely,

Statistical Clerk

Dear Ms. Amos:

Arlene Arnold is a precise statistical clerk; her work is fast and accurate. She is consistently pleasant, tackling all assignments with a smile. She usually comes to work early, and she was absent only five days in the four years she worked here.

She learns quickly but is not really analytical or research minded. On the other hand, after being shown step-by-step how to do a report or assignment, few can better her performance.

I recommend her highly for a position working with numbers.

Sincerely,

Billing Clerk

Dear Mr. Hansen:

I am happy to recommend Norma Bellson, who has worked under my supervision for the past four years as a billing clerk. She does her work on schedule and is more accurate than most billers. In addition, her work is neat and thorough. She is always on the job a little ahead of time and her absenteeism is nearly zero.

Norma grasps new ideas and instructions quickly. She has a book-keeping background and would be excellent as a billing clerk or junior accountant.

Sincerely,

Domestic Service

Dear Mrs. Watson:

Annette Winton has worked for me two days a week for almost twelve years. She is punctual and a hard worker. In my opinion, her work is better than average. I have found her steady and cooperative — two qualities I appreciate.

I am sorry she is leaving, and I sincerely feel that whoever is fortunate to have her will be rewarded with work well done.

I have found Annette loyal to those she serves. My best wishes go with her.

Sincerely,

Inexperienced Worker

Dear Mr. Bishop:

I gladly recommend John Harley for work in your garage. He has been a neighbor all his life, is a hard and steady worker, and is a friendly person.

John has helped me with my car a few times and has demonstrated a good basic understanding of automobile mechanics.

Regards,

High School Graduate

Dear Ms. Wilson:

The best I can say may not be a sufficiently good re[...] for Joanne Grebner. She will be an excellent executive [...] ee. She had the highest rating in my senior typing class [...] years I have taught here. Joanne is punctual, accurate, ...oc w.....g, and quick to grasp new ideas.

In whatever she tries, she will rise to the top.

UNCOMPLIMENTARY REFERENCE

You may be asked for a reference about a former employee of whom compliments cannot honestly be given. When this occurs, be careful about what is written. In a period of emphasis upon individual rights, all precautions must be taken to prevent a legal suit against your company. An attorney or your company's legal department should be consulted before you put in writing anything derogatory about a person.

Some personnel departments give references by phone only. Even then, any uncomplimentary statements are general and vague. Such mild words as, "John Allison has worked here for seven years and except for some personal problems his work has been satisfactory," could be the basis for a legal suit by John Allison, and, although true, the "personal problems" statement would have to be proved in court. Litigation could be avoided by writing, "John Allison was employed here from January 15, 19__ to March 31, 19__ ," ignoring any reference to character or performance.

If you feel the need to write a negative recommendation, don't write any!

REPRIMAND

A reprimand should include constructive criticism, and constructive criticism starts with a compliment. Show appreciation for some part of the other person's work that has been good or for some event he or she has participated in. A phrase like "Your work record in the past has been excellent," "We appreciate your willing attitude," or "You have been with us a good many years," lets the person know that he or she is being treated with consideration. The complimentary attitude should not be overdone, however, or the turnabout to a reprimand will seen contradictory.

Make a letter of reprimand short: there is no reason to prolong the agony. Shortness will also prevent a tendency to ramble around the fringes of the subject. Make the fact of a reprimand direct, but in a tactful and considerate way. There is no need for abusive language. This would arouse defensiveness, resentment, and even anger, causing the reader to become completely unreceptive to suggestions for improvement. To keep criticism easy to take, criticize indirectly. Rather than saying, "Don't smoke in the lunchroom," say, "Please smoke outside." Replace "You are late all the time" with "Please try to be more prompt." The critical "You make too many mistakes" would be more receptively received with the less direct "We believe a little more effort will improve the quality of your work."

The Oriental concept of saving face is applicable to a letter or criticism. Let the reader keep his or her ego; don't grind the reader into the ground with overcriticism or derogatory statements; let the reader know you too are not without fault — that you are human. A word or two of praise now and then in the letter will let the person retain his or her good image. This leads to a cooperative attitude on the part of both parties. Then, corrective action can be suggested. Tell the reader how errors can be corrected, what action needs to be taken, and how you will help. Offer encouragement so corrective steps will seem easy to take. One easy step begins a journey of 1,000 miles (paraphrasing the Orientals again).

Set goals that can be reached, not grand goals of an improved self or a happier life ahead, but specific goals, as 95 percent attendance, 200 units per hour, only 4 errors next month, or a report completed by the 9th of the month. Aided by the idea that improvement of one person's performance will help the whole company, this person will feel happy about following your suggestions.

How to Do It

1. Start with a compliment or a straightforward statement of what is wrong.
2. Use indirect criticism.
3. Set definite goals for improvement.
4. Offer encouragement.

Poor Work

Dear Jim:

Cintex plant reports sent to Headquarters during the past six months have been on time and have raised no significant questions, with one notable exception: the sales invoice processing has steadily deteriorated. This has delayed receipts of data for the Sales Statistics Reports. It is also delaying our cash receipts because customers are getting their invoices late.

While some of the problems can be attributed to the Headquarters Data Center, the major problems are being created by the Cintex plant. The problems at Headquarters will be resolved, and I am confident that the future support from the Data Center will meet our standards.

The problems being created by the plant are in three categories: (1) late receipts past cutoff date, (2) month-end bunching of sales invoices, and (3) other problems such as illegible documents and invalid data.

The attached schedule details the receipts in the Data Center for the month of February. As you will note, 22 percent of February's invoice volume was apparently billed on the last two days of the month. With 20 billing days, the expected percentage of billings on the last two days should not have exceeded 10-12 percent. Additionally, over 3 percent of the month's invoices were received after the cutoff date.

I am going to monitor future closings more diligently. Each month we will publish a report on the prior month's closing to highlight problems and take corrective action as necessary.

Please give this your personal attention. We must resolve this problem.

Sincerely,

Poor Attendance

Dear Howard:

Your work during the past four years has been excellent, but is becoming offset by your absentee record. I am aware that your health has not been the best, but regular attendance is one requirement of your job. Something must be done to improve your attendance, because we cannot schedule our workloads efficiently when we cannot depend on you to be here.

If you need to see a doctor, we can easily schedule time from work for you to do that. Please give this serious thought; we need you on our team.

Sincerely,

Improper Language

Dear Jim:

I have a complaint from H&H Pallet Co. that you used abusive language toward their purchasing agent when asked to clear up a mistake on one of their orders.

Who was at fault is of little importance, but what is of importance is that you violated a company policy and came close to destroying a potentially profitable relationship. There is nothing you need to say to a customer that cannot be said politely.

I have straightened out the difficulty, and Mr. Johnson is reasonably pacified. Now that you both have had time to cool off, I want you personally to apologize to Mr. Johnson — and remember the importance courtesy plays in persuasive selling.

Sincerely,

Outside Activities at Work

Dear George:

Your work record in the past has been excellent, but now it has come to my attention that you have been spending a lot of working hours campaigning for new officers. I haven't been there to observe, but reports have come to me from several sources. Since this interferes with the amount of work you are doing, I would suggest you devote less time to campaigning and more to Company work.

Sincerely,

Lack of Cleanliness

Dear Betty,

You have a lot of good friends here. We all like your smile and your cheery greeting in the mornings. There is one area, however, in which we feel there is room for improvement. We would like to suggest a stronger deodorant and perhaps more frequent washing of your blouses. You no doubt have been unaware of this need, but your co-workers would appreciate your considering the problem.

Keep smiling and please hold on to your cheerful ways.

Sincerely,

Bad Behavior

Dear Employees:

We had a minor fender bender accident in the parking lot yesterday at quitting time between an employee and one of our customers. Our employee disregarded the directional arrows in his rush to leave.

Our customer was astounded that so many employees were dashing out against the arrows. He was more than unhappy, and threatened to take his business elsewhere.

Not only because of loss of business, but also for your own physical safety, DIRECTIONAL ARROWS IN THE PARKING LOT MUST BE OBEYED. If you cannot correct this type of behavior, strong measures will be taken to insure that you do.

Safety requires not only care but also courtesy and consideration for others.

Sincerely,

Travel Expense

Dear Ms. Rundell:

The executive committee has reviewed your travel expense account for the past year. Your overall expenses seem reasonable, and although we have not established a budget for each salesperson, we plan to have one developed for use next year.

One facet of your travel strikes us as probably uneconomical. You appear to be covering the western states in a disorganized way. For example, in May you made calls in cities in this order: Portland, San Francisco, Oakland, San Diego, Los Angeles, Boise, Denver, Portland, Seattle, Salt Lake City, Sacramento, and Oakland.

Looking at a map of the western states, this schedule involves a lot of skipping and backtracking. The Committee believes that money and travel time could be saved if you traveled in a roughly circular route to prevent backtracking. Is this thought correct, or is there a good reason for not following a more direct route from city to city?

Please let me have your comments on this by April 30.

Regards,

Lack of Cooperation

Dear Mr. Bell:

Reports on the attractiveness of your displays in our midwestern stores and favorable comments by customers indicate you are doing an excellent job of displaying our merchandise.

These reports come to me from our department buyers who also bring up a situation that needs correcting. They report that you often appear on the selling floor during busy periods and request too much help from the salespeople. There is no reason why you should need help from the sales staff. Disruptions in the sales area could be minimized by organizing all your materials and tools in the work areas before bringing anything onto the selling floor. This will also lessen your time on the floor. You should be able to schedule your work on the sales floor so that most of it is done before customers arrive and after the store is closed.

Please give this some thought and let me know by March 20 your plans for closer cooperation with the department buyers. I know they tend to be difficult at times — but they do have a point.

Sincerely,

Fire Insurance Increase

Dear Mr. Benjay:

The January 31 report from our fire insurance company states that the fire insurance on the Belson plant will increase 30 percent next year. The reason stated is unsafe conditions, supported by two citations from the fire marshall for the *same* violation within four months.

This is poor management. You are risking the lives of the Belson employees.

By February 27, I want to have on my desk a compliance certification from the Belson County fire inspector.

Regards,

Exceeding Budget

Dear Mr. Harbor:

I have been studying the September and year-to-date cost statements for your plant. Overall, your cost-cutting has improved since my review of the first six months, but one thing disturbs me: the reductions have been in the small-cost categories. If you are to meet the budgeted goal by year-end, costs of finishing supplies and maintenance materials must be cut considerably. We discussed this in/July. The time for action is fast disappearing. Please send me a plan by November 1 for reducing costs in the last two months.

Continue the good work on the small items; we can't lose any ground already gained.

Regards,

Trespassing

Dear Al:

A situation has recently come to my attention that must be corrected. Evidently some employees' families and friends are coming in to the plant, particularly on the second and third shifts.

As you know, this is strictly against company policy, because of the liability we could incur if someone were hurt. Any tours of the plant must be arranged through the Personnel Department.

Effective immediately, please take whatever steps are necessary to secure the manufacturing area from unauthorized persons.

Sincerely,

Inventory Records

Dear Dick:

The discrepancy in our small motors physical inventory of November 20, compared to our book inventory, amounted to approximately $39,000 (975 units). On a percentage basis this amounted to .8 percent. The Division average is .2 percent, making our variance four times the Division average.

In this particular case, I must approve of the favorable effect of the variance. However, in the future, it will be mandatory that we take steps to get this variance in line with the Division average.

After you have had a chance to review this, please report, by December 15, the procedural changes you will make.

Regards,

Sales Falling

Dear Dave:

I know you have been trying, but upon reviewing the first three months of 19_3, we find ourselves running 20 MM units behind our Budget, and your short-range forecast shows no improvement in the next few months. Last January, I suggested you consider 19_1 costs for 19_3 rather than your budgeted figures, since your volumes for 19_1 and 19_3 are similar. For the first three months of 19_3 you are behind 19_1 by 6 MM units; therefore your costs should be as low as or lower than 19_1.

If you will evaluate your Profit Analysis Report, you will see how the loss of volume has lowered your profit. Besides the loss of profit from the loss of volume, your salesmen are not obtaining last year's average price level, let alone the price level they projected for this year.

Comparing the first three months of 19_3 with the first three months of 19_1, you have spent $7,000 more for printing, $19,000 more for cutting tools, and $18,000 more for packaging — all of these are higher expenses with lower volume.

The only area in which you have reduced costs is wrappings, and that is to the tune of $930. This is the only sales-controlled item in which any improvements have been realized.

I would like to know by May 7 what steps you have taken to:

1. Bring your sales volume up to your 19_3 Budget level
2. Bring up your depressed average price levels
3. Decrease your printing costs and bring them in line with 19_1 costs
4. Decrease your cutting tool costs and bring them in line with 19_1 costs
5. Decrease your packaging costs and bring them in line with 19_1 costs

Also, please advise me by May 7 when these objectives will be accomplished.

Sincerely,

PRESENTING GIFTS

The purpose of sending a letter with a gift is to indicate that the giver is really a part of the gift; it is a way of giving oneself. Use individuality of expression as much as possible because it will put your own personality into the message. The letter should be short and friendly and reveal pleasure in the giving.

How to Do It

1. Mention the occasion for the gift.
2. Express pleasure in the giving.

Companionship

Dear Kathy,

This gift is only a token of how much your friendly companionship this summer has meant to me.

There will always be love in my thoughts of you.

With affection,

Friendship

Dear Don,

This gift is just a small thank-you for the friendship you showed me this summer.

I will always think of you as a kind friend who took a real interest in both my work and play.

Sincerely,

Advice

Dear David:

I am sending you a Chinese puzzle. It is a small thank-you for the consultation and advice you offered Tuesday. I felt much better about approaching the problem after discussing it with you. Your interest is appreciated.

Sincerely,

Funeral Officiating

Dear Reverend Thomas:

Please accept the enclosed check for conducting the funeral service for my father. We deeply appreciate the extra time and effort you devoted to making this a memorable service.

Sincerely,

Baptismal Officiating

Dear Reverend Thomas:

Thank you for the beautiful baptismal service for our daughter, Becky. Please accept the enclosed check as a personal gift for the thought and work you put into making the service so beautiful and meaningful.

Sincerely,

Hospital Patient

Dear Jo Ann,

Please accept this robe as a gift to someone special. I am sure you will find use for the robe now that you are doing a little walking each day. I hope it buoys up your spirits enough for you to leave the hospital soon.

Sincerely,

Dear Joe,

Here is a book from your old friend Jack Hoskins. It should help to wile away the long daytime hours as you recuperate in the hospital. I'll drop by to see you the next time I'm in town, and I hope that by then you will be home. If not, I'll stop by the hospital.

Regards

Eightieth Birthday

Dear Mr. Winslow,

For your eightieth birthday, the bunch at the Neighborhood Center thought we would give you a reason to relax a little — about time.

The reclining chair you will receive this Thursday is a gift to show our appreciation for all the little things you do at the Center to make life more pleasant for your many friends.

Please enjoy the chair for many years to come.

Your friends,

Illness

Dear Ron,

Your friends at Elton Corporation are sorry to learn of your wife's serious illness. Please accept the flowers we have sent as sincere wishes that she will have a fast and complete recovery.

Sincerely,

Dear Alan:

Please accept this book from the office group. We hope it is not too exciting while you are recovering from your operation. If the book is too exciting, it is good enough to keep until your stitches heal over.

Sincerely,

Retirement

Dear Doug:

The Company, we are sure, will present you with a watch upon your retirement. If you are going to watch the time go by, we thought you might appreciate a place to relax while doing so. That is why we in the Production Department are sending to your home a high-back reclining chair. Lean back and enjoy your retirement in comfort.

We have all benefited from working with you and your presence
will be sorely missed.

Congratulations,

ACCEPTING GIFTS

Accepting a gift graciously can be disquieting at times. The receiver may feel an obligation to reply while being unable to think of
an appropriate expression of thanks for a gift that is really not wanted.

In spite of this seeming difficulty, one can write an appropriate
gift acceptance letter by starting with a statement of what the thank-
you is for:

> We wish to thank you for the book . . .
>
> Your box of goodies arrived yesterday . . .
>
> Your recent contribution of $ . . .
>
> The watercolor chosen by you for my office arrived today.

After the opening statement, make some comment about the
gift; try to do a little better than merely saying, "It is just what I always wanted." Try to be original with a few words about the gift's desirability, beauty, usefulness, appropriateness, or some distinctive
phase of the gift. For example:

> The refrigerator you gave us has upgraded the cooler department
> to the point where I may have to trade in the boat for a larger one.
>
> Your care in selecting a gift which coordinates so well with my of-
> fice decor, serves to further increase my enthusiasm.
>
> Your gift of the finely crafted glass unicorn, so fragile in appearance
> yet strongly made, is distinctive.
>
> We shall treasure the gift for its beauty and craftsmanship, but even
> more as a constant reminder of your friendship.

The gift acceptance letter should express gratitude and pleasant
expectancy in a courteous and tactful way.

How to Do It

1. Mention the gift received.
2. Make an original comment about the usefulness, desirability,
   beauty, or other distinctive phase of the gift.

Chess Set

Dear Mr. Danforth,

Your gift was waiting for us when we returned home. It reminded us of your gracious and pleasant hospitality.

We shall treasure the chess set for its beauty and craftsmanship, but even more as a constant reminder of your friendship.

Sincerely,

Food Snacks

Dear Len:

Your letter and box of goodies arrived yesterday and I have to return the thanks. It was nice of you to send along the snacks, and everyone here at Albany will partake of the treats.

We are glad you enjoyed the golf game with Brenner; he is a very personable young man.

Since I know you will forgive the photography, I am enclosing some photographs of you, Brenner, and the gang that played golf together.

Please let me know if you have a day while in San Francisco and maybe you and I can play golf at the Olympic Course.

Sincerely,

Book

Dear Ms. Vaughn,

The arrival of your gift was a pleasant beginning for my day, expecially since the book was so unexpected. I admire greatly the works of Victorian authors but have never anticipated actually owning a signed first edition.

The volume will remain among my treasured displays to bring me pleasure and to remind me of your consideration.

Sincerely,

Dear Mrs. Kleinfeld,

The small brown package that came in today's mail was really an understated way in which to send such a valuable book. You must have known how thrilled I'd be as the wrappings were unfolded and the book appeared.

You know that I'll cherish this gift and you can expect to see it in a place of honor next time you visit. I'm not sure that I'll even dare read it — just look at it in wonder.

Thanks so much for indulging me. I'll take good care of my new treasure.

Sincerely,

Money

Dear Mr. Dodson:

Your recent contribution of $12,000 to the fund for aid to battered wives was a long-needed boost to our program. The money will be put to use in providing temporary shelter and protection to abused wives and their children, and in generating further contributions.

Your gift is an affirmation of the kindness and humanity that still exists in this world.

Sincerely,

Dear Mr. Gough:

Your gift to the battered wives' fund is a real start for us. A few months ago, none of use knew whether the project could even get off the ground, let alone survive all the red tape and expense.

Now, thanks to you, things will begin moving. We can do a lot with $12,000 to make people aware of the problem and to set up facilities.

Once the program has a real home, don't be surprised if we name it after you. Many women are in your debt.

A big thank you from them — and from me.

Sincerely,

Oil Painting

Dear Mr. Cowden·

While admiring your fine work last Wednesday, I never anticipate⸱ actually owning an original oil painting for my personal collection. You have an eye for color and proportion, and the work fits in beautifully with the decor of my office.

Stop by the office and see just how good a choice you made.

You can expect that whoever enters the office will notice the work and leave familiar with your name.

Thank you for your kindness.

Sincerely,

Watercolor Painting

Dear Ms. Meadows:

The watercolor that you chose for my office arrived today. The quality of your work, of which the gift is an excellent example, has long been familiar to me.

Your care in selecting the gift, which coordinates so well with my personal work surroundings, serves to further increase my enthusiasm.

Thank you once again.

Sincerely,

Art Object

Dear Mrs. Skeen:

Although Annie is still too weak to thank you herself, I wanted you to know immediately how much your concern and your generous gift is appreciated.

Seriously ill children often receive many gifts from kind yet impersonal well-wishers. Your gift of the finely crafted glass unicorn, so fragile in appearance yet strongly made, was different. The care and love which you took in selecting the gift for Annie are visible, just as your concern for her well-being can be felt. It may only be our imagination, but we can see her gain strength daily as she gazes upon the tiny creature, knowing that many people love her.

Thank you for caring.

Sincerely,

Statuette

Dear Mrs. Skidmore:

Your considerate holiday gift arrived today and renewed my good feelings about our recent decision to collaborate.

The marble statuette, placed where it is always in my line of vision, remains a constant reminder of the quality and the enduring nature of our work.

I appreciate your effort.

Sincerely,

Free Product

Dear Mr. Bauer:

The shipment of cartons with a "No Charge" invoice and your best wishes arrived today. Rarely does one business provide anything, even merchandise that it doesn't need, to another fledgling company free of charge.

Your effort and the merchandise are both greatly appreciated.

Sincerely,

Cooler

Dear Don:

The food cooler for our boat arrived here in Sausalito yesterday, and I can't thank you enough for the wonderful gift. You have actually upgraded the cooler department to the point where I may have to trade the boat for something larger and more appropriate.

We are glad you enjoyed your day with us and hope that you will return to San Francisco for some more sailing. Should Betty and I get to New Orleans, we will take you up on your offer to do some lake sailing.

Sincerely,

DECLINING GIFTS

Declining a gift is a delicate task, but at times a refusal may be necessary. Company policy may forbid accepting gifts that could be valued at more than a very few dollars; a gift from a near stranger may be expensive; a gift may be a duplicate and of no use to you, but of value to the giver; you may feel your position could be compromised; or public opinion may be opposed to your accepting gifts.

Whether accepted or declined, a gift should always be acknowledged. However much you dislike the gift or the giver, never criticize either. You received the gift because of a kind thought, and there is no reason to indirectly criticize the thought by directly criticizing either the gift or the giver.

Make the letter brief to avoid drawing out the disappointment of a refusal.

How to Do It

1. Agree on some point with the giver, or apologize, or offer thanks for the thought.
2. State the refusal.
3. Offer an explanation.

Company Policy

Dear Ms. Sylvan:

I am sorry I cannot accept the case of champagne you sent me. Although the thought is gratefully accepted, company policy prevents me from accepting a gift of this value.

The gift has been returned, but not my appreciation of your thoughtfulness.

Sincerely,

Dear Ms. Carrell:

The company appreciates your offer to provide free service and supplies for the copying equipment in return for an agreement to deal exclusively with Aabco.

Regrettably, the offer must be refused. Our long-standing policy is that no one company may be dealt with on an exclusive basis. While the reputation of Aabco and the quality of your product are well known, company policy must be followed.

Sincerely,

Must Maintain Image

Dear Mr. Torres:

Your recent gift of appreciation as a result of the court decision last Tuesday was a kind gesture.

However, I must decline your offer, although I know it was well meant.

As a civil court judge, I take great pains to maintain my image of impartiality. Acceptance of gifts in this manner could compromise that image. Nonetheless, your kindness is appreciated.

Sincerely,

Duplicate Gift

Dear Mr. Luddy:

Thank you for so thoughtul a gift. You are right. Every writer should have a typewriter of such quality.

I am sorry that I must return the typewriter, because, you see, my parents have the identical belief and good taste, and they bought a similar typewriter for my last birthday. Once again, thank you so much for caring.

Sincerely,

Gift Too Valuable

Dear Mr. Scott,

Once again you show that your taste in gifts is impeccable. Thank you so very much for the lovely, and valuable, antique silver vase.

I regret that I must return it; a sincere regret because of its great beauty.

It is unfortunate but my frequent business trips make my home vulnerable, and several area homes have recently suffered burglaries. Although insurance would provide financial reimbursement, the irreplaceable nature of the vase would leave me forever guilty. Please allow me to return it.

Sincerely,

Expensive Gift

Dear Mrs. Byers:

The painting you sent is well suited to the decor and mood of the office.

I regret, however, that it must be returned.

It is my policy not to accept expensive gifts from clients, and an original painting by Picasso certainly fits the category of "expensive."

Sincerely,

INDEX

A

Aabco, company, 388
Aames Company, 16
A and S Associates, 353
Abbott Company, 25
Abbott's, 31
Abel Paint Company, 340
Ableson Corporation, 309
Absentee record, 236
Academic assistance, 326
Accepting gifts, 382
Accepting invitations, 329
Accepting job applicant, 334
Accountant, junior, 335
Accounting:
　Help, 312
　Position, 345
　System, 186
Accounts payable clerk, 369
Ace Manufacturing Company, 178
Acknowledgment of gift, 186
Action taken, 178
Action words, 49
Activities at work, 374
Adam-Sloop Company, 209
Address change, 183
Additional information provided, 343
Additional information requested, 342
Adjustments, customer, 41
Advice, 303, 379
Advertising, 328
Agreeing while refusing, 23
Agreement, 24
　Ended, 322
　For signature, 338
Alameda Real Estate Board, 310
Alamo Business Women, 15
Alcove, J., Inc., 229
Alderwild Machine Shop, 182
Allergies, 239
Allen Company, 66
Allen's, 34
Alumni solicitation, 124
American Chicken, franchise, 35
American Heart Association, 94

American veterans, 95
Amsterdam, Inc., 286
AMVETS, 95
Analyses, viii
Anniversary, 295
Ansell's, company, 312
Answering complaints, 214
Answer delayed, 271
A O Pi, 26
Apology, 21, 24, 267
　Reasons, 268
　Sentences, 268
Appeal:
　Ego, 119
　Faith, 110
　Religious, 128
　Secular, 106
Appley Building Supplies, 42
Applicant, accepting, 334
Appointment, making, 190
Appointment missed, 278
Appreciation, 299, 306
Arthritis, 100
　Foundation, 100
Art object, 76, 385
Ashton Warehouse Company, 339
Assistance, expert, 362
Association president, 295
Atchison project, 279
Atlanta, 326, 327
Attendance, poor, 373
Attending, 313
Attention devices, 49
　Collection, 138
Attention openings, collection, 138
Attitude, 366
Atwater Shoe Company, 240
Australia, 314
Auto defect, 220
Auto insurance, 59
Auto World, 207
Availability of item, 27
Award:
　Industry, 294
　Service, 291
AZE Corporation, 228
Aztec Hotel, 328

B

Bad behavior, 269, 375
Bad risk, 34
Baker and Hamilton, company, 344
Baker's Dozen Bakery, 286
Bakery, 286
Ball game, 329
Baltimore, 362
Bangladesh, 99
Bank of California, 303
Baptismal officiating, 380
Bardahl's, store, 352
Barking dog, 213
Barrow's, business firm, 32
Barrows, college, 130
Basker Company, 259
Bay Area Youth Council, 24
B. C. Manufacturing, Inc., 191
Beginning sentences, vi
    Accepting gifts, 382
    Accepting job, 332
    Collection, 138
    Complaint answer, 214
    Encouragement, 357
    Fund raising, 83, 129
    Sales, 50–52
    Thank you, 300
Behavior, bad, 375
Being our customer, 311
Belated condolences, 257
Belmont Boys Home, 37
Benefits, v
Better truck loading, 362
BFG Shoe Company, 229
Bid:
    Construction, 364
    Price, 176
Billing:
    Clerk, 370
    Error, 209, 223, 270
Birthday, 381
Birth defect, 261
Blue Cross health plan, 59
Board a relative, 17
Boise, 375
Bonner Bridge, 250
Book, 383
Book Club, 60
Boulder River Hospital, 28
Bowen's Department Store, 30
Boys, troubled, 89
Bradford Associates, 275
Bread, 69

Buchannan University, 128
Budget:
    Can be met, 109
    Exceeding, 376
    Limitation, 38
Building fund, 127
Bulletin, free, 321
Business:
    Account delinquent, 153–155
    Collection letter, 135
    Forecasts, 12
    Guidance, 11
    Letters, 319, 349
    Location, 13
    Magazine, 56
    Meeting, 44
    New, 351
    Opportunities, 13
    Statistics, 12
Business Elders, 314

C

California, 198
Cambodian relief, 102–106
Camera, 64
Canada, 323
Candidate, 322
Cantebury Hospital, 118
Canvassing, fund raising, 108
Capper's, 29
CARE, 98
Career helps, 303
Carl & Henderson, 24
Cash discount, 41
Catalog order, 210
Categories, 319
    Letter, v
Celebration, football, 330
Central Freight Payments, Inc., 33
Central Trailer, 36
Centrex, company, 315
Cerebral palsy, 96
Cerebral Palsy Center, 96
Certificate of incorporation, 339
Change:
    Address, 183
    Items used, 183
    Policy, 183
    Procedural, 194
Charge account, 147–151
    Inactive, 343
    Requested, 311

Charitable help, 86
Charity, disagree with, 38
Chemical hazards, 197
Chess set, 383
Chicago, 315
Children:
    Crippled, 91
    Destitute, 90
    Handicapped, 92
    Runaway, 86
Children's Fund, 37
Christmas Seals, 101
Churches, fund raising, 106
City councilman, 296
City information, 186
City clerk, 333
Claim:
    Against city, 181
    Follow-up, 199
    Freight, 46
    Review, 188
Clarity, 173
Classroom:
    Performance, 235
    Procedure, 231
Cleanliness, lacking, 374
Clerk:
    Accounts payable, 369
    Billing, 370
    City, 333
    Office, 335
    Statistical, 369
Cleveland Dental School, 125
Closing sentences (see ending sentences)
Club, Book, 60
Colfax, company, 97
Collection letters:
    Business, 135
    Final, 166–170
    First, 155
    General, 142
    Middle, 160–166
    Series, 141–155
Collection, personal, 137
Collection service, 72
College degree:
    Handicapped, 289
    Music, 288
    Specialized teacher, 289
College training, 238
Commodity codes, 339
Companionship, 305, 379
Company cutbacks, 228
Company hotel room, 328

Company merger, 229
Company policy, 37, 387
Company procedure, 270
Complaints:
    Answering, 214
    Making, 203
Compliments, 361
Comply with request, 177
Computer error, 210
Computer systems, 65
Condolence, 245
Confidence, expressing, 4
Confirmation, 178, 180
Confusing word usage, 270
Congratulations, 285
Construction bid, 364
Consulting, income tax, 70
Consumer survey, 7
Contest, sales, 358
Continue procedure, 179
Contra Costa County Crippled Children's
    Society, Inc., 92
Contract, TV service, 71
Convalescing, 356
Cooler, 386
Cooperation, lacking, 376
Cornwall, college, 131
Corporate name, 191
Correct an error, 193, 342
Cost of purchases, 204
Cost savings, 78
Costs, expansion, 115
Councilman, 296
Cover letter, 337
Credit:
    Business, 32
    Card, 189
    Delayed, 273
    Information, 36, 186
    Late pay, 33
    Limited, 33
    Personal, 29, 74
Credit memo, using, 194
Credit Union, 240
Credit Union loan, 159
Crippled children, 91
Cupertino, 351
Customer, 311, 368
    Adjustments, 41
    Disturbed, 215
    Inactive, 72
    Ignored, 276
    New, 286, 352
    Specific, 66

D

Damaged merchandise, 219
Damaged product, 41
Dartmouth Alumni Fund, 124
Data for newsletter, 187
Data no longer needed, 177
Deadline:
  Meeting, 9
  Shorten, 9
Death:
  Belated, father, 258
  Brother, 256
  Business associate, 249
  Business firm, 259
  Business friend, 250
  Daughter, 255
  Father, 254
  Husband, 250
  Mother, 253
  Others, 256
  Relative, 253
  Sister, 256
  Son, 255
  Spouse, 250
  Suicide, 258
  Use of the word, 245
  Wife, 253
Declining:
  Dinner invitation, 271, 331
  Gift, 387
  Requests, 21
  Responsibilities, 222
Delayed answer, 271
Delayed credit, 273
Delayed dinner, 273
Delayed order, 218, 273
Delayed paper work, 274
Delayed thank you, 275
Delinquent account, 153
Delinquent pledge, 110
Delivery, late, 217
Delivery method, 218
Delivery person, 212
Deloitte, Haskins & Sells, 71
Delta Cost Accountants, 26
Denver, 279, 324, 375
Departing employee, 315
Destitute children, 90
Diesel, A. C. Company, 336
Dinner:
  Declining, 271
  Delayed, 273
  Invitation, 304, 331

Dinner (cont'd)
  Guest, 329
  Postponed, 273
  Retirement, 331
Direct mail, 85
Disadvantaged girl, 88
Disagree with goals, 240
Disease, lung, 101
Distribution of reports, 180
Disturbed retail customer, 215
Divorce, 261
Doctors as business persons, 117
Doctors, giving, 116
Doctors, last appeal, 118
Domestic service, 370
Donation, 36
Dun & Bradstreet, 34
Duplicate gift, 388

E

Earth Grains, 69
East Bay Accounting Society, 329
Easton, company, 364
Effect of strike, 181
Ego, appeal to, 119
Eightieth birthday, 381
Election, public, 73
Elitist magazine, 57
Ellsworth College, 130
Elton Corporation, 249, 381
Emerson Society, 43
Emphatic position, 22
Employment, declined, 39
Employee:
  Departing, 315
  New, 352
  Notice of leaving, 231
Employee's parents, 322
Employment:
  Information, 40
  Short, 30
  Unsuitable, 39
Encouragement, 24, 357
Ending paragraph, 174
Ending sentences, vi
  Accepting gifts, 382
  Collection, 139–141
  Complaint answer, 215
  Favors, 5
  Information, 174, 185
  Invitations, 329
  Job acceptance, 332

Ending sentences *(cont'd)*
Recommendation, 366
Refusals, 23
Sales, 51, 54
Sending invitations, 327
Thank you, 300
Enjoyed meeting you, 322
Enterprise, 93
Entertaining a friend, 16
Equal Employment Opportunity Commission, 227
Equipment:
Hospital, 114
Replacing, 119
Error:
Billing, 209, 223, 270
Computer, 210
Correction, 342
Finding, 363
Manufacturing, 207
Pricing, 222
Quote, 279
Shipping, 209, 218, 279
Statement, 224, 282
Etching, metal, 76
Evaluation, personnel, 195
Every bit helps, 129
Every member canvass, 108
Exceeding budget, 376
Exceeding goal, 287
Executive recruiter, 74
Expansion costs, 115
Expenditures, 338
Expense, travel, 375
Expensive gift, 389
Expert assistance, 362
Explanation, inadequate, 205
Exxon, company, 306

F

Face, saving, 372
Facts, getting, 363
Failure of project, 279
Fairfield, 363
Faith appeal, 110
Falling sales, 378
Farnsworth, Inc., 352
Favors, 3
Fear, alleviating, 17
Fibreboard, company, 314
Fibre Containers, 292
Final sentences *(see* Ending sentences)

Final collection letters, 166–170
Financial condition, 32
Financial disadvantage, 129
Financial problems, 229
Financial statements, 11
Finding error, 363
Fire insurance increase, 376
Firing, 227
First collection letter, 155
Fishing trip invitation, 323
Follow-up, 341
Follow-up, claim, 199
Food, foreign object in, 222
Food gift, 68
Food snacks, 383
Football celebration, 330
Football game, 26
Fordham's, 30
Ford Motor Company, 220
Ford's, 31
Foreign object in food, 222
Foreman, 336
Franchise refused, 35
Free bulletin, 321
Free product, 386
Friend, 326
For sales position, 325, 326
Helping, 18
Personal, 230
Friendship, 305, 379
Freight bill, 143
Freight claim, 46
Fund:
Building, 127
Drive, 360
Fund raising:
Canvassing, 108
Charities, 86
Churches, 106
Hospitals, 111
Preparation, 107
Sales techniques, 85
Schools, 121
Series of letters, 101
Funds limited, 37
Funeral officiating, 380
Furniture Mart, 8
Furniture, retail, 75

G

General collection letters, 142
General Electric, 182

Georgia-Pacific, 260
Getting the facts, 363
Gift, 301
  Accepting, 382
  Acknowledgment, 186
  Declining, 387
  Duplicate, 388
  Expensive, 389
  Food, 68
  Presenting, 378
  Received, 323
  Small, 130
  Valuable, 389
Girl, disadvantaged, 88
Giving:
  Doctors, 116
  For love, 111
  Haven't yet, 124
  Increase, 107
  More, 121
Goal, exceeded, 287
Going away party, 305
Golf invitation, 321
Golf tournament, 294
Good salesman, 364
Goodwill, 21, 319
Good wishes, 354
Good work, 321
Graduate, 367
Graduate, high school, 371
Graduation, 288
Grande Company, 18
Granger Graduate School, 126
Greetings, seasonal, 320, 355
Group, joining, 26
Guarantee, merchandise, 220
Guarantor, 33
Guest, dinner, 329

H

H & H Pallet Company, 374
Handicapped:
  Children, 92
  College degree, 289
  Youth, 93
Hanukkah, 320
Hamilton Heavy Hardware, company, 311
Harcourt College, 121
Hard sell, vii
Harper Clean Air, company, 237
Harry and David, 69
Hastings-Allison, 278

Health:
  Illness, 238
  Insurance, 59
Heart:
  Disease, 94
  Fund, 93
  Problem, 239
Help:
  Orientation, 362
  Unusual, 363
H. H. H. Associates, Inc., 339
How to Do It:
  Accepting gifts, 382
  Accepting invitations, 330
  Accepting job applicant, 335
  Apology, 267
  Collection, 137
  Complaint answers, 214
  Complaint making, 204
  Compliments, 361
  Congratulations, 285
  Cover letter, 337
  Declining gifts, 387
  Encouragement, 358
  Favors, 5
  Follow-up, 342
  Fund raising, 86
  Goodwill, 320
  Good wishes, 354
  Introduction, 325
  Invitation, 328
  Job acceptance, 332
  Presenting gifts, 379
  Providing information, 174
  Recommendation, 366
  Reprimand, 372
  Requesting information, 185
  Requests, 23
  Resignation, 237
  Resignation acceptance, 241
  Sales, 51
  Sympathy, 245
  Termination, 227
  Termination warning, 233
  Thank you, 301
  Welcome, 350
Highland Estates, 314
Highland Hospital, 315
High school graduate, 371
Homes, 62
Homes, real estate, 62
Homeowner's insurance, 58
Honorary sorority, 295
Honourman Medical Center, 28

Hoskins and Halloid, company, 238
Hospital:
  Equipment, 114
  Foundation, 120
  Fund raising, 111
  Patient, 380
Hospitalized:
  Accident, 249
  Illness, 248
  Injury, 249
Hotel room, 328
Houston, 278
How to's, v
Humboldt College, 127
Huston power lawn mower, 343

I

IBM, 65
Ignoring customer, 276
Ill Health, 238
Illness, 249, 308, 381
Image, 388
Improper language, 374
Inactive charge accounts, 343
Inactive customer, 72
Inadequate explanation, 205
Increased sales, 365
Income tax consulting, 70
Incomplete files, 192
Incomplete instructions, 216, 277
Incomplete project, 277
Incorporation certificate, 339
Incorrect mailings, 205
Index explained, viii
Indiscretion, 230, 276
Individual Financing, 74
Industry award, 294
Inexperienced worker, 370
Inflation, fund raising, 107
Information, 302
  Additional, 342, 343
  City, 186
  Credit, 36, 186
  Employment, 40
  Exchange, 10
  Lacking, 29, 32
  Provided, 173, 343
  Requested, 5, 27, 184, 324, 342
  Sending, 324
  Wrong, 282
Inland Steel, 23
Inquiry, response to, 7

Instructions:
  Incomplete, 216, 277
  Repeated, 180
Insurance:
  Auto, 59
  Fire, 376
  Health, 59
  Homeowner's, 58
  Increase, 376
  Life, 77
  Mortgage, 57
  Policy transfer, 181
  Questions, 193
  Renewal, 340
Intermediate collection letters, 160–166
Internal Revenue Service, 9
International Business Machines, 65
Interview:
  Job, 341
  Obtaining, 14
Introduction, 324
Inventory:
  Physical, 198
  Records, 377
Investigate, 192
Investment, real estate, 55
Invitation, 25, 327
  Accepting, 329
  Declining, 271, 331
  Dinner, 25, 304, 331
  Fishing trip, 323
  Sending, 327
  To speak, 25

J

Jacobs Company, 292
JCPenney, company, 59
Job, 327
  Accepting, 331
  For friend, 18
  For relative, 18
  Interview, 341
  Part-time, 334
  Promotion, 367
  Resumé, 341
  Well done, 309
Job applicant, accepting, 334
Johnson Corporation, 66
Johnson's Hardware, 238
Join a group, 331
Jones & Hamilton, 40
Jones Simpson Company, 344

Junior accountant, 335
Junior Chamber of Commerce, 38
Juveniles, 326

K

Keep records, 195

L

Lack of cleanliness, 374
Lack of cooperation, 376
Lambert Company, 353
Language, improper, 374
Last collection letters, 166–170
Late delivery, 217
Late report, 278
Lawn mower purchase, 343
· Layoff, 182
Lease instructions, 177
Lenkurt Company, 290
Letter:
  Categories, v
  Sample, 14
Letter series, fund raising, 101
Levitz, 75
Library, needs, 123
Life insurance, 77
Life insurance questions, 193
Lions Club, 333
Lists, 338
Loan paid, 296
Loan past due, 146
Long's Department Store, 311
Lord and Taylor, 370
Los Angeles, 375
Love is reason for giving, 111
Low productivity, 358
Low sales, 206
Luncheon for old friend, 328
Lung disease, 101

M

Magazine:
  Elitist, 57
  Subscriber, 44
Mail, misdirected, 217
Mailings incorrect, 205
Maintain image, 388
Maintain service, 116
Making an appointment, 190

Manager, store, 336
Manufacturing errors, 207
Manufacturing plant visit, 10
Manufacturing problem, 208
Marriage, 296
Marriage separation, 261
Martinez Boy's Club, 302
Master Card, 77
Materials received, 302
Matson's Department Store, 31
MEDICO, 98
Meeting:
  Missed, 278
  Out of control, 212
Menson Accounting System, 27
Mentally retarded, 90
Merchandise guarantee, 220
Messy work area, 206
Metal etching, 76
Middle collection letters, 160–166
Mills College, 288
Minneapolis, 326, 328
Minolta Corporation, 65
Minorities program, 126
Misdirected mail, 217
Misfortune, 262
Misrepresentation, 211
Missed appointment, 278
Missed meeting, 278
Missing a caller, 279
Mistake, ours, 216
Misunderstanding, 36, 216
Models:
  Easy to follow, viii
  Standards, viii
Money, 384
Monte-Atlanta Corporation, 187
Morgan Hill Toastmasters, 26
Mortgage insurance, 57
Morton, Martin, and Grove, 308
Mountain property, 63
Mt. Zion Hospital and Medical Center, 111
Muddy newspaper, 212
Music, college degree, 288
Music Teacher's Conference, 304
Must maintain image, 388

N

National ALS Foundation, 95
National Labor Relations Board, 227
National Office for Social Responsibility, 88
Negative phrases, 214
Negative words, 136

New business, 351
New challenge, seeking, 237
New customer, 286, 352
New employee, 352
New England, 302
New member, 351
New position, 237, 291
New resident, 350
New sales representative, 325
Newsletter data, 187
New York, state, 320
Noisy driver, 211
Norcross Development Company, 238
Norfork University, 127
No, saying "no," 21
Notice of employee leaving, 231
Notice of retirement, 232
Number code changes, 179

O

Oakland, 375
Occurrence, future, 182
Office:
    Clerk, 335
    Furniture, 193
    Visit, 10
Official, public, 73
Officiating:
    Baptismal, 380
    Funeral, 380
Oil painting, 385
Old equipment, 190
Olin College, 126
Onward Civic Club, 327
Opening sentences (*see* Beginning sentences)
Opening store, 295
Opinion asked, 198
Orders:
    Delayed, 218, 273
    Rescheduling, 8
Organization, 173
    Explained, vi
    Illustrated, vi
Orientation help, 362
Outside activities, 374

P

Pacific Northwest Medical Center, 116
Painting:
    Oil, 385
    Watercolor, 385

Pamphlet, 302
Paper work delayed, 274
Paragraphs, ending, 174
Parents of young employee, 322
Parking in driveway, 211
Past due freight bill, 143
Part-time job, 334
Patient, hospital, 380
Payment, 312
    Instructions, 178
    Loan, 296
    Slow, 281
Performance, 231
    Classroom, 235
    Poor, 233
Personal collection letter, 137
Personal credit, 74
Personal friend, 230
Personal information, 40
Personal letters, 349
Personal problems, 233, 239
Personal referral, 368
Personal reverses, 262
Personnel agency, 74
Personnel evaluation, 195
Persuasive words, 49
Phoenix, 275, 309
Phrases:
    Negative, 214
    Positive, 214
Physical inventory, 198
Pierce Tractor, company, 352
Plant closed, 228
Pleasant Hill Medical Center, 119
Please investigate, 192
Pledge:
    Delinquent, 110
    Not received, 130
Policy:
    Change, 183
    Company, 387
Political candidate, 322
Politics, 73
Pollution check, 191
Poor attendance, 373
Poor pay, 34
Poor performance, 233
Poor work, 372
Portland, 370, 375
Position:
    Accepting, 331
    Accounting, 345
    New, 291
    Purchasing, 344
Positive phrases, 214

Positive words, 137
Postponed dinner, 273
Power lawn mower purchase, 343
Power words, 49
Postscript, 85
Preparation for fund raising, 107
Presenting gifts, 378
President:
    Association, 295
    Rotary, 294
Price increase, 175, 340
Price quote, 196
Pricing error, 222
Problem:
    Financial, 229
    Manufacturing, 208
    Personal, 233, 239, 357
Procedural change, 175, 194
Procedure:
    Changing, 7
    Classroom, 231
    Company, 270
Product:
    Damage, 41
    Free, 386
    Slow selling, 43
    Special, 42
Productivity, low, 358
Project:
    Completed, 230
    Failure, 279
    Incomplete, 277
    Worthy, 131
Promotion, 289, 359
    Job, 368
    Sales, 68
Prompt reply, 137
Property, mountain, 63
Providing information, 173
Psychology Association Workshop, 14
Publication:
    Editorial program, 45
    Needs reworking, 45
    Specialized, 45
Public official, 73
Purchasing:
    Agent, 333
    Policy, 176
    Position, 344

Q

Questionnaire, using, 6
Questions answered, 5

Quote error, 279
Quote, requesting, 14

R

Ralph's, company, 311
Rankin's, 29
Reader, consideration for, 22
Reader's viewpoint, 22, 349
Real estate:
    Homes, 62
    Investment, 55
    Mountain property, 63
    Service, 323
Receiving hours, 193
Recent graduate, 367
Recent sales activity, 187
Recognition, 304
Recommendation, 304, 366
Records:
    Inventory, 377
    Telephone, 194
Recruiter, executive, 74
Redwood Girls Club, 21, 37
Reed & Barton, 76
Reference, uncomplimentary, 371
Referral, 313
    Personal, 368
REFUGE, 86
Refusal, 22, 24
Regan Department Store, 334
Relative, helping, 18
Religious appeal, 128
Ren Bearing Company, 339
Repeated instructions, 180
Repetition, 173
Reply, prompt, 137
Report, 185
    Distribution, 180
    Late, 278
Reporting period changed, 195
Requesting information, 184, 324
Requests, 3
    Declining, 21
Reprimand, 371
Research paper, 359
Resident, new, 31, 350
Resignation, 236
    Acceptance, 241
    Notice, 232
Respect for reader, 245
Response:
    Positive, 4
    Willing, 3

Responsibility, declining, 222
Restricting receiving hours, 193
Resumé, job, 341
Retail customer disturbed, 215
Retail furniture, 75
Retail Hardware Association, 13
Retail selling, 344
Retarded, mentally, 90
Retirement, 292, 381
    Dinner, 331
    Notice, 232
Review of claim, 188
Reward, small, 281
Roofing tile, 66
Rotary president, 294
Runaway children, 86

S

Sacramento, 350, 375
Safety news, 196
St. John's University, 38
Sale, Christmas, 79
Sales, 49
    Activity, 187
    Agreement ended, 322
    Control, 358
    Falling, 378
    Forecast, 206
    Fund-raising techniques, 85
    Increase, 365
    Letter, 319
    Position, 325
    Presentation, 312
    Representative, 325
    Volume, 206, 286, 364
Sales Promotion Book, 67
Salesman, good, 364
Salesman's wife, 321, 353
Salesperson, top, 287
Salt Lake City, 375
Salvation Army, 90
Sample letter, 14, 43
Sampson's, 35
Samuelson Company, 309
S & A Parts, 333
S & S Corrugated Paper Machinery Co., 320
Sanders Company, 192
San Diego, 324, 375
San Francisco, 279, 375, 383
San Jose, 312
San Jose State University, 345
Saving face, 372

Savings:
    Cost, 78
    Statement, 340
Saxxon Company, 290
School teacher, 336
Schools, fund raising, 121
Sclerosis, 95
Seasons greetings, 320, 355
Sear's Lumber, 249
Seattle, 350, 370, 375
SEC, 178
Secretary, 368, 369
Secular appeal, 106
Security Pacific Real Estate, 63
Seeking new challenge, 237
Seiko, 64
Selling, retail, 344
Sending information, 324
Sending invitations, 327
Sentences (*see also* Beginning sentences and
    Ending sentences)
    Apology, 268
Separation, marriage, 261
Series collection letters, 141–155
Service award, 291
    Five years, 292
    Twenty years, 292
Service Club, 304
Service contract, 71
Service, domestic, 370
Service, maintaining, 116
Seymour Port Company, 368
Share experience, 11
Sheraton Hotel, 15
Shipping:
    Error, 209, 218, 279
    Instructions, 175
Simon, A. and Co., 335
Simplified organization, vi
Slow pay, 31, 151–153, 281
Slow-selling product, 43
Small reward, 281
Smith Manufacturing, company, 207
Snacks, 383
Society of Historical Businesses, 29
Soft sell, vii
Sorority, honorary, 295
Speaker:
    Getting, 15
    Requesting, 15
Speaking, 330
Special assignment, 44
Special product, 42
Specific customer, 66
Specific example, fund raising, 118

Staff help, 361
Stanford Corporation, 39
Stanford Law School, 18, 367
Stanford University, 288
Stanley Company, 342
Staples Family Store, 79
Starting sentences (*see* Beginning sentences)
State Farm insurance, 58
State of California, 198
Statement error, 224, 282
Statement of future occurrence, 182
Statements requested, 339
Statistical clerk, 369
Statuette, 386
Stewart City, 181
Stop light, 213
Store:
    Manager, 336
    Opening, 295
    Sale, 79
Strength analysis, 187
Strike, effect, 181
Student funding, 129
Student Union Building, 127
Style, wrong, 221
Subscriber, magazine, 44
Success story, 113
Suggestions requested, 199
Sundstrom, J. P., company, 335
Sun Ray Distributors, 353
Support, continuing, 114
Surgery, fear of, 17
Survey:
    Consumer, 7
    Consumption, 198
Sympathy, 245, 307
    Sentences, 246
    Thanking for, 247

T

Tardiness, 235
Tax consulting, 70
Teacher:
    College degree, 288
    School, 336
Teaching, 360
Termination, 227
    Warning of, 232
Terry's TV, 71
Test run assigned, 182
Texon University, 124
Time extension, 8

Thanking in advance, 4
Thanks for sympathy, 263, 264
Thank you, 299
    Delayed, 275
    With refusal, 23
Todd Valley, 63
Token, A. J., 207
Tomkin's, company, 309
Top salesperson, 287
Tournament, golf, 294
Tractor Mechanics, Inc., 27
Tragedy, 262
Transit damage, 204
Travel:
    Expense, 375
    Less, 240
Trespassing, 377
Troubled boys, 89
Truck loading, 362
TV service contract, 71
Tylenol, 72

U

Uncomplimentary reference, 371
United States Steel Company, 302
United Parcel, 312
United Way, 97
United Way Campaign, 97
University of California, 288
University of Oregon, 129
University of Washington, 14, 76, 123, 326, 353
Unnamed tragedy, 262
Unsatisfactory chair, 221
Unsatisfactory recorder, 221
Unusual help, 363
Updating facilities, funding for, 112
Using credit memo, 194

V

VA, 95
Valco Cincinnati, 78
Valuable gift, 389
Veterans Administration, 95
Veterans, American, 95
Victory, 26
Viewpoint, reader's, 349
Visiting, 314
Visual aids, 49
Volume, sales, 286, 364

Volunteer, refusing, 46
Vote getter, 365

W

Wadsworth University, 125
Want less travel, 240
Ward Company, 274
Warehouse report, 339
Warner Bros., J&J, 343
Warning of termination, 232
Warranty questions, 190
Washington, state, 315
Watch, wrist, 64
Watercolor painting, 385
Water Resources, State of California Department of, 198
Watson Company, 184
Webster Technical Institute, 129
Welcome, 349
Wellington College, 122
Wells Fargo Bank, 77
Western Core Division, 293
Western Management Association, 295
Western States, cities of, 375
Wheeler Hospital, 120
Where is report, 197
Whittington College, 127
Wife of salesman, 321, 353
Wiley Company, 237

Will contact you again, 184
Willow Pass Company, 206
Wilson Publishers, 45
Women's Hospital Auxiliary, 331
Words:
  Negative, 136
  Positive, 137
  Power, 49
Word usage, confusing, 270
Work:
  Good, 321
  Poor, 372
Work records lacking, 30
Worker, inexperienced, 371
Workmanship, 42
Worthy project, 131
Wrist watch, 64
Writer's Digest Book Club, 61
Wrong information, 282
Wrong style, 221

X

Xerox, 66

Y

"You" attitude, 319
Youth, handicapped. 93